With many th...
for your support in
making these stories
known.

March 2008

MW00635138

Southeast Asian Refugees and Immigrants in the Mill City

Southeast Asian Refugees and Immigrants in the Mill City

Changing Families, Communities, Institutions—
Thirty Years Afterward

EDITED BY

Tuyet-Lan Pho, Jeffrey N. Gerson, and Sylvia R. Cowan

University of Vermont Press
Burlington, Vermont

PUBLISHED BY
UNIVERSITY PRESS OF NEW ENGLAND
HANOVER AND LONDON

University of Vermont Press
Published by University Press of New England,
One Court Street, Lebanon, NH 03766
www.upne.com

© 2007 by Tuyet-Lan Pho, Jeffrey N. Gerson, and Sylvia R. Cowan
Printed in the United States of America
5 4 3 2 1

All rights reserved. No part of this book may be reproduced in any form or by any electronic or mechanical means, including storage and retrieval systems, without permission in writing from the publisher, except by a reviewer, who may quote brief passages in a review. Members of educational institutions and organizations wishing to photocopy any of the work for classroom use, or authors and publishers who would like to obtain permission for any of the material in the work, should contact Permissions, University Press of New England, One Court Street, Lebanon, NH 03766.

Library of Congress Cataloguing-in-Publication Data

Southeast Asian refugees and immigrants in the mill city : changing families, communities, institutions-thirty years afterward / edited by Tuyet-Lan Pho, Jeffrey N. Gerson, and Sylvia R. Cowan.
    p.   cm.
Includes index.
ISBN-13: 978-1-58465-662-3 (cloth : alk. paper)
ISBN-10: 1-58465-662-x (cloth : alk. paper)
1. Cambodian Americans—Massachusetts—Lowell—History.
2. Cambodian Americans—Massachusetts—Lowell—Social conditions.
3. Cambodian Americans—Cultural assimilation—Massachusetts—Lowell.
4. Lowell (Mass.)—History. 5. Lowell (Mass.)—Emigration and immigration.
6. Lowell (Mass.)—Social conditions. 7. Cambodia—Emigration and immigration. I. Pho, Tuyet-Lan. II. Gerson, Jeffrey N., 1956- III. Cowan, Sylvia.
E184.K47S68 2007
305.8959'3207444—dc22   2007034271

University Press of New England is a member of the Green Press Initiative. The paper used in this book meets their minimum requirement for recycled paper.

Contents

Part III. Reflections

Photographs follow page 38

Foreword

Peter Nien-chu Kiang

Following a multilingual parent-organizing meeting in Lowell, Massachusetts, two decades ago, I interviewed several Southeast-Asian-refugee community members about their efforts to challenge what they perceived to be separate and unequal treatment of their children in the local public school system. A Lao community leader at the time observed, "When they say 'Americans', they don't mean us. Look at our eyes and our skin. We are minorities, but we have rights, too." Referring to the remarkable efforts of Latino and Southeast Asian immigrant/refugee/minority parents, who had joined together that year to form the Minority Association for Mutual Assistance (affectionately abbreviated as MAMA), she affirmed the importance of conducting the meeting in Spanish, Khmer, Lao, and Vietnamese, as well as in English—despite the patience and stamina required—by asserting, "We have to support each other." She went on to note an obvious difference in the expressive cultural and political style of the coalition's Latino parents:

It's so easy for them [the Latino parents] to get up there and raise their fists and say, 'WE WANT THIS!!!' But for us Asians, it's different. We're like [hiding her face behind a piece of paper and weakly raising her hand while whispering], 'we want this . . .'"

She paused briefly and then added in a firm, clear voice, "But give us a few years. We're still learning."[1]

One hundred Latino and Southeast Asian parents had already come to the previous month's official school board meeting to voice concerns about their children's education. Having requested to speak with the assistance of interpreters who accompanied them, the parents had been quickly rebuffed by a senior member of the School Committee, who declared that they were in "an English-Only meeting in an English-Only town in an English-Only America."[2]

When the first wave of refugees fleeing from Vietnam, Laos, and Cambodia began to resettle in the United States in 1975, less than 5 percent of students in Lowell's public schools were children of color. But by 1987 when I conducted my interviews, Latino and Southeast Asian students had become 40 percent of Lowell's school-age population; half were English language-learners. Throughout that year, as many as 35 to 50 new

Southeast Asian students arrived and enrolled in school each week. Forced to address these drastic demographic shifts while complying with state bilingual education mandates at that time, the city had allowed Spanish, Lao, and Khmer bilingual classes to be established in makeshift settings such as hallways, cafeterias, basements, storage areas, and even a converted bathroom that still had a toilet stall in it.

The Lao community leader's reflexive commentary on social justice, identity politics, and civic engagement—particularly in her collective self-assessment that "We're still learning"—begs the basic question that this book seeks to answer: In the thirty years since Southeast Asian refugees first came to Lowell, Massachusetts, and began to transform their own and others' families, communities, and institutions in this historic mill city, what have we all learned?

Tuyet-Lan Pho, Jeffrey N. Gerson, Sylvia R. Cowan, and their colleagues have compiled an important, multi-disciplinary analysis of the recent history of Southeast Asian American populations in Lowell—a city always of great interest to scholars, policy makers, and the public because of its significance in U.S. history since industrialization more than 150 years ago. Overall, this volume provides a useful set of contemporary lenses with which to examine current public-policy challenges related to immigration, race relations, and urban community development, as well as important theoretical directions and methodological challenges in the social sciences, ranging from human and social capital analysis to thick description of secondary migration, transnationalism, and diasporic cultural citizenship.

Researchers and practitioners in applied policy fields such as education, health, law, and politics who focus on Asian American populations often lament the lack of studies that disaggregate Asian American data by ethnicity, language, religion, migration wave, and so forth. Moreover, the need for in-depth studies of Southeast Asian American populations, in particular, has long been noted by many in the field of Asian American Studies.[3] This volume, therefore, will be welcomed across many fields because of the disaggregated analyses provided and the numerous concrete examples and empirical data, often based on longitudinal participant observation by both insiders and outsiders among Lowell's local/global Southeast Asian American communities.

Embedded in the framework of the overall volume is the value, not only of using multidisciplinary approaches (authors representing disciplines across political science, community psychology, education, anthropology, education, sociology, etc.), but also of exploring multiple domains of community life (families, religion, education, culture, health, mental health, etc) and their intersections with a city's institutions (schools, police, courts, temples, businesses, media, etc). In the process, the authors are also making a compelling case for college/university engagement with immigrant/refugee community development. Though individual authors have their own specific rationales and purposes for engaging with Southeast Asian communities in Lowell, their activities and insights over time—when brought together—suggest the importance of developing university commitments and models/methods for collaboration with and investment in immigrant/refugee communities as sites of not only service and development, but also knowledge production.

Indeed, as American Studies/Asian American Studies scholar Shirley Tang has modeled through her own work on public health and community development in Lowell's Khmer American community:

By taking into account the specific history of an immigrant/refugee community, including the complex ways in which "things changed" over time, one can design effective community-based programs and research that not only produce fresh, meaningful knowledge, but also contribute directly to the community's capacity-building and development process.[4]

Co-editors Pho, Gerson, and Cowan would be the first to recognize the conceptual and methodological value of developing long-term, organizational and research capacities of local refugee/immigrant communities to document, analyze, and develop their own stories beyond that which is reflected in this volume. Interestingly, for example, despite the school board member's exclusionary challenge to refugee/immigrant parents in 1987 that "this is an English-Only town," Chanrithy Uong was elected to Lowell's City Council a short twelve years later—becoming the first non-white elected official in Lowell's long history and, just as important, the first Cambodian American elected city councilor in the United States. By taking stock of these past 30 years of what Linda Silka describes in the book's penultimate chapter as Lowell's transformation from "host" to "home" for Southeast Asian refugees/immigrants and their children, the collaborating editors and contributing authors have provided an invaluable service to the communities and the fields represented here.

Yet, the three decades of history documented collaboratively in this volume is not finished, and also has broader meaning across time and place, especially in light of raging public debates over larger issues of race, class, immigrant assimilation, and legacies of war in the United States. This volume echoes what historian Mark Scott Miller asserted in his 1988 study analyzing the impact of World War II on Lowell:

At each step of the city's history, Lowell's citizens experienced the extremes of the advance of American society and its social and economic structures. Because Lowell's life as a city is so dramatic, changes in this archetypical community clarify trends that more moderated experiences in other communities might obscure.[5]

As concerns over U.S. involvement in Iraq have intensified and comparisons to the war in Vietnam are increasingly referenced,[6] I am well aware that public awareness and policy-making efforts are beginning to focus on the possibility that thousands of Iraqi refugees may soon resettle in the United States. Certainly, there are relevant lessons that need to be shared by those who have learned from an earlier generation of non-white, non-Christian refugees who fled civil war and socio-political chaos due, in part, to U.S. military intervention. Writing for this purpose was not at all the intent of the authors, but we are, nevertheless, fortunate to have access to their insights. Hopefully it is not too late to say once again: *Give us a few years. We're still learning.*

Notes

1. *Personal interview*, June 11, 1987.
2. Diego Ribadeneira, "School Panelist in Lowell Accused of Racism," *Boston Globe*, May 8, 1987; and Nancy Costello, "Kouloheras Sparks Racial Clash at Meeting," *Lowell Sun*, May 7, 1987.
3. Peter N. Kiang, and Shirley Suet-ling Tang. "Electoral Politics and the Contexts of Empowerment, Displacement, and Diaspora for Boston's Vietnamese and Cambodian American Communities." *Asian American Policy Review* 15 (2006): 13–29; Kiang, P. N., "Checking Southeast Asian American Realities in Pan-Asian American Agendas," *AAPI Nexus: Policy, Practice and Community* 2, no. 1 (2004): 48–76.
4. Shirley Suet-ling Tang, Community Development as Public Health/Public Health as Community Development: A Report on the HIV/AIDS Needs Assessment Among Cambodian Americans in Lowell, MA, Boston: Massachusetts Asian AIDS Prevention Project, 2001.
5. Marc Scott Miller, *The Irony of Victory: World War II and Lowell, Massachusetts*, Urbana: University of Illinois Press, 1988, viii.
6. See, for example, Andrew Lam, "Iraq Replaces Vietnam as Metaphor for Tragedy," *New America Media*, Commentary, Posted and retrieved Feb. 21, 2007, from http://news.newamericamedia.org/news/view_article.html?article_id=0057cc2 8807ff9160f0688e6ofe9a11e.

Preface and Acknowledgments

Hai B. and Tuyet-Lan Pho owned a home on the 700 block of Broadway Street in Lowell and worked at the University of Massachusetts Lowell, from 1968 until their recent retirement and move to California. During their tenure at the university, in addition to their teaching they also volunteered, mentored, and were advocates for Southeast Asian refugees in the city. Hai was a Humanities Scholar for the National Endowment for Humanities and served on the Massachusetts State Advisory Board on Refugees and Immigrants under Governors Dukakis, King, Weld, and Cellucci. He brought to Michael and Kitty Dukakis's attention the Khmer Killing Fields survivors and advocated their support in Lowell. Hai and Lan also worked with the City of Lowell for more than two decades to see that Southeast Asian refugees' needs were accommodated. Together the Phos brought more than three million dollars in grants from state and federal agencies to the city and Lowell schools.

On an institutional level, for more than fifteen years since the establishment of the Center for Family, Work, and Community, the Department of Regional, Economic, and Social Development and the Center and Council on Diversity and Pluralism, the University of Massachusetts Lowell, has encouraged its faculty, students, and administrators to engage in numerous projects in collaboration with community-based organizations, social services agencies, public schools, and colleges for the Southeast Asian population in Lowell. The council's diversity grants and the Joseph P. Healey and Public Service endowment grants have provided financial and academic support for several studies about this population. They have also facilitated conferences and community seminars to promote a better understanding of the plight and resettlement of Cambodian, Lao, and Vietnamese refugees and immigrants in the Greater Lowell area. It was a Council on Diversity and Pluralism workshop on cross-cultural communication in the late 1990s that brought the editors of this volume together. The council brought together members of the community and contributors to this volume in June 2005 for an energizing and informative exchange on our work and research with Southeast Asian communities. The council continues to support faculty research and community-university partnerships. Over the years the initial casual linkage between the university and the communities has become a long-term commitment that benefits both the institution and the people it serves.

This book has been a collaboration in the truest sense of the word. Each of the editors was centrally involved in the research and writing and editorial work of the collection. The original idea for *Southeast Asian Refugees and Immigrants in the Mill City* came from Maura Doherty and Jeffrey Gerson in the late 1990s, but the driving force since the early 2000s was Lan Pho. Without her leadership, the book would not have come to fruition.

We also thank and appreciate our contributors who have made this a pioneering work, laying the foundations for future scholars of Southeast Asians in America to build upon. Their dedication and tireless efforts to communicate their ideas, observations, and research have formed the core of the work.

For advice and feedback, we are especially grateful to the following: Mehmed Ali, Phala Chea, George Chigas, Mitra Das, Maura Doherty, Arlene Dallalfar, Gene Diaz, Jill Hackett, Samkhann Khoeun, Peter N. Kiang, Paul Marion, Martha Mayo, Nick Minton, Vesna Nuon, Pere Pen, Hai B. Pho, Sonith Peou, Chath pierSath, Thel Sar, Linda Silka, Susan Thomson, David Turcotte, Douangmany Malavong-Warren, and Cheryl West.

A special thanks to Paul Watanabe and the faculty and staff of the University of Massachusetts Boston's Asian American Studies Institute and the Asian Americans in New England Research Initiative (AANERI) for nurturing the study of Asian Americans in the region and Asian American scholars.

For technical assistance, many thanks to Mitch Shuldman, librarian and head of the University of Massachusetts Lowell's Media Services and the always helpful Media Services' crew: Paul Coppens, Rick Harvey, Dave Ambrose, and Fred Kallus. Kudos as well to Arlene Huard of Duplicating, David Driscoll and David McSwain from the Centers for Learning, the University of Massachusetts Lowell's, interlibrary loan staff, Debbie Friedman and Rose Patton, and the Lesley University research librarians and Kresgee Center staff, especially Kathy Holmes, Robin Ferrero, and Robin Fineland.

We are most grateful for the financial support of the Theodore Edson Parker Foundation and its dedicated administrator, Phil Hall; the Mogan Center Cultural Committee and the Lowell National Historical Park; the University of Massachusetts Lowell's then provost, John Wooding, and the dean of humanities and social sciences, Charles Carroll; and the leadership of the Council on Diversity and Pluralism, past and present: Carolyn Caci, Nicole Champagne, Brenda Evans, Suzanne Gamache, Jeanne Keimig, Anne Mulvey, Charles Nikitopoulos, and Larry Siegel, dean of student affairs, University of Massachusetts Lowell.

We are indebted to James Higgins and Joan Ross of Higgins and Ross, and Rady Mom for contributing their wonderful photos; and to Dan

Toomey of the Center for Family, Work, and Community for his map of the Asian American population of Lowell.

Our editor, Ellen Wicklum, and production editor, Ann Brash, at UPNE were a pleasure to work with.

We dedicate this book to our families and colleagues who have generously provided guidance and support to this book project, and to all who shared their amazing and heartfelt stories with us.

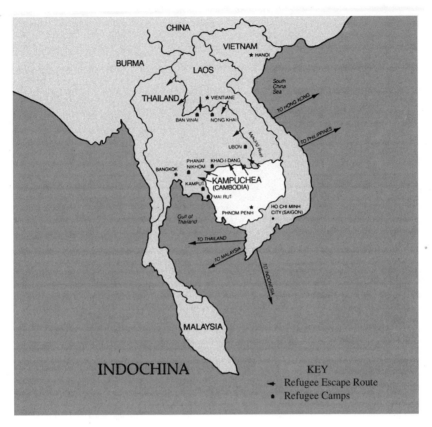

Indochina Map with Refugee Migration Routes
Source: Southeast Asians—A New Beginning in Lowell

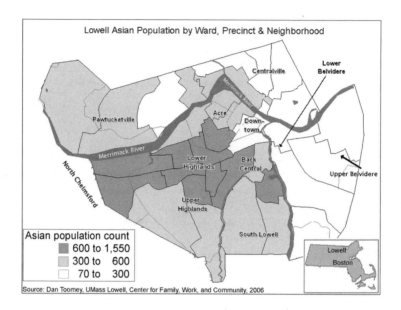

Lowell Asian Population by Ward, Precinct and Neighborhood
Source: Dan Toomey, University of Massachusetts Lowell Center for Family, Work, and Community

Part I

MIGRATION AND SETTLEMENT

I   *Jeffrey N. Gerson, Sylvia R. Cowan,*
and Tuyet-Lan Pho

Introduction

Southeast Asian Refugees and Immigrants in the Mill City: Changing Families, Communities, Institutions — Thirty Years Afterward is a collection of original, previously unpublished essays (except for one) that chronicles and investigates the experiences of a New England midsized city that has supported a major migration of refugees and immigrants from Southeast Asia. This immigrant population consists primarily of refugees who fled genocide, war, and oppression in Cambodia, Laos, and Vietnam in the late 1970s and resettled in the United States in the 1980s.

Numbering some 1.8 million in 2004, Southeast Asian refugees are geographically distributed throughout the country.[1] Yet, owing to a combination of U.S. refugee policy and voluntary secondary migration, they are concentrated in California, Texas, Washington (State), Pennsylvania, Wisconsin, Minnesota, and Massachusetts. The Southeast Asian community in Lowell has been estimated at approximately 20,000 (out of a total population of 105,000). The Cambodians of Lowell represent the second-largest community in the United States (Long Beach is the largest). Nationally, Cambodians are the smallest of the Southeast Asians, yet in Lowell they constitute an overwhelming majority of the Southeast Asian immigrants. Southeast Asians come from various religious, ethnic, linguistic, and historical backgrounds, and their contribution to cultural life in the United States is rich. A focus on Lowell provides a unique opportunity for learning more about the Southeast Asian refugee population.

While the Lowell experience is not singular (half a dozen cities can claim similar experiences), nevertheless, this book contributes to a broader understanding of such areas as U.S. refugee policy, migration, identity and group formation, political adaptation, social acculturation, transnationalism, and community conflict. This volume chronicles the pain, the struggles, and the victories of this distinctive population as its members re-create their community and identity amid economic disparity, discrimination, and pressures to assimilate. To date, there is no edited volume that examines Southeast Asians who arrived in one city via the phenomenon of voluntary or secondary migration. This collection of essays utilizes interdisciplinary perspectives (anthropology, political science, economics, sociology, education, and community psychology) to address relevant debates concerning Southeast Asians in the United States, such as the rising high school dropout rate, Buddhist temples as sites of cultural renewal and political conflict, and whether post-traumatic stress disorder continues to damage large numbers of Cambodians or whether, despite such mental health distress, the community is resilient and thriving.

Most authors utilize qualitative research methods, such as oral history, in-depth interviews, focus groups, participant observation, and case studies, to shed light on a changing community and its new residents, to trace demographics and historical events, and to explore how these events influenced individuals, families and communities in the last thirty years. Participants with a history of trauma often seek to avoid thoughts, feelings, conversations, and interactions with others that could remind them of their past. Care was taken to minimize potential retraumatization in the process of collecting data.

The interplay of multiple factors weaves a dynamic tapestry with many threads: the politics of migration on local and national policy levels; the psychosocial effects of past trauma and transition on the newcomers themselves; the social and economic impact on the community (education, social services, businesses, civic engagement); and the changes that occur within the communities (new projects, ideas, businesses and employment, emerging conflicts, intersection of cultures, and so forth). By bringing together in one volume these various perspectives, the totality of the experience becomes more apparent, the layers of complexity are revealed, and plausible resolution may emerge.

Most of the book's authors have lived and/or worked in Lowell over several decades and know the community intimately. Some were instrumental in helping to bring and settle Southeast Asians in Lowell. Others have developed close relations with its people and institutions, such as the Cambodian Mutual Assistance Association, the Lao Family Association, the area's Cambodian and Lao Buddhist Temples, the Angkor and Lao Dance Troupes, as well as the Asian-American Business Association, the Cambodian American Voter Project, the Southeast Asian Water Festival and the Cambodian Artists Association. The authors are academics, lawyers, community activists, and social service program managers: all are connected to the community by participating in the numerous civic associations; many served as members of boards of directors. Several have written previously on the community and have made the study of Southeast Asians a major part of their research and teaching.

Trends in Asian American Studies

Only in the last ten years has the field of Asian American Studies begun to focus attention on the Southeast Asians in the United States. Prior to the 1990s, the literature almost exclusively centered on the experience of Chinese, Japanese, and Korean immigrants. Of the works that address Southeast Asian groups, most focus on the adaptation and mental health status of the refugees during their years of resettlement. This volume will begin to fill this gap in the literature.

In this volume we follow the lead of the Asian American Studies Institute at the University of Massachusetts Boston, which recently established the Asian Americans in New England Research Initiative (AANERI) to facilitate the studying and documenting of Asian Americans in New England. The contributors have been participants in AANERI; in addition, they were partners with the institute's leading scholars at the university—such as Paul Watanabe, Connie Chan, and Peter N. Kiang—long before AANERI began. AANERI has paved our way by promoting conferences (held biannually at various participating colleges and universities), workshops, scholars in residence, meetings at universities and colleges throughout New England, and encouraging scholarly publication. To gain a sense of the tremendous growth in this scholarly field, one can consult the complete listing of works on Asian Americans in New England in AANERI's "A Resource Guide to Researching Asian American History and Culture in New England."[2]

In 2005 and 2006 the first-ever conferences on Lao and Hmong studies were held in Illinois and Minnesota, respectively. A second international conference on Lao Studies was held in May 2007 in Arizona. In fall 2004, the University of Michigan published the first number of a special double issue on Vietnam, *Viet Nam: Beyond the Frame,* in its *Michigan Quarterly Review.* In February and August 2006, the University of California Press published its first two issues of the *Journal of Vietnamese Studies.*

The year 2005 marked the thirtieth anniversary of the end of the war (variously called the "American War" in Asia or the "Vietnam War" in the United States), as well as of the coming to power of the Khmer Rouge in Cambodia and the communist government in Laos. Subsequent events in Southeast Asia have captivated the world: for example, the United Nations reached an agreement in 2003 with the Cambodian government for an international criminal tribunal to try former Khmer Rouge leaders; United States and Vietnam exchanged ambassadors in 1997; and in November 2003, the first U.S. Navy ship since the American/Vietnam War docked on the Saigon River. These events and others contribute to the growing interest in the plight of refugees from this region. Moreover, Southeast Asia remained in the news as President George W. Bush attended the APEC (Asia-Pacific Economic Cooperation) meeting in Vietnam in November 2006, evoking mixed feelings among the Vietnamese American population.

The story of the Southeast Asians of Lowell is told here from migration (part 1), through the contemporary period of resettlement, and cultural adaptation, and transnationalism (part 2), and finally to reflections on the transformations that both refugees and their host communities undergo (part 3). In chapter 2, "Lowell, Politics, and the Resettlement of Southeast Asian Refugees and Immigrants, 1975–2000" Hai B. Pho—an active participant in the resettlement of the first wave of Southeast Asians in Lowell and professor emeritus of political science at the University of Massachusetts, Lowell—discusses the important role that voluntary agencies and the federal government played in the early phase of resettlement for Southeast Asians in the city. The work of these agencies, combined with the efforts of private citizens, local organizations, churches, and political leaders (as well as low-cost housing and employment opportunities in the booming electronic industry) did much to ease the difficulties of the resettlement process.

In chapter 3, "Public Policy and Local Economics: The Phenomenon of Secondary Migration," Jean Larson Pyle, a senior associate at the Center for Women and Work and a professor emerita in the Department of Regional Economic and Social Development at the University of Massachusetts Lowell (RESD at UML), examines the factors that influenced the Southeast Asian chain migration from cities and towns of original settlement in the United States to Lowell. Pyle found that a host of factors laid the foundation for the great secondary migration to Lowell, including burgeoning networks, mutual assistance associations, small businesses, and Buddhist temples, along with job availability and attractive relative wages.

In chapter 4, "Reflections on the Concept of Social Capital," Dr. David Turcotte, program manager, and Linda Silka, professor of RESD and director of the Center for Family, Work, and Community at the University of Massachusetts Lowell, indicate the need for researchers to focus on the practices of community economic development and social capital development that immigrant and refugee groups implicitly use in building a presence in the region. Without a full understanding of these views, they argue, efforts by university partners and others are likely to be unsuccessful because they will not be attuned to the complex perspectives on community development that drive efforts among newcomers to enhance the community. Turcotte and Silka examine the impact of "transnationalism" and the clashes of models of community economic development between immigrants and nonimmigrants on local community development.

In chapter 5, "Family Education and Academic Performance among Southeast Asian Students," Tuyet-Lan Pho, director emerita of the Center for Diversity and Pluralism at the University of Massachusetts Lowell, and visiting professor of ethnic studies at the University of California, San Diego, writes that Southeast Asians (like other immigrants who came before them) brought their own cultural values and traditional ways of educating children from their home country to the new land. In this chapter Pho describes (1) the foundation upon which Cambodian, Lao, and Vietnamese parents formulate their family education; (2) explores how cultural values and family life may have influenced the academic performance of their children; and (3) examines the nature of parents and school relationship.

In chapter 6, "Does the System Work for Cambodian American Students? The Educational Experiences and Demographics of Cambodians in Lowell, Massachusetts," Khin Mai Aung and Nancy Yu, a staff attorney and policy analyst, respectively, with the Asian American Legal Defense Fund in New York, explore various interconnected factors impacting the educational experience of Cambodian youth in Lowell. They examine the challenges faced by these students in completing their education, owing to cultural, educational, and linguistic barriers and a shortage of resources and infrastructure. They also look at difficulties faced by Lowell's overcrowded public high school in trying to meet student needs, as well as a number of resulting effects—including the increased likelihood of involvement with the criminal justice system.

In chapter 7, "Along the Path to *Nibbana*: Civic Engagement, Community Partnerships, and Lowell's Southeast Asian Buddhist Temples," Susan Thomson, a cultural anthropologist teaching at Middlesex Community College and an associate at the Center for Women and Work at the University of Massachusetts Lowell, looks at Middlesex Community College and the Lowell National Historical Park's partnership launched as the Lowell Civic Collaborative. Begun in 2003, the collaborative was an ambitious three-year project aimed at increasing civic engagement opportunities for students. Given the large Southeast Asian population both in the college itself and the surrounding city of Lowell, a key question is, how is civic engagement defined and implemented within this particular cultural framework? To address this question, Thomson reviews civic engagement in Theravada Buddhism and provides an in-depth look at two activities at Lowell-area Buddhist temples: a joint venture with the Lowell Police Department called "Operation Middle Path," and the Lao New Year's celebration.

Lao immigrants in Lowell are less visible than other Southeast Asians, yet Lao have shared a point in history with the United States that is little known. Recruited by the CIA (Central Intelligence Agency), highland Lao (Hmong) fought alongside American soldiers in the mountains and along the Ho Chi Minh trail. In chapter 8, "Lao Refugees in Lowell: Reinterpreting the Past, Finding Meaning in the Present," Sylvia Cowan, intercultural relations program director and associate professor in the Graduate School of Arts and Social Sciences, Lesley University, provides crucial background information on Lao arrival in Lowell and significant events in their history that form the context for greater understanding. Meeting challenges in adaptation, Lao develop social networks and maintain culture and traditions. The diversity within the community reveals a variety of ways by which individuals make meaning of their experiences and their current lives—and the resulting divisions that occur as they reinterpret their past and connections with the homeland.

In chapter 9, "The Battle for Control of the Triratanaram Cambodian Temple," Jeffrey N. Gerson, a scholar of ethnic politics at the University of Massachusetts Lowell, examines the conflict between two groups of Cambodian monks that has languished in the Massachusetts courts since 1999. Below the surface of the legal conflict are broader issues that the study explores: Cambodian homeland politics, different notions of how power should be structured (centralized versus decentralized) and differing religious philosophies. The best theoretical framework for understanding the current conflict is also assessed.

Medical sociologist Leakhena Nou, on the faculty of California State University, Long Beach, uses a sociological stress process model in chapter 10, "Exploring the Psychosocial Adjustment of Khmer Refugees in Massachusetts from an Insider's Perspective," to explore the Khmer adult refugees' experience. The analysis is based on the responses of three focus groups in the Khmer communities of Lowell, Lynn, and Revere, Massachusetts. The focus groups provide an exploration of Khmer understanding of sources of stress, stress mediators, and psychosocial adjustment/adaptational patterns for refugees who had experienced the Cambodian genocide. Symptoms and reactions associated with underlying causes of mental health problems had culturally specific relevance to concepts of physical illness and mental health. The results of the analysis are used to formulate suggestions for policy changes in community services.

In chapter 11, "Transforming Experiences: When Host Communities Become Home Communities," Linda Silka—Director, Center for Family, Work, and Community at the University of Massachusetts Lowell; professor of RESD; and special assistant to the provost for community outreach and partnerships—indicates that refugees and immigrants often face the challenge of being perceived as outsiders in the communities in which they settle and start their new lives. In the case of Lowell, Massachusetts, the ubiquitous questions that arise when communities move from being host communities to home communities and some of the ways in which transformation may occur both to the newcomers and to the community itself are examined. These oft-difficult transformations provide opportunities for growth but also challenge past practices. The Lowell, Massachusetts, example identifies some of the issues most communities are likely to face and must address.

In the final chapter, the major themes that interweave throughout the chapters are highlighted. We examine contemporary problems that were raised and some of the solutions suggested. We explore partnerships and collaborations that have, in many cases, been mutually beneficial. We identify policy implications that affect any city receiving large numbers of immigrants. Cities and towns, community agencies, immigrant communities, activists, professionals, educators, social service workers, and health care providers are guided toward practical options and stimulated with ideas and insights. Ways of anticipating challenges and struggles inherent in the experiences of first- and second-generation immigrants moving to a new place are cited. Equally important are ways of engaging newcomers' energies and incorporating aspects of their rich cultures as contributions that make the city more vital and dynamic. Not all the answers have been discovered; nevertheless, this exploration both points in important directions and raises questions about future research that needs to be undertaken by and with immigrant communities, as Southeast Asian immigrants continue to sort out their histories and contribute to their new home.

Notes

1. Southeast Asian Resource Action Center, Washington, D.C. Retrieved on December 3, 2005, from www.searac.org.
2. Retrieved on December 5, 2005, from http://www.iaas.umb.edu/research/resource_guide.shtml; other volumes include *Latinos in New England* (Temple University Press, 2006), edited by Andres Torres, and *A Cultural History of Asian/Americans in New England* by Monica Chiu (forthcoming).

Lowell, Politics, and the Resettlement of Southeast Asian Refugees and Immigrants, 1975–2000

Lowell, Massachusetts, is currently considered a model of urban revitalization (Vaznis 2006). Yet few Lowellians know that this planned industrial city, once a leading center in textile production, became in the postindustrial era a rundown rust-belt mill city with abandoned factories and boarded-up commercial properties. The economic downturn also led to the drain of its younger and potentially more productive population from the area. By all accounts, Lowell hit rock bottom in the middle 1970s, when it led the country in unemployment (Gerson 2005). The slow revival process of Lowell that began in the late seventies is the result of many factors, not the least of which was the influx of Southeast Asian refugees into the area that started in 1975.[1]

The United States, in taking up the role of the free-world leader to stop Communist expansion during the cold war, engaged in a long-drawn-out conflict in Southeast Asia, particularly in Vietnam. Shortly after the end of this Vietnam War in 1975, approximately 130,000 South Vietnamese refugees were admitted for permanent resettlement into the United States. Among them were two Vietnamese families (I and my wife were not among them) with altogether fifteen persons who came and resettled in Lowell, Massachusetts (Pho n.d.). By the end of 1975 there were, perhaps, no more than two hundred Vietnamese refugees in all of Massachusetts: with only a handful of our friends and with the help of the Bethany Congregational Church in Quincy, Massachusetts, we were able to organize for these refugees their first New Year's party in the United States. Some of these first Vietnamese were sponsored by American veterans or workers who had befriended them while on assignment in South Vietnam. Some were sponsored by their own children who, as international students, were attending universities in Massachusetts.

The resettlement and integration of the first 130,000 refugees across the United States proved to be fast and successful, leaving hardly an impact on the local host communities. Most were either trained professionals or ranking officers in the South Vietnamese army and possessed a working command of the English language. With limited help from their sponsors they quickly found permanent housing and employment, and became economically self-sufficient and independent. The members of some families who settled in Lowell initially had to live in small, cramped apartments, working for minimum wage at full-time menial jobs that were far below their skills. They spent additional long hours in English as a Second Language (ESL) classes and/or technical training programs to enhance their job opportunity and mobility. Their rapid and successful resettlement was in fact documented by a study made by the United States Office of Refugee Resettlement (ORR) in 1990. The ORR *Report to the Congress* stated: "The Southeast Asian refugees who arrived between 1975 and 1979, who comprise about 22 percent of all refugees admitted between 1975 and 1987, were paying over $185 million yearly in federal income taxes by 1987. These tax filing data show that the 1975 arrivals had achieved incomes equivalent to those of other United States residents by 1985. Refugees as taxpayers and entrepreneurs are making a substantial and growing contribution to the United States economy" (United States Department of Health and Human Services, Office of Refugee Resettlement [ORR], 1990, 99).

In Lowell the inflow of Southeast Asian refugees only started after 1979. In 1978 a large number of South Vietnamese fled by boat and arrived in refugee camps in the neighboring countries of Thailand, Malaysia, Singapore, Indonesia, and the Philippines. Tens of thousands of Cambodians also sought refuge in neighboring Thailand as the Khmer Rouge rulers began to lose their control of Cambodia to the invading Vietnamese Communist army. The plight of Vietnamese boat people and the Cambodian holocaust victims attracted worldwide sympathy; in the United States, with broad popular support, Congress passed the 1980 Refugee Act. Although refugee *admission* policy was a federal program, refugee *resettlement* in the United States was primarily a local and state matter.

Between 1979 and 1980 the first one hundred Cambodian and Lao-Hmong families were resettled as a cluster in the Greater Lowell area. They were sponsored by the Boston branch of the American Fund for Czechoslovakian Refugees and hosted by local churches (Anderson 1980). In the 1980 U.S. Census, Southeast Asians constituted less than 1 percent of the city's population—604 out of 92,418 (as cited in Massachusetts Municipal Profiles 1992).[2]

Under the Family Reunification Provisions of the Refugee Act hundreds more were resettled between 1981 and 1985. After 1985, however, as the result of an unanticipated *secondary migration*, a larger influx of Southeast Asian refugees from other resettlement clusters moved, on their own, into Lowell.[3] For a time, this migration overwhelmed various social and educational services of the city.

The Massachusetts Office for Refugees and Immigrants (MORI) estimated that in 2000 about 20,000 Southeast Asians (officially, 17,371) lived in Lowell, or about one-fifth of the city's population. Of this population, about 90 percent were Cambodian, 5 percent Laotian, and 5 percent Vietnamese. Like some immigrant groups that previously came to the United States, the Southeast Asians came as singles as well as families with able-bodied adults, single parents with young children, and adults in their late fifties or older. Most had an inadequate command of functional English and few or no employable skills; many were disabled veterans deeply traumatized by persecution and warfare (Higgins and Ross, 1986).[4]

At first the Southeast Asian refugees and immigrants who came to Lowell experienced little hostility from the host community. Perhaps many people who supported the U.S. war effort against the Communists in Vietnam felt a keen sense of responsibility for having let the South Vietnamese people down. They shared a sense of responsibility for the destruction of Cambodia and indirectly for the subsequent rise of the Khmer Rouge and the Cambodian holocaust. Even those Americans who opposed the war believed that because the United States had destroyed many of the countries of Indochina, it had to give its local allies who suffered the loss of their homeland and the wrath of the Communist victors the asylum and support they so desperately needed.

This initial phase of resettlement of Southeast Asian refugees in Lowell was made somewhat easier with generous federal government cash and medical assistance for up to 36 months (Pho 1991). In addition, there was a broad-based voluntary sponsorship by private citizens and local churches and nonprofit organizations (U.S. Department of Health and Human Services, retrieved on January 25, 2007, from http://www.acf.hhs.gov/programs/orr/programs/rcma.htm).

The economic boom of the eighties also made resettlement easier, in particular, the growth of high-tech industries along the I-495 corridor, such as Data General, Digital Equipment Corporation, and Wang Laboratories. Electronic circuit-board assembly jobs that required more dexterity than physical stamina or communication skills were readily available (Gittell 1992). Southeast Asian refugees filling the gap in the labor pool required minimum on-the-job training and, once hired, they were prized for their adroitness, hard work, and compliance. Refugees and immigrants also filled many manual labor jobs and cash-only piecework that most American-born residents were not willing to take. Many Southeast Asians took on two or more jobs and, in a short period of time, saved enough money to buy a car, a house, or open a store with the combined resources from family members and friends.

In the seventies the efforts of many farsighted city leaders such as Pat Mogan (city manager) and Paul Tsongas (U.S. senator) to create the Lowell National Historical Park and the Heritage State Park also facilitated the integration of Southeast Asian immigrants in Lowell. The parks restored Lowell's pride as a mill town and the nation's first planned industrial city. In the process of reclaiming the past, the history of the Irish, French, and Greek immigrants who came to build the canals and operate the mills was documented and celebrated. Articles on ethnic food and folk arts were daily features in local presses. A widespread attitude of tolerance of diversity and promotion of collaboration among ethnic communities pervaded the city. The Cambodian, Laotian, and Vietnamese groups with their distinct appearance, customs, languages, religions, and cultures were publicly recognized and readily accepted both by local officials and civic leaders (Gerson 1998).

Of course, there were incidents of prejudice and discrimination against the Southeast Asians by individual residents. Tension soon emerged as the sudden surge in demand for services found many public agencies unprepared. From the mid-1980s on, as public school classrooms in the Acre neighborhood became overcrowded, the Lowell School Department sought to rent spaces in the Boys' Club and in parish halls as makeshift classrooms to house the newcomers. When more children arrived, the School Department, claiming the lack of space, sent the children home. And it was only after much protest and the threat of a civil rights lawsuit that the elected school committee voted to authorize a central registration and busing system both to provide access to classrooms available elsewhere in the rest of the school district and to integrate the Southeast Asian children into the school system (Kiang 1994).

The proactive stand by some city and state leaders contributed to the climate of tolerance and acceptance of new immigrants to the region. Four months into his second term of office, on April 26, 1983, Massachusetts Governor Michael Dukakis signed Executive Order no. 229, which established a Governor's Advisory Council for Refugees (the first chair was his wife, Kitty Dukakis). On October 4, 1985, he signed the more far reaching Executive Order no. 257, which, in effect, committed his administration to make all state agency services available, accessible, and appropriate to the growing refugee population across the state (Pho 1991). As a result of these measures, nine state agencies developed formal plans to review and revise their Eligibility Intake Forms to ensure refugees' access to their services. This trend that recognized and supported Southeast Asian immigrants as valuable to the state continued under the administration of Governor Bill Weld. In 1991 Governor Weld created an Asian-American Commission (chaired by his then wife, Susan Weld); in 1992, he signed into law the permanent establishment of the Massachusetts Office for Refugees and Immigrants (MORI) and the Governor's Advisory Council for Refugees and Immigrants. These units were placed in the Executive Office of Health and Human Services. In April 1994, when the Cambodian community in Lowell invited the governor and his wife, the Middlesex district attorney, as well as the Lowell city mayor and the city manager to its traditional New Year celebration, they all came and participated in the community festivities.

Yet despite these notable successes, a large number of Southeast Asian immigrants continued to face a long and painful road to full integration. Those who gained a satisfactory competence in English and employable skills were able to achieve economic self-sufficiency. But many others who did not sufficiently develop these skills continued to require basic support services, such as English as a Second Language courses, job and employment training, and interpreter/advocacy services sensitive to their cultural and linguistic need. During the second term of the Reagan administration, federal funding for refugee cash medical assistance was reduced from twelve months to an eight-month eligibility period—after which the states were financially responsible for those who had not gained economic self-sufficiency.

There were also a host of state and local programs to help youths and disadvantaged adults overcome employment barriers. Many of these programs were also funded in part by different federal agencies. According to the Massachusetts Office for Refugees and Immigrants (Massachusetts Office for Refugees and Immigrants n.d.), fourteen different federal departments and agencies managed approximately 125 programs with a budget totaling $16.3 billion to train adults and out-of-school youths. Many of these programs, however, such as the Job Training Partnership Act (JTPA) and the Job Opportunities and Basic Skills Program (JOBS) were not easily accessible to refugees and immigrants because of the language and literacy requirements and because of the funding policies that screened out those who were hardest to serve. In order for these programs to serve the new immigrant population, agency officials had to revise their regulations and guidelines that would take into consideration refugees' and immigrants' special conditions. They had to consider certain policies that called for options such as refugee funding "set asides," special outreach services, and services specifically targeted to the newcomer communities.

In the recession of the early nineties, when the economy suffered a downturn and job opportunities were scarce, some Americans wrongly believed that refugees and immigrants took jobs away from the natives and that most newcomers abused the welfare system (American Friends Service Committee n.d.). A majority of Americans also could not distinguish the difference between the undocumented aliens and refugees and those immigrants who were legal residents of the state. As a result an increase in anti-immigrant sentiment spread across the state. A significant number of hate crimes were committed against Asians because of their ethnicity.[5] At one time in Boston, for instance, almost 15 percent of victims of hate crimes were Vietnamese, even though they made up only 2 percent of the city population (Kelly 1989). In addition, various ethnic gangs began to emerge and vie for territorial control. In Lowell the intraethnic gang struggles not only threatened public safety; they also undermined the viability of the burgeoning Southeast Asian business community and disrupted schools and neighborhoods. With the rising concern for public law and order—a concern raised by both the Southeast Asian immigrant community and the general public—city leaders and the Middlesex district attorney took a highly visible leadership role. With the participation of Southeast Asians in Lowell, these leaders created a Southeast Asian Task Force and opened communication with the Southeast Asian communities (Davis 1998). They also successfully opened up four police department positions for candidates with Southeast Asian bilingual and bicultural competence. To gain a voice, some Southeast Asians ran for public office, including the public school committee and the city council. The leadership of public officials and their collaboration with Southeast Asian communities made Lowell a more secure and economically prosperous place to work and live in. In 1999 a milestone was reached with the election of Chanrithy Uong as the nation's first Cambodian-American city councilor. Uong was subsequently reelected in 2001 and 2003 (Gerson 2004).

Prospects for Lowell after 2000

Lowell had gone through several phases of face-lifting and soul-searching with events such as the opening of the first federally supported urban national historical park in the mid 1970s. Also contributing to the revival were several federal block grants for employment, job training, and school improvement, and several major state capital investments for the University of Massachusetts Lowell, and Middlesex Community College. For twenty-five years the loss of population in Lowell—and Massachusetts generally—was stemmed by the increase in immigrant and refugee migration.[6] The city's 2004 population stood at 103,000, a rise of 11 percent from 92,418 in 1980 (Sutner 2006). Since 2004, Lowell, like many cities and towns of the Commonwealth of Massachusetts has lost jobs (Massachusetts has lost 260,000 jobs since 2001) and population (losses from July 1, 2004, to July 1, 2005, were some 8,600) as single-family home and condominium prices soared to heights that made the state un-friendly to young individuals and families who wished to fulfill the dream of home ownership. Since 2000, "Massachusetts had lost roughly 230,000 more residents to other states than had moved here from other parts of the country, according to census figures." Michael Goodman of the University of Massachusetts Boston, said, "that deficit . . . had been offset by an influx of more than 160,000 immigrants" (both quotations in Helman 2005, 1). Despite that loss of population and jobs, Lowell continued to hold its own, in large part owing to the recent influx of the latest wave of immigrants and refugees from Brazil and West Africa (Sum, Uvin, Khatiwada, and Ansel 2005). A fruitful avenue for future research would be an examination of the continued relationship between public officials and the new and newest immigrants and refugees, as post-1960 immigrants now form a majority of Lowell's population.

Notes

1. I thank Jeffrey Gerson for his helpful remarks and supplemental contribution.
2. I was fortunate to study the process of resettlement in Lowell by serving as a participant observer and advocate for the Southeast Asian newcomers. I myself had immigrated to Lowell in 1968 to teach at Lowell State College; I returned briefly to Saigon to teach and conduct research in 1973, only to flee the country after the fall of Saigon in 1975. In the late 1970s I attended many meetings with city, state, and federal officials, including local elected representatives. I volun-teered for several of the resettling agencies, such as the American Fund for Czech-oslovakian Refugees and the Lowell International Institute. I came to know all of the key participants on a personal as well as a professional basis.
3. For a lengthy discussion of secondary migration, see chapter 3 in this volume.
4. See chapter 10 in this volume for a discussion of the Cambodian geno-cide and the subsequent development of post-traumatic stress disorder among Cambodian refugees, and its ability to impede their adjustment to life in the United States.
5. Reviewing statistics of acts of violence committed against Indochinese, Hein (1995) found that the percentage of Indochinese conflicts in New England (Massachusetts and other states) between 1985 and 1990 was disproportionate to the population of Indochinese in that region. Seventeen percent of the total conflicts reported occurred in New England, which had only 5 percent of the In-dochinese population, while 17 percent of the total conflicts occurred in the Cali-fornia, Nevada, and Arizona region, which had 41 percent of the Indochinese population. (Statistics gathered by the U.S. Community Relations Service, 1985–1990, reported in Hein 1995.)
6. The population increase of Southeast Asians by some three thousand from 1990 to 2000 is largely due to family migration. Since 2001 the numbers have lev-eled off. New immigration regulations following September 11, 2001, make it harder for Cambodians to immigrate to the United States via legal means. In fact, the Cambodian population in the United States may now be shrinking due to a

new deportation law. An agreement between the United States and Cambodia signed in 2002 makes it easier for the United States to deport Cambodians who had gone to prison here. According to the Southeast Asian Resource Action Center in Washington, D.C., in 2002 Cambodia and the United States signed an agreement making it possible to deport noncitizens to Cambodia: "As of December 2004, 126 people had been deported to Cambodia. As far as we know, no deportations of refugees to Laos or Vietnam have taken place yet, although the U.S. and Southeast Asian governments are negotiating agreements." There are 1,400 more Cambodians in the United States who have been marked for deportation, most of whom have already served their prison terms and have been released (retrieved on January 12, 2007 from http://www.searac.org/seadeptconcern3–14–05 .html). Cambodians across the country joined together to challenge the deportation agreement. Although the anti-deportation movement was unable to overturn the agreement between Cambodia and the United States it did create a new core group of young activists, who in Lowell have remained involved in civic affairs.

References

American Friends Service Committee. N.d. Immigrants' Rights in the United States: Understanding Anti-Immigrant Movements. Retrieved January 13, 2007, from http://www.afsc.org/immigrants-rights/learn/anti-immigrant.htm.

Anderson, L. 1980. For Indochinese: A New Land. *Lowell Sun*, July 31, p. 10.

Davis, E. 1998. Community Policing in Lowell: Partnerships is Our Key to Success. Retrieved on January 13, 2007, from http://www.popcenter.org/Library/Goldstein/1998/98-40.pdf .

Gerson, J. 1998. Cambodian Political Succession in Lowell, Massachusetts *New England Journal of Public Policy* 13, no. 2.

———. 2004. Cambodian-Americans of Lowell: A Cautionary Tale of Refugee Political Incorporation. Unpublished paper.

———. 2005. Lowell and Lawrence, MA: A Tale of Two Massachusetts Cities. Unpublished paper and PowerPoint presentation.

Gittell, R. 1992. *Renewing Cities*. Princeton, NJ: Princeton University Press.

Hein, Jeremy. 1995. *From Vietnam, Laos, and Cambodia: A Refugee Experience in the United States*. New York: Twayne.

Helman, S. 2005. Census Estimate a Concern for State. Seats in Congress, US Funding at Risk. *Boston Globe*. Retrieved on December 23, 2006, from http://www.boston.com/news/local/articles/2005/12/23/census_estimate_a_concern _for_state/.

Higgins, J., and J. Ross. 1986. *Southeast Asians: A New Beginning in Lowell*. Lowell, MA: Mill Town Graphics.

Kelly, H. 1989. Seminar on Hate Crimes in Boston. Retrieved on January 12, 2007 from http://main.wgbh.org/ton/programs/6407_02.html. Kelly noted that Vietnamese residents were victimized at a rate far out of proportion to their population. Kelly's story is based on a presentation by Professor Jack McDevitt, Center for Applied Research, Northeastern University. McDevitt now heads Northeastern's Institute for Race and Justice. He authorized the first study of hate-motivated violence, which became the basis of *Hate Crime: The Rising Tide of Bigotry and Bloodshed*, coauthored with Jack Levin. He also authored the first national report on hate crime: *The 1990 Hate Crime Resource Book for the FBI*.

Kiang, P. N. 1994. When Know-Nothings Speak English Only: Analyzing Irish and Cambodian Struggles for Community Development and Educational Equity." In *The State of Asian America: Activism and Resistance in the 1990s*, edited by Karin Aguilar-San Juan. Boston: South End.

Massachusetts Municipal Profiles. 1992. Lowell, Middlesex Country, Lowell Public Library.

Massachusetts Office of Refugees and Immigrants. See their Web site at http://www.mass.gov/?pageID=eohhs2agencylanding&L=4&L0=Home&L1=Government&L2=Departments+and+Divisions&L3=Office+for+Refugees+and+Immigrants&sid=Eeohhs2.

Pho, H. B. N.d. The Families of Tien Dinh Ta and Gia Thai Pho. Author's private conversations.

———. 1991. The Politics of Refugee Resettlement in Massachusetts. *Migration World* 19, no. 4. For the most up-to-date information on the immigrant population in Massachusetts today, see "The Changing Face of Massachusetts," prepared by Andrew M. Sum, John Uvin, Ishwar Khatiwada, and Dana Ansel, June 2005, published by Mass INC, The Massachusetts Institute for a New Commonwealth and the Center for Labor Market Studies at Northeastern University, Boston, MA.

Sum, A. M., Johan Uvin, Ishwar Khatiwada, Dana Ansel, Paulo Tobar, Frimpomaa Ampaw, Sheila Palma, and Greg Leiserson. Research Report: The Changing Face of Massachusetts: Immigrants and the Bay State Economy. *Commonwealth Magazine*, published by MassINC.org. Retrieved on December 3, 2006, from http://www.massinc.org/fileadmin/researchreports/changingface/changing_face_report.pdf.

Sutner, S. 2006, p. 1. MassINC.org. Retrieved on February 3, 2006 from http://www.massinc.org/index.php?id=500&pub_id=1771. Special Issue of *Commonwealth Magazine*, published by MassINC.org: Urban Re-Renewal: No Longer the Mothballed Commercial and Industrial Districts of a Time Gone By, Downtowns in Lowell and Worcester are Emerging as Places to Live and Play.

United States Department of Health and Human Services, Office of Refugee Resettlement. N.d. Retrieved on January 25, 2007, from http://www.acf.hhs.gov/programs/orr/programs/rcma.htm).

———. 1990. *Report to the Congress*. Washington, DC, p. 99.

Vaznis, J. 2006. Lowell's Third Act. Following Efforts to Attract Visitors, City's Latest Renewal is Bringing in Homeowners. *Boston Globe*. Retrieved March 7, 2006, from http://www.boston.com/realestate/news/articles/2006/03/05/lowells_third_ act/.

3   Jean Larson Pyle

Public Policy and Local Economies

The Phenomenon of Secondary Migration

There has been considerable concern about the effect of flows of the foreign-born on the U.S. economy. Correspondingly, even though national immigration policies[1] have been altered several times in the last thirty years, there is recurring debate over what additional changes may be needed. The issues regarding legal immigrants revolve around the total number of such immigrants permitted each year and their demographic and economic profiles (family relationships, national origin, education, skills, or financial resources). With respect to undocumented immigrants, the key issue is how to restrict their numbers. Resources are increasingly devoted to curtailing their inflow at the borders and deporting them when discovered—with the warning of steep fines and prison sentences if they attempt reentry without permission of the U.S. attorney general.[2]

These issues have arisen for a number of reasons: increases in the absolute numbers of the foreign-born flowing into the United States during this period; doubling of the percentage of the foreign-born in the population from 5 percent in 1970 to 10 percent in 2000; changes in their demographic profiles; fears that they might take jobs that otherwise could be held by native-born citizens; apprehensions that they may depress wages in certain sectors, and perceptions that providing them with needed social services is a net drain on the economy. These concerns were exacerbated by fluctuations, particularly downturns, in the national economy.

The foreign-born are not evenly dispersed throughout the United States. Therefore, several key issues emerge: What are their effects on the particular areas in which they settle? How will any proposed changes in national immigration policy affect such localities? Most immigrants settle initially in six gateway states: California, New York, Texas, Florida, Illinois, and New Jersey (U.S. Census Bureau 2001; 2003).[3] This initial settling is often followed, however, by a process of secondary migration[4] whereby large numbers of immigrants or refugees move from initial locations to different cities or states. They can converge in a relatively short period of time on particular localities. These movements of the foreign-born are outside the control of national immigration policy, yet substantially influence the effect of national immigration policy on a local economy. According to the U.S. Census: "Internal migration of the foreign-born had a dramatic impact on several areas of the country" (2003, 4). It also states that "these moves may potentially result in changes to the demographic, social, and economic make-up of those destination areas" (U.S. Census 2003, 4). This report concludes: "As the size of the foreign-born population in the United States increases in numerical and percentage terms, understanding the migration patterns of this mobile and fast-growing group will become increasingly important for understanding the country's overall migration picture" (9).

Secondary migration is important to the immigrants and of concern to government officials, social service agencies, and citizens in localities to which they move. The ability to move from one locality or region in the United States to another is and has been very important to refugees and immigrants, who often can relocate quickly. Localities into which they relocate, however, have expressed concern about how to accommodate inflows that are relatively large for the size of the community into the social fabric. Although many studies concentrate on the impact of foreign-born populations on labor markets and social service networks in particular cities or states, the reasons *why* they are disproportionately represented in certain areas and *how* this clustering mediates the impact of national immigration policy on local communities has not been adequately recognized and explored. I draw on the case of Lowell, Massachusetts—where secondary migrations of Southeast Asian refugees[5] were particularly dramatic in the 1980s—to illustrate the importance of the phenomenon of secondary migration and to outline some of its causes. I suggest that what is missing in understanding the effect of national immigration policy on regional or local economies (and what may therefore hamper efforts to use changes in national immigration admission criteria to produce desired outcomes in local or regional economies) is analysis of the process of secondary migration.

The essay proceeds as follows. The first section begins by summarizing the main issues in the debate over national immigration policy, briefly surveying scholars' divergent points of view regarding the issues, policies that could address the issues, and the problems accompanying different strategies. I utilize a simple figure to represent the traditional view of the relationship between immigration policy and economic outcomes. It indicates that policymakers believed that changes in national immigration criteria would substantially address the problems of undesirable economic outcomes, wherever they occurred.

The second and third sections describe the flows of Southeast Asian refugees into Lowell, Massachusetts, that occurred in the 1980s and examine the available evidence regarding the reasons for this secondary migration. I point out how the experience in Lowell during this decade differs from traditional approaches to migration in the economics literature. In the fourth section I suggest an alternative framework of analysis that (1) incorporates the phenomenon of secondary migration into the broader study of the impact of immigration and immigration policy on local economies (for example, their labor markets and social service networks); and (2) delineates the economic, social, and institutional factors that influence the secondary migration of immigrants and refugees.

The concluding section points out that although secondary migration was recognized in the 1970s and 1980s, it has not received the sustained attention from researchers and policymakers that immigration policy has. The complexities and contradictions it involves for immigration policy have thus been subsequently overlooked. I discuss the importance of secondary migration for policy analysis and formation at both the local/regional and national levels; that is, to fully understand the impact of immigration and immigration policies on particular areas (their labor markets, social service systems, and economies) it is necessary to incorporate the secondary migration of the foreign-born within the host country and the factors influencing it into the analysis. This reconceptualization would provide a broader and more accurate framework of understanding upon which to evaluate the implications of proposed changes in national immigration policies for local communities. Alterations in national immigration policies that do not fundamentally understand the process of secondary migration may be ineffective in attaining their desired goals in areas with large populations of immigrants. In fact, the impact of immigration on local areas may depend more on the variables that motivate secondary migration than on the structure of national immigration policy. Finally, an analysis incorporating secondary migration provides a basis for the development of other types of policy interventions to alleviate stresses that occur in particular areas.

National Immigration Policy: Debates, Perspectives, and Policy Implications

There has been increased debate over the past thirty years regarding the impact of flows of the foreign-born into the United States on labor market outcomes, social service systems, and the larger economy. For example, there has been considerable controversy over whether the foreign-born are taking jobs that natives would otherwise obtain, therefore raising unemployment rates (particularly for certain ethnic groups or low-skilled workers), or whether they are filling jobs that would otherwise be vacant because of labor shortages in particular occupations or sectors. There is also much contention over whether immigrants cost the country more in their utilization of social services—such as education systems, health care, and other public assistance programs—than they contribute to the country by paying taxes, spending their wages (and thereby creating jobs), and establishing businesses that hire and spend.

Immigration policy has been changed several times: the Refugee Act of 1980, the Immigration and Reform Act of 1986, the Immigration Act of 1990, and the Illegal Immigration Reform and Immigrant Responsibility Act of 1996 (Briggs and Moore 1994; DeSipio and de la Garza 1998). Put simply, these policy changes either involve methods to reduce undocumented immigration or alter the criteria for legal immigration (including refugee status, increases in income requirements for sponsorship, changes in criteria for immigration from being almost totally based on family reunification needs to approximately 20 percent based on skills needed, or the potential immigrants' financial ability to become entrepreneurs).

Nevertheless, in spite of these changes, there is still debate over what further changes may be necessary to address the controversial issues outlined above. The debate has been exacerbated by the problems following the bursting of the Internet bubble in the early 2000s: recurring economic uncertainty, rising inequality, and the contrasting interests of businesses and state governments. On the one hand, state governments seek to reduce their costs for social services for immigrant populations. U.S. welfare reform in 1996 took a national position on restricting immigrants' access to many benefits of public assistance programs. Of course individual states were still able to provide social services exceeding this national limit for immigrants; nonetheless, some are chafing under what they consider a burden. On the other hand, employers on both the high and low ends of the labor market have lobbied for admission of increased numbers of immigrant workers into the United States (to work in the high-tech industry in electronics and software or for employment in lower-skilled jobs in agriculture, food processing, or apparel).

The points of view of some well-known scholars of immigration illustrate the major themes of recent debates and the questions arising for policymakers. George Borjas (2001) believes the United States should reduce the number of immigrants allowed annually to the levels of the 1970s (approximately 500,000) and shift from the current emphasis on family reunification to the objective of admitting more skilled workers. Based on his detailed analyses of the data, he argues that the benefits of immigration have been overestimated and that, because immigrants in recent years have less education, they lower wages of less-skilled native workers.

Borjas has long been criticized for being a Cuban refugee who benefited from U.S. policy while becoming a harsh critic of a U.S. immigration policy that historically allowed many groups (such as his) a chance in a growing economy. In his more recent publications, he has based his restrictionist point of view on the argument that current U.S. immigration policy has allowed an enormous transfer of wealth from workers to employers ($160 billion a year). His analysis is wholly based upon the effects on U.S. workers, taxpayers, and businesses—and on immigrant workers' economic outcomes relative to U.S. workers (rather than relative to the economic outcomes of comparable workers in their native countries).

By contrast, Hanson et al. (2001) take a broader point of view that includes interests of stakeholders in the United States plus the economic interests of immigrants themselves and the countries from which they originate. They characterize the debate over immigration in the United States as having three major components: "the level and composition of immigration, the public-finance impact of immigration, and how to control illegal immigration" (94). They explore several key policy questions that address these concerns: "whether to replace family-based immigration with skills-based immigration, whether to continue to exclude immigrants from access to public assistance, whether to expand temporary immigration, and how to balance border and interior policing in enforcing against illegal immigration" (96). In examining potential strategies, they work through the possible consequences to native U.S. citizens, workers, and businesses as well as to the immigrants themselves and their home countries. In so doing, they highlight the complexities involved in setting immigration policy goals and objectives, the contradictions and intricacies of policy formation, and the political difficulties of making changes.

The orthodox/prevailing view of the relationship between immigration policies and economic effects of the foreign-born can be illustrated in figure 3.1. National immigration policy is the filter through which potential immigrants must pass. Different types of people are admitted according to what national policies are in place. In turn, as figure 3.1 illustrates, the foreign-born have a variety of effects on the economy: labor market impacts, the utilization of social services, the development of businesses, the payment of taxes, and so on. Feedback loops exist. Depending on the results of empirical studies regarding these effects, immigration policy can be altered to try to attain desired goals. For example, to the extent that one of the objectives of immigration policy is to accommodate labor market needs, the results of studies regarding the labor market impact of immigrants can be utilized in reformulating immigration policy.

As shown in figure 3.1, the consequences of current and future policy are viewed primarily in terms of the effects that admission of different types of persons at national borders has had or is likely to have on the

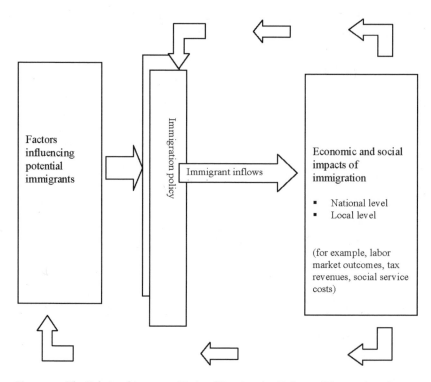

Figure 3.1: The Relationship among National Immigration Policy and Economic and Social Outcomes: The Traditional View

U.S. economy. However, many of the consequences of immigration for local communities—as well as for the U.S. economy in general—are influenced not only by who is admitted, but also by where and in what numbers they settle via initial and secondary migrations. As we shall see, the economic and social impact of the Southeast Asian immigrants in Lowell, Massachusetts, was influenced by the interaction of local economic factors and local institutional arrangements on the one hand, and the speed and size of the in-migration flows relative to the size of the community on the other hand.

Initial and Secondary Migration of Southeast Asians into Lowell, Massachusetts, in the 1980s

Lowell, Massachusetts, has a renowned industrial history. It was internationally known in the 1820–1830s as the first site for the integrated mass production of textiles in the industrial United States. It was again internationally highlighted in the 1980s for its renaissance from a decaying mill town into a vital city that included the headquarters of a major computer firm and a unique national park based on its industrial history. Although its overreliance on textiles in the nineteenth century and mini-computers in the 1980s proved unsustainable, Lowell diversified to its present status as a multifaceted regional industrial and service center. Throughout this span of time, Lowell has had a rich history as a city of immigrants. Beginning with the Irish in the 1820s, at least a score of different nationalities of immigrants have located in Lowell in search of a better life, including French Canadian, Greek, Polish, Jewish, Swedish, Lithuanian, Armenian, Puerto Rican, Italian, Portuguese, and Hispanic immigrants.

In the 1980s, Lowell became known as one of the main locations where Cambodians settled in the United States. Although there were some Southeast Asian refugees, chiefly Vietnamese, arriving in Lowell in the late 1970s, the census of 1980 reported only 594 Asian/Pacific Islanders (a broader category than Southeast Asian) in the Lowell Metropolitan Statistical Area (MSA). This group constituted less than 1 percent of the population of Lowell (92,500 at that time). In the six-year period from 1984 to 1990, secondary migrations of Southeast Asian refugees, chiefly Cambodians, flowed into Lowell in such numbers that in early 1990 it was estimated they constituted at least 22 percent of the population of this city of 115,000. Most of this growth occurred in two major waves of in-migration after 1984.

It is difficult to assess the exact timing and extent of the influx of Southeast Asians into Lowell because it occurred in intercensal years and the size and speed of the in-migration often overwhelmed the ability of social service organizations to collect accurate figures. Interviews with a number of community organizations and leaders, however, provide the following profile. Although the Southeast Asian population in Lowell throughout this decade consisted of Cambodians, Vietnamese, and Lao, by far the largest proportion were Cambodian. Their immigration began in 1979 when the Vietnamese invaded Cambodia and some Cambodian refugees were able to flee the oppression and genocide that had occurred under Cambodia's Pol Pot regime (Pho 1986). Relocation into the United States was facilitated by the Refugee Act of 1980 (Pho 1986). By 1983 it was estimated that Lowell's Southeast Asian population was 1,400. Most of these initial immigrants came directly from Southeast Asia and were part of the federal refugee resettlement program. A stipulation of this program was that anyone in this category of immigrant had to have a sponsor in the host area. This gave the Lowell community some control over the size of the incoming immigrant population.

Table 3.1

The Two Major Waves of In-migration

First major wave of Cambodians (late 1984 to September 1986)

	December 1984	September 1986
Number of Families	412	1,363
Number of Individuals	2,225	7,360

The First Six Months of the Second Major Wave of Cambodians (mid-1987 to early 1990) *

	June 1987	January 1988
Number of Families	1,496	2,215
Number of Individuals	8,078	11,961

* Records were not kept for December 1986 and March 1987.

In contrast to this, the subsequent in-migrations differed in their size and speed, the previous residence of in-migrants, and the control the city had over the numbers involved. The two major waves of in-migration are generally characterized as occurring from late 1984 to September 1986 and mid-1987 to early 1990. Table 3.1 is constructed from the records of the Cambodian Mutual Assistance Association (CMAA) for the first wave and the first six months of the second wave.

During the first major wave of Cambodians, the number of families more than tripled, increasing from 412 to 1,363. Given the assumption that a Cambodian family averaged 5.4 individuals, this translated into an increase in the number of individuals from 2,225 to 7,360. During the first six months of the second wave, the number of families increased from 1,496 to 2,215, while the number of individuals rose to 11,961.

It was estimated that in January 1990 the population of Southeast Asians in Lowell reached 25,000.[6] Cambodians constituted 18,000 of this total, while the Lao numbered 5,000, and Thai and Vietnamese totaled 2500. In terms of absolute numbers, Lowell then had the second-largest population of Cambodians in the country (following Long Beach, California). In percentage terms (the percentage of the total population of the city that was Cambodian), however, it ranked first.

All of the social service organizations interviewed indicated that, in contrast to the earliest newcomers (who were placed directly in Lowell from refugee camps in Southeast Asia), these large waves consisted chiefly of secondary migrants, refugees who originally settled elsewhere in the United States and later moved to Lowell. Many came from the West Coast (California and Washington) but others moved from New York, Minnesota, Georgia, and Detroit. In contrast to the control that the community had over the number of refugees directly relocating to it, there were no controls over this secondary migration process. The city found itself inundated with groups of Southeast Asians—people needing housing and space in the school systems, and placing unexpected and immediate demands on other social service systems.

That a sizable immigration of Cambodians to the United States occurred in the 1980s is easily explainable. That so many subsequently relocated to Lowell in a process of secondary migration requires further analysis. Clearly, flows of such size had an impact on the local economy. For example, it would affect the local labor market, whether by providing a source of workers in what was a tight labor market (until late 1988) or by augmenting unemployment rates (which only began rising from their exceptionally low levels in early 1989).[7] It is beyond the scope of this essay to assess such impacts. My point is simply that, when a group of immigrants (in this case refugees) has risen from 0.6 percent of the population to 22 percent in a decade, the impact of national policies regarding immigration or refugees on particular local economies is clearly mediated by the size and speed of the secondary migration.

Reasons for the Secondary Migration to Lowell, Massachusetts

What were the factors influencing the Southeast Asians relocating to Lowell? What does the Lowell case suggest as variables to include in a model that incorporates secondary migration when examining the impact of national immigration policy (and changes in it) on local areas?

Many of the immigrants arriving in the early 1980s came to Lowell as part of the effort to directly resettle refugees. Two national organizations assisted in this relocation as did a number of local churches and associations in Lowell. Organizations such as the American Fund for Czechoslovak Refugees and the American Council for Nationalities Service were active in sponsoring members of this initial influx, as were local churches, the Cambodian Mutual Assistance Association (MAA), the Laotian MAA, the Vietnamese MAA, and the International Institute (Pho 1986). Once this small nucleus was settled in Lowell, however, a variety of economic and social factors combined to attract the numerically and proportionately enormous inflow of secondary in-migrants of Southeast Asians who had been originally resettled in other parts of the country.

Information gathered from interviews with city officials and personnel in community service institutions (assisting with employment, housing, and other social services for the new in-migrants) provides insights regarding the primary factors affecting the secondary migration into Lowell. The interviews suggest that this secondary migration occurred because of the following three factors: job availability and attractive relative wages; a growing Southeast Asian community (burgeoning networks, including shops selling items familiar to Southeast Asians, mutual assistance associations, a religious facility); and policies and programs of state and local government (educational system, self-help programs) as well as those of private, nonprofit institutions.[8]

Economic factors such as relatively high entry-level wage rates and job availability during the mid-1980s—compared to wage levels and opportunities in the areas of original resettlement—were important. For example, interviewees told me in late 1987 that entry-level wage rates in Lowell were approximately $6.20 an hour to start, with the likelihood that they would increase in two months to $6.60 or $6.70. This contrasted sharply with such areas as California, where wages were $3.75; or Michigan, where, to obtain employment, immigrant workers had to accept less than the minimum wage (at that time, the minimum wage was $3.35 an hour, according to the U.S. Department of Labor). This factor, however, is not an entirely satisfactory explanation of the in-migration: many other areas of New England and the Middle Atlantic had similar or better wages and job growth during this period.

While it has been thought that many may have relocated to Lowell because of the relative attractiveness of public assistance in Massachusetts, the evidence does not support this. The initial newcomers exhibited low rates of reliance on public assistance: in early 1990, approximately 24 percent of the welfare families in Lowell were Southeast Asian—a percentage equivalent to their proportion of the Lowell population.

Many of the interviewees suggested that once the small basic community of Southeast Asians was present in Lowell, the development of an ethnic community with Southeast Asian–owned shops (grocery, auto repair, jewelry, video), restaurants, and community organizations (such as the Cambodian Mutual Assistance Association) was a major factor in the attraction of secondary migrants. In addition, the immigrants' construction of a Buddhist temple (one of the few in the United States) in the adjoining town of Chelmsford, provided further impetus to the continued migration. Southeast Asian cultures are communally focused (rather than focused primarily on the individual, as in the United States), making the existence of a viable ethnic community highly attractive to prospective secondary migrants.

The communal approach serves as an economic survival strategy in addition to meeting social needs and preserving cultural perspectives. For example, there were virtually no Southeast Asian street people because everyone was taken into a home, even though it may have resulted in overcrowding of facilities. This cooperative strategy for economic survival extended to pooling financial resources in loan clubs (from which funds are often used to establish small businesses) or to make major purchases such as a car or house.

Secondary migration was also influenced by the provision in the Lowell community of a variety of social services for education (including English-language courses), job training and placement, assistance in finding housing and processing necessary immigrant paperwork, and personal and social growth. A number of new institutions were established by the local community to assist with the in-migration and existing organizations adapted their strategies to help with the integration of the new arrivals. These included immigrant groups such as the mutual assistance associations, community development corporations working under contracts (such as the Coalition for a Better Acre), offices in Lowell City Hall, local offices of regional organizations (International Institute), and the Massachusetts State Employment Security or Welfare Offices.

With respect to employment, there were several distinct types of opportunities for these immigrants in the late 1980s. Reports from personnel in the community service organizations suggest that several major firms willingly employed Southeast Asian immigrants in the mid-1980s in spite of language barriers. Some firms made specific adaptations to accommodate this supply of workers, such as providing bilingual supervisors and instituting ESL (English as Second Language) classes in-house.

Other major sources of employment for immigrants were in the local service industries (such as gas stations and hotels) and in the rapidly growing sector of Southeast Asian–owned businesses. It was estimated that in 1987 there were approximately forty such enterprises, whereas the number grew to approximately eighty-five by early 1990. In 2002, they had grown to almost 750 (Reid 2006). In addition, there have been anecdotal reports of an active informal employment network that operated in addition to the formal employment placement agencies run by the state or private agencies under a variety of contracts. This informal backroom network was run by middlepersons using immigrants who congregated on a walk-in basis. For a portion of the workers' wages, the middlepersons provided a supply of laborers to employers who came from as far away as central Massachusetts.

How do these reasons for the secondary migrations of the Southeast Asians into Lowell compare to traditional explanations for internal migration? These preliminary results suggest a broader range of causal factors. The theories of migration that appear most relevant to the rapidity of the movement of the Southeast Asian immigrants within the United States are those developed in a Third World context. Because of the mobility of populations in much of the developing world, migration takes place with greater speed than in most industrialized countries. Michael Todaro's well-known model of migration focuses largely on wage differentials (Todaro and Smith 2006). He argues that migration occurs between rural and urban areas based upon expected differences in wages and incomes rather than actual differences (the expected differences take into consideration the probability of actually getting a job). The framework of analysis is wider in Shrestra's (1987) survey article as he examines how past institutional policies in developing countries affected people's migratory behavior, the problems that arose from this, and the ways Third World governments adopted alternative policies to address the problems.

These approaches, however, deal mainly with the movement of a group of people within their native society, rather than with the migration of people of one nationality within the borders of a new country to which they have recently immigrated. Therefore, these approaches have not incorporated the impact of closely interwoven economic and cultural factors that influence the movement of such populations as the Cambodians in Lowell.

An Alternative Approach, Incorporating Secondary Migration

The alternative framework I suggest for understanding the economic and social impact of U.S. immigration policy (illustrated in figure 3.2) indicates that the effect of national immigration policy, both in general and locally, is mediated by the secondary migration process. People are motivated to emigrate from their home countries by a variety of factors—economic, political, and sociocultural—all of which involve institutional arrangements. Although they have been screened by the criteria of the national immigration policy of the host country, the immigrants still bring these diverse reasons with them. These factors will further influence their actions once in the country, including their patterns of internal migration. These economic and sociocultural institutional factors (and how they fit into the overall understanding of the impact of immigration policy developed in this chapter) can be summarized in Figure 3.3, which elaborates on a section of figure 3.2.

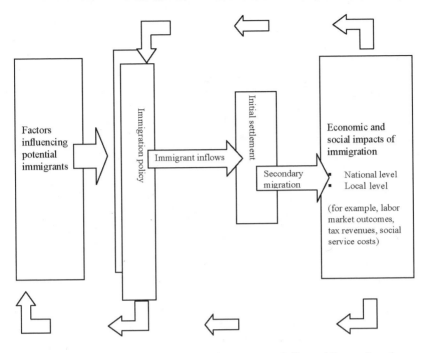

Figure 3.2: The Relationship among National Immigration Policy and Economic and Social Outcomes, Including Secondary Migration

By illuminating the process of secondary migration *and* the factors influencing it, this framework provides a basis for recognition of how this phenomenon can influence the impact of immigration policy on economic and social outcomes. It encompasses a broader set of variables than traditional economic analyses because it includes political and cultural factors and the institutional factors surrounding them. This approach suggests that it is not only the numbers of in-migrants involved in secondary migration that impact on communities but also the configuration of local institutions that shapes outcomes. This framework can provide a basis for addressing the scope of the social problems posed by rapid secondary migration and for formulation of policies to alleviate them.

In addition, there are other factors not illustrated in figure 3.3 that are important. Immigrants may make their migration decisions collectively as a family or a household rather than as individuals. Differences by social class and gender must also be examined in understanding this process. Space constraints preclude discussion of them here, but future development of this model must explore them further.

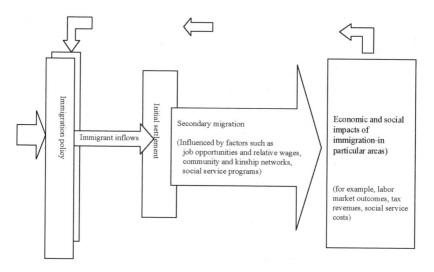

Figure 3.3: Factors Affecting Secondary Migration

Implications for Immigration Theory and Policy

The nature of the secondary migration process, the factors that influence it, and the challenges it presents for policymakers at national and local levels have not received the sustained research attention or policy deliberation over the last three decades that the process of initial immigration has received.

The secondary migration of Southeast Asian refugees *was* recognized in the late 1970s. It was analyzed for a few years and some policy change experiments were briefly implemented; nonetheless, the relevance of this phenomenon for understanding wider flows of immigrants was not pursued. It was thought that immigrant populations would settle in stable communities after initial movements—rather than participating in subsequent moves from one area to another in response to conditions deemed important to them. It is only more recently that government officials have understood the magnitude of these secondary migration flows among broader groups of the foreign-born and have become concerned with the ramifications for areas into which the immigrants move. It is timely to reexamine the earlier process and factors influencing it to see what insights it provides for the present. The secondary migrations of Southeast Asians illuminate the complexities that exist and the contradictions that can arise in designing national policies to address flows of the foreign-born that, although national in range, have very local consequences.

During the second half of the 1970s Southeast Asian refugees were placed with sponsors throughout the United States using a scatter approach that was thought to simultaneously aid in their assimilation and minimize their impact on the host communities (Mortland and Ledgerwood 1987). According to policymakers, refugees would be successfully integrated by having sponsors who could assist them in accessing services that would instruct them in English, guide them in achieving economic self-sufficiency, and help them acclimate generally (Mortland and Ledgerwood 1987).

Policymakers, resettlement organizations, and sponsors were not, however, taking into consideration the agency of the refugees themselves—what their interests and motivations were and how they were dealing with resettlement (Haines 1982). The refugees soon began secondary migrations and developed concentrations in certain key areas (Forbes 1985, 11; Kelly 1986).[9] Secondary migration was considered a failure of refugee resettlement policy in several ways. The "success" of refugees (measured in terms of assimilation and economic self-sufficiency) was thought to be impaired because sponsoring organizations could not provide services for large concentrations. In addition, the communities in which they concentrated could be adversely impacted (Mortland and Ledgerwood 1987). Further, groups such as congregations of Lutheran Social Services (a major sponsor in some areas) were personally hurt and angered by the sudden departure of many refugees and decided against further sponsorships (McInnis 1983). Control of the process of resettlement was not totally in the policymakers' hands. The refugees themselves significantly shaped outcomes.

In turn, there was some analysis of *why* the refugees migrated secondarily. Around 1980, discussion regarding why refugees clustered arose at the state and regional level among directors of the Offices of Refugee Resettlement (ORR), organizations that worked directly with the resettlement of Southeast Asian refugees in the United States. Some changes in policies were advocated. In March 1981, the Select Commission on Immigration and Refugee Policy recommended to Congress and the president of the United States that

refugee clustering be encouraged in appropriate circumstances. . . . Mechanisms should be developed, particularly within the voluntary agency network, to settle ethnic groups of similar background in the same areas. . . . The initial resettlement of Indochinese refugees followed a pattern of dispersal that has led to a great deal of secondary migration. In order to minimize the impact of refugees upon communities, refugees were placed in many different areas of the country, but, with time, many of them moved to a few areas that ended with high concentrations of refugees. Experts now believe that ethnic coalescence is not only a fact of life, but that it can be a beneficial development as long as clusters are not so large that they overburden local services. The development of refugee communities, they argue, provides support systems for newcomers, eases the shock of adjustment and transition, and through the development of ethnic associations and cultural centers, reduces the motivation for secondary migration to areas of high concentration of refugees. (Select Commission on Immigration and Refugee Policy 1981, 84–85)

By the beginning of 1982, the ORR, which specified several criteria for refugee resettlement (that refugees be placed to reduce their negative impact, that the private sector continue to be involved in their settlement, that refugees be settled in communities with conditions favorable for them to achieve economic self-sufficiency), also stipulated that this resettlement be done with awareness of the refugees' desires for cultural and familial integrity (Mortland and Ledgerwood 1987, 299; Forbes 1985, 11–12). The potential contradictions among these criteria (that is, the possible conflict between the placement of refugees in a way that reduces their adverse impact on a community while simultaneously meeting their needs to cluster) appeared to have gone unnoticed.

A demonstration project known as the Cambodian Cluster Project was developed and briefly implemented.[10] Mortland and Ledgerwood (1987) report that eight thousand Khmer refugees were resettled over a six-month period into twelve sites considered favorable.[11] According to Mr. Khoa Le, former executive director of the Indochinese Refugee Action Center in Washington, D.C., and Mr. Ha V. Vo, former deputy regional director for ORR Region IV, there are no published studies analyzing the cluster community approach.[12] Isolated comments regarding the success of this short-lived project, however, were mixed. Mortland and Ledgerwood (1987, 300–302) concluded this project was unsuccessful and that secondary migration rates of those resettled during this project were high. Yet Forbes (1985, 12–13) argued that it *did* alter Cambodian patterns of resettlement. Although policymakers had been forced to recognize immigrants' needs to be together, once again those crafting policy were trying to maintain control over the resettlement process, resulting in problematic outcomes.

Analysis of secondary migration was difficult in the following years because of data limitations. Nevertheless, as quoted in the introduction to this essay, the U.S. Census Bureau has recently refocused on the multiple effects of the secondary migration of the foreign-born and the importance of understanding it. Recognition of the existence of secondary migration, its importance, and the challenges it presents is particularly important when policymakers seek to use changes in immigration policy as a primary means to achieve particular goals (for example, different labor market outcomes). The success of such policy reformulations will be influenced substantially by the internal movement of the foreign-born in secondary migrations and the manner in which they are integrated economically and socially in the localities to which they choose to locate. Therefore, understanding the range of factors affecting such secondary migrations is necessary in assessing whether changes in national immigration policy will, in fact, result in the desired economic and social outcomes.

The Lowell case suggests that changes in national policy regarding admission into the United States alone will *not* adequately address the issues facing communities with large secondary concentrations of the foreign-born. The Lowell experience shows that the impact that immigrant flows have on local economies is strongly affected by processes outside the control of immigration policy. Secondary migration and the potentially large clusterings of the foreign-born influence how these immigrants will be absorbed into a community and the impacts they will have. These concentrations place disproportionately large economic and social pressures on local areas relative to the nation as a whole. In addition, the Lowell case suggests that there is much more involved in these migrations than simply wage differentials: the existence of an ethnic economy and society (network of religious institutions, ethnic stores, community self-help organizations) is also widely regarded as important.

The framework developed in this essay assists in moving toward a fuller understanding of how immigration policy impacts local economies (their labor markets, social service networks, small businesses, and tax revenues) and the U.S. economy in general. The lessons of the past reveal that policymakers must understand the wants and needs of those migrating secondarily and build them into their construction of policies. Policymakers do not have total control. Identifying which groups of immigrants are likely to be involved in secondary migration and the influences of their secondary migration can shed more light on the probable effects of national-level policy changes.

With an understanding of factors shaping secondary migration, more carefully integrated policies can be developed at the national and local levels to influence desired outcomes. On the one hand, subsequent revisions in national immigration policies must be based on an understanding of the potentially substantial impact of immigration and secondary migrations on particular areas. On the other hand, systematic policies that address the serious economic and social stresses that can accompany such secondary migrations at a more local level can be formulated. At present, such problems are considered on an ad hoc basis, if at all. Federal policy to compensate localities for refugee and immigrant relocation can be rethought in light of the phenomenon of secondary migration.

The recognition of the importance of secondary migration and the preliminary construction of an explanation of the factors that influenced it in Lowell in the 1980s suggest an agenda for future research. In other areas experiencing secondary migration, research teams could administer a large-scale household survey and a survey of relevant businesses and construct a community network analysis (1) to understand the secondary migration more fully; (2) to assess the labor-market impact of this secondary migration (for example, whether these workers met labor shortages, how their skills matched those of the jobs they obtained) as well as the overall impact of these immigrants on the entire local economy, including the area's social infrastructure; (3) to explore whether decision-making is done by individuals, families, or households and incorporate gender and class variables into the analysis; and (4) therefore, to contribute more specifically to the debate regarding national immigration policy. Such concrete studies could provide more information upon which to formulate an integrated set of policies to ease the immediate strains of secondary migration.

Notes

1. I use the phrase "national immigration policies" to refer to U.S. policies regarding immigrants and refugees.

2. There is also debate over whether to reduce the number of illegals by allowing larger numbers of temporary workers (Hanson et al. 2001).

3. The six gateway states—California, New York, Texas, Florida, Illinois, and New Jersey—had 70.4 percent of the foreign-born population in 2000. Almost one-half of all foreign-born lived in five metropolitan areas in 2000 (Los Angeles, New York, San Francisco, Miami, and Chicago) (U.S. Census Bureau 2001).

4. The term *secondary migration* will be used to refer to any migrations within the recipient country, subsequent to the initial in-migration to the country. Therefore, it may in fact be secondary, tertiary, and so on.

5. The Southeast Asians were refugees, one of the subclassifications of "immigrant." A refugee is any person fleeing his or her country "because of persecution or a well-founded fear of persecution on account of race, religion, nationality, membership in a particular social group, or political opinion" (Refugee Act of 1980, quoted in Higgins and Ross 1986, 14). Although they were refugees, not immigrants, analysis of their secondary migration, the reasons for it, and the policy initiatives to shape it sheds light on the phenomenon as it occurs in the larger immigrant populations.

6. These estimates of total numbers of Southeast Asians furnished by social service providers differ from the official census numbers. Substantial undercounting occurred because of the refugees' great fears of the government and language barriers.

7. The unemployment rate in Lowell in the second quarter of 1988 was 3.1 percent, rising to 4.9 percent by the third quarter of 1989.

8. Personnel (in all applicable cases, the director) were interviewed at the following community institutions: the Cambodian Mutual Assistance Association, the International Institute, the Affirmative Action Office of Lowell City Hall, the Department of Employment Security, the Coalition for a Better Acre (which focuses on housing and community land issues), and the Gateway Cities Program.

9. See Forbes (1985), pp. 7–11, for an overview of the studies of Southeast Asian secondary migration.

10. Another short-lived project (Favorable Alternate Sites Project, or FAST, which settled fewer than six hundred refugees in four cities in Arizona and North Carolina) was set up by the U.S. government to address the problems of the Cambodian Cluster Project; it too, however, experienced high secondary migration rates (Mortland and Ledgerwood 1987, 301–2).

11. According to Smith-Hefner (1994), one of these was Boston. The identities of the others were not specified and the source she cited cannot be located.

12. Conversation between Mr. Khoa Le, former executive director of IRAC in Washington, D.C. (Indochinese Refugee Action Center) and Mr. Ha V. Vo, former deputy regional director for ORR Region IV, on November 15, 2006.

References

Borjas, George J. 2001. *Heaven's Door: Immigration Policy and the American Economy.* Princeton, NJ: Princeton University Press.
Briggs, Vernon M., Jr., and Stephen Moore, eds. 1994. *Still an Open Door? U.S. Immigration Policy and the American Economy.* Washington, DC: American University Press.
DeSipio, Louis, and Rodolfo O. de la Garza. 1998. *Making Americans, Remaking America: Immigration and Immigrant Policy.* Boulder, CO: Westview.
Forbes, Susan S. 1985. Residency Patterns and Secondary Migration of Refugees. *Migration News* 1 (January): 3–18.
Haines, David W. 1982. Southeast Asian Refugees in the United States: The Interaction of Kinship and Public Policy. *Anthropological Quarterly* 55, no. 3, 170–81.
Hanson, Gordon H., Kenneth F. Scheve, Matthew J. Slaughter, and Antonio Spilimbergo. 2001. *Immigration and the U.S. Economy: Labor-Market Impacts, Illegal Entry, and Policy Choices.* Document prepared for the Third European Conference of the Fondazione Rodolfo Debenedetti (Immigration Policy and the Welfare State), Trieste, Italy.
Higgins, James, and Joan Ross. 1986. *Southeast Asians: A New Beginning in Lowell.* Lowell, MA: Mill Town Graphics.
Kelly, Gail P. 1986. Coping with America: Refugees from Vietnam, Cambodia, and Laos in the 1970s and 1980s. *ANNALS of the American Academy of Political and Social Science* 487: 138–49.
McInnis, Kathleen M. 1983. The Resettlement Approach. *Migration Today* 11, nos. 2–3: 21–25.
Mortland, Carol A., and Judy Ledgerwood. 1987. Secondary Migration among Southeast Asian Refugees in the United States. *Urban Anthropology* 16, nos. 3–4: 291–326.
Pho, Hai B. 1986. Introduction to *Southeast Asians: A New Beginning in Lowell.* By James Higgins and Joan Ross. Lowell, MA: Mill Town Graphics.
Refugee Act of 1980, Pub. L. No. 96–212. U.S. Department of Health and Human Services. Retrieved on March 24, 2007 from http://www.acf.hhs.gov /programs/orr/geninfo/index.htm.
Reid, Alexander. 2006. Leading Lowell's Asian Boom; Cambodian Entrepreneurs Finding Success, Trying New Ventures in the City. *Boston Globe*, September 3.
Select Commission on Immigration and Refugee Policy. 1981. *The Final Report and Recommendations of the Select Commission on Immigration and Refugee*

Policy to the Congress and the President of the United States—March 1, 1981, sec. V.C.2.

Shrestha, Nanda R. 1987. Institutional Policies and Migration Behavior: A Selective Review. *World Development* 15, 329–45.

Smith-Hefner, Nancy J. 1994. Ethnicity and the Force of Faith: Christian Conversion among Khmer Refugees. *Anthropological Quarterly* 67, no. 1: 24–37.

Todaro, Michael P., and Stephen C. Smith. 2006. *Economic Development.* 9th ed. Boston, MA: Pearson.

U.S. Census Bureau. 2001. Profile of the Foreign-born Population in the United States: 2000. Available at http://www.census.gov/prod/2002pubs/p.23–206 .pdf.

———. 2003. *Migration of Natives and the Foreign Born: 1995 to 2000.* Census 2000 Special Reports. Issued August 2003. Available at http://www.census.gov/prod/2003pubs/censr-11.pdf.

U.S. Department of Labor. History of Federal Minimum Wage Rates Under the Fair Labor Standards Act, 1938—1996. Available at http://www.dol.gov/esa/minwage/chart.htm.

Newly-arrived Cambodian Refugees at Logan Airport in Boston, 1985. © *James Higgins, Higgins & Ross*

Children at Moore Street School, 1986. © *James Higgins, Higgins & Ross*

Artist depicts escape by boat from Vietnam. The raised fists symbolize the refugee's will to survive. © *James Higgins, Higgins & Ross*

Lao family at home. © *James Higgins, Higgins & Ross*

Work in Banking. © *James Higgins,*
Higgins & Ross

Graduation! © *James*
Higgins, Higgins & Ross

Fashion Show. © *James Higgins,*
Higgins & Ross

Preparing food dishes for
ancestors on Vietnamese
New Year. © *James Higgins,*
Higgins & Ross

First wedding of an American man and Cambodian woman in Lowell. © *James Higgins, Higgins & Ross*

Angkor Dance Troupe. © *James Higgins, Higgins & Ross*

Water Festival Race 2006. © *Rady Mom*

Celebrating Cambodian New Year. © *Rady Mom*

Monks at Water Festival program. © *Rady Mom*

Vibrant Teens! © *James Higgins, Higgins & Ross*

Part II

CULTURAL ADAPTATION AND TRANSNATIONALISM

Reflections on the Concept of Social Capital

A paradox pervades discussions of the impact of immigrants and refugees on communities. Many commentators reporting on struggling communities highlight the daunting obstacles faced by these cities because of an influx of immigrants and refugees who bring with them a host of needs. Yet others point to the importance of immigrants and refugees in bringing vibrancy to otherwise stagnant local economies. These are not idle differences. They shape whether community residents see immigrants and refugees as in urgent need of social services or as bringing resources likely to improve a city's prospects. These differences in perspective also tap into many current discussions, such as what constitutes viable social capital and how we can best build and maintain a civil society. At their least refined, these differences reflect whether refugees and immigrants are seen as a problem or a promise.

Still another paradox emerges in discussions of immigrant and refugee communities within the United States. On one side, traditional analysis of these communities examine why migrants leave their native countries and how they integrate into their new host country. More recent research, however, is analyzing the new phenomenon of the ongoing transnational relationships of immigrant and refugee communities between their country of origin and their new home. The existence of this new phenomenon has generated considerable debate and controversy within the study of immigration.

Too often the above positions are argued in the abstract. Our experiences at the University of Massachusetts Lowell's (UML) Center for Family, Work, and Community (CFWC) have shown the need to become immersed in concrete activities aimed at community building and economic development if one is going to address these issues with care. Over the last few years we have engaged in many community development and social capital ventures with newcomers. These initiatives have included leadership training, development of new business opportunities linked to environmental activities, development of communication tools, and support for the development of business networks and mutual assistance associations. All of these initiatives reflect in-depth partnerships with refugee and immigrant leaders. These initiatives have helped us explore three questions: (1) What innovative infrastructure developments in the newcomer community have taken place in the Merrimack Valley? (2) What strengths of the newcomer community typically go unrecognized by traditional approaches to community economic development? (3) What clashes in models of community economic development emerge between immigrants and planners engaging in traditional planning practices?

In this essay we point to the need to focus on the practices of community economic development and social capital development that immigrant and refugee groups implicitly use in building a presence in the region. Without a full understanding of these complex views, efforts by university partners and others are likely to be unsuccessful; they will not be attuned to the complex perspectives on community development that drive efforts in newcomer groups to enhance the community.

To set the stage for our discussions of the local scene, in the next section we consider the social capital analysis that is increasingly being used to understand what is "missing" in poor communities and to explain how communities can strengthen their economic base by focusing on social capital formation. This body of work provides an important framework from which to think about communities that are home to growing numbers of immigrants. Social capital analysis is of interest in part because it brings to the forefront questions about certain skills and approaches that immigrants may bring to their communities, but also because the implications of this analysis for understanding the impact of newcomers remains contested.

Social Capital and Community Economic Development

Increasingly the notion of strengthening a community's economic base is being framed in terms of the language of social capital. Community development efforts have increasingly adopted the language of social capital as a way to understand what communities must do to prosper (Briggs 1997; Callahan 1996; Chang 1997; Fettig 1995; Flora and Flora 1993; Gardner 1996; Irwin 1998; Kawachi, Kennedy, and Lochner 1997; Kingsley, McNeely, and Gibson 1998; Laws 1997; Miller 1997; Messer 1998). Although disagreements remain about the exact nature of social capital, it is generally described as civic engagement, as formal and informal civic structures such as schools, neighborhood associations, and churches. These structures are seen as enhancing a community's ability to compete for jobs and residents (Irwin 1998). The links to business and economic development are seen as relatively straightforward. As Irwin (1998) notes: "Small, locally owned establishments reinforce civic engagement because the owners are heavily invested in the community. Owners and managers of small production firms participate in local community institutions in order to maintain networks of local business contacts and supporters. Community involvement means that these small businesses may be less likely to pull out of the community in an economic downturn, and more likely to support and lead local nonprofit institutions" (17).

This construct of social capital has become important within community development discussions. Okagaki (1998) focuses on community development as an antipoverty strategy, which in turn is seen as a comprehensive opportunity-oriented approach; he argues that true economic opportunity depends on both an internal process of individual development and the external support provided by *social capital*. Flora and Flora (1993) emphasize openness, ease of entry, optimal utilization of available resources, and strong networking as key to community development. Strong networking is often touted as an important component of social capital.

Some researchers and development specialists focus on whether a particular community has social capital, whereas other analysts concern themselves with the question of whether it is possible to create and increase social capital through appropriate interventions. Gardner (1996), for example, charts the progress of a region that has attempted to revitalize itself by investing in social capital and taking active steps to reestablish a healthy and growing civic society. At the start of a community-driven intervention, the area was high in social instability and low on job creation. Rather than working on these problems directly, the community worked indirectly through the development of social capital. Community leaders noted: "We needed to develop social capital, putting a new emphasis on the 'we' relative to the spirit of community. If we were to be competitive, we needed to concern and involve as many citizens as possible in the solution of common problems" (61).

With regard to social capital creation, Kingsley, McNeely, and Gibson (1998) talk about community building focused on creating social capital. They differentiate community building from the neighborhood-based, poverty alleviation programs that have been predominant over the past half-century. Kingsley et al. notes that the primary aim of building social capital is not simply giving "more money, services, or other material benefits to the poor" (3). Instead, "the central theme is to obliterate feelings of dependency and to replace them with attitudes of self-reliance, self-confidence, and responsibility" (3). "[T]hese are not ideas being imposed from the outside—they are what the leaders of distressed neighborhoods across the nation themselves are saying that they want to see accomplished" (4).

The extent to which a social capital analysis has value in explaining community economic development in immigrant and refugee communities remains a point of contention. Many see problems in taking the ideas of social capital and applying these concepts to diverse immigrant neighborhoods. For example, Chang (1997) points out that focusing on dominant Anglo-European norms can smother the norms and practices of minority groups and with them the development of social capital within that group. The difficulties of language loss are also pointed out by Chang. Elders have difficulty offering support and norm development if they speak a language that children in the family are not learning.

Laws (1997) focuses on immigrants who have relocated as a result of changing conditions associated with globalization: "At the heart of this linkage is an economic restructuring across societies and in the U.S. that has potent social consequences for immigrant populations. Such people, induced to migrate by changing economic circumstances, find growing ghettoization, isolation, and cultural antipathies in their new settings. In this new globality, immigrant populations are commonly fingered as the other, the invading and ominous people threatening time-tested social norms and economic principles" (89).

Yet many strengths of the newcomer communities—strengths that bear considerable resemblance to operational definitions of social capital—typically go unrecognized by local business and economic development professionals. The strong family and social bonds that provide the ability to generate financial capital within ethnic communities go unrecognized in many cases. As Portes and Zhou (1992) have described, immigrants often pool their saving into an informal "rotating credit association" that is used as a source of financing for entrepreneurial members of newcomer communities. According to Portes and Zhou, most immigrants feel more comfortable with informal verbal agreements than with going through the process of obtaining a time-consuming and selective bank loan. They contend that the former informal approach functions well, even without a legally enforceable agreement, because members of these newcomer communities would risk ostracism if they failed to follow through on their verbal commitments. In addition to the fear of expulsion from one's safe community, immigrants usually place a high value in honoring commitments to their close family and social networks. The strength that this "social compact" brings to a local economy usually goes unnoticed by a society where businesses on a regular basis file for bankruptcy in order to avoid the obligation to repay debt.

These brief examples suggest the need to know more about the infrastructure development in immigrant communities—often highly impoverished communities—that is perhaps not quite what would be expected.

These developments seem to fit under social capital, but they also appear to involve something "more," something not fully captured by standard social capital analyses and that calls for new analyses such as of transnationalism. In the next section we describe some of the infrastructure developments that have emerged in Lowell's large Southeast Asian community and that raise intriguing questions about how local communities are building a viable economic base by creating much more than just businesses (that is, deep social networks and community links).

Innovative Infrastructure Developments in a Newcomer Community

A number of infrastructure developments have emerged within the Southeast Asian community in Lowell over the last decade or so. Organizations and associations have proliferated: the Asian American Business Association, the Cambodian Mutual Assistance Association (CMAA), the Cambodian American League of Lowell, the Cambodian Women's Organization, and the Lao Family Mutual Association. Programs such as UML's CIRCLE (Center for Immigrant and Refugee Community Leadership and Empowerment) program have also emerged.

These organizations, associations, and projects focus in part on social services but many also attempt to serve as engines of economic growth. CMAA, for example, has provided training programs to increase the workforce skills among refugees and immigrants, has worked to become a microincubator for start-up immigrant businesses, and, through its acquisition of a former mill, has attempted to become a site for growth and revitalization in a depressed neighborhood of Lowell.

Other "engines" of immigrant economic development have emerged as well, and their diversity speaks to the diverse skills and resources immigrants bring to the region. The New Farmers, New Beginnings program funded by the Farm Services Administration and jointly sponsored by Community Teamwork, Inc., and Tufts University has involved American farmers leasing land to Cambodian farmers and then mentoring these farmers so that they can employ their traditional farming skills to develop viable businesses raising Asian crops that families cannot currently buy in the United States or can only buy at great expense. Associated with this work are attempts to start an Asian Farmers' Market in Lowell that would draw Cambodian and other Southeast Asian families as consumers. Others have focused on urban aquaculture and the possibilities of developing a viable industry that would blend the traditional skills people bring from

Cambodia with new technologies based on new environmental models. To explore this possibility, the CMAA and UML received funding from the Department of Food and Agriculture to develop a demonstration program and a business plan. As yet another example of bringing together recent environmental innovations with traditional practices, UML's CFWC and Center for Sustainable Production worked with local immigrant restaurants to investigate nutrient cycling and the possibility of linking local businesses to the farmers through composting.

Another innovative way that the immigrant and refugee communities have pushed economic development is through celebrations. The Southeast Asian Water Festival directly and indirectly promotes economic development in the immigrant community; in each case, the underlying themes of small business and economic development animate these events. The festival, Celebrating Diverse Traditions, further exemplifies this approach. This event brought together immigrant leaders with officials from the Executive Office of Environmental Affairs to address, in part, issues of economic development. The focus of Celebrating Diverse Traditions was placed on identifying the best economic development practices from the home countries of Lowell's newcomers; these practices could then be used to transform Lowell into an economically vibrant city that does not neglect environmental safety. Many examples emerged in the focus groups leading up to the festival, including one by a Cambodian community leader, who presented a plan for an Asian cultural center that would be housed in a building designed to integrate East and West and that would draw together established businesses, start-up businesses, and cultural and museum space to capture the integration of Cambodian and American approaches to transforming Lowell.

By no means has the creation of traditional businesses been neglected. A university-funded study of minority businesses in Lowell pointed to the emergence of many new immigrant businesses; this survey documented their needs and infrastructure concerns. The impact of this strength on small business development can be seen in many areas. If one looks at the downtown and neighborhoods of Lowell, one can see the number of newcomer businesses that are now in operation. In many respects, Lowell's storefronts would be ghost towns were it not for the immigrant entrepreneur.

Yet other examples of economic development in immigrant and refugee communities emphasize alternative ways immigrants in the area access capital. Money sharing and the development of informal loan funds (particularly with the Southeast Asian community in Lowell) has propelled considerable small business development. In addition, this small business development has forged strong commercial links with suppliers from native countries. As a result, potential export links with native countries could provide additional economic development opportunities.

These businesses apparently benefit from the many existing social links. One of the reflections of these social links is the high *multiplier effect* in immigrant communities such as Lowell. The multiplier effect quantifies the degree to which each dollar continues to circulate, thus creating a "multiplied effect" (Harrison 1974). Studies indicate that within newcomer communities, the multiplier impact is typically greater—and sometimes much greater—than in the larger community. In a study in Miami, for example, it was determined that in the Cuban refugee community the additional income generated by the multiplier effect was 4.5 times higher than in the nonimmigrant community (Wilson and Martin 1982). Why might this be the case? Immigrant communities tend to buy products and services within their social networks in part as a result of language and cultural familiarity and comfort. There is also recognition within the community of the importance of supporting newcomer businesses. This has been termed "bounded solidarity" and increases the opportunity of success of these ethnic enterprises; newcomers experience heightened cultural identity and regularly prefer services and products associated with their native country (Portes and Zhou 1992). In addition, these newcomer businesses often emphasize "high value added retailing" through offering such benefits as convenient hours, informal credit, fluency in native languages, and check-cashing services (Bendick and Egan 1991).

Factors that increase the multiplier effect take on particular importance because much in the region actually works against the recirculation of resources. As a community close to New Hampshire's border and its many commercial malls, Lowell has had to struggle to avoid the fate of most downtown commercial districts, which have been decimated over the last thirty years because of competition from large commercial malls. For downtown districts in border communities, the impact has been more devastating; for example, consumers have a larger incentive to shop in New Hampshire in order to avoid sales tax. The importance of newcomers' propensity to purchase services and products from local immigrant businesses has likely enhanced this multiplier effect within Lowell.

Any study of how local immigrants and refugees impact the host communities must also consider how the unique relationships between immigrant communities in the United States and their country of origin influence local communities. Understanding the nature of the above relationships has become more important. One phenomenon, *transnationalism,* is increasingly the focus of efforts to understand the dynamics between immigrants in their host country and their relationships with their home country. Transnationalism is the term used to describe the process by which immigrants forge and sustain multistranded social relations that link together their societies of origin and settlement (Basch, Schiller, and Blanc-Szanton 1994, 6). This is a process by which "transmigrants, through their daily activities, forge and sustain multi-stranded social, economic, and political relationships that link together their societies of origin and settlement, and through which they create transnational social fields that cross national borders" (Basch et al. 1994, p. 6). Prior to the study of transnationalism, researchers focused their attention on why immigrants leave their country of origin and how they subsequently adapt to their new host country (Portes, Haller, and Guarnizo 2002). Emphasis is now being placed on understanding the continuing relationship between immigrants and their country of birthplace and how this changing interplay evolves into complex political, economic, and social interaction.

From the economic perspective, researchers have suggested that the success of transnational immigrant entrepreneurs is dependant on their ability to forge social networks between the country from which they came and the country in which they settled (Guarnizo 1992; Zhou and Bankston 1994). However, whether transnationalism is commonplace or whether transnational entrepreneurs are limited to certain groups or types of individuals remains to be seen. Transnational entrepreneurs may be "a distinct class of immigrants who engage in these activities on a regular basis and who rely on them as their primary livelihood" (Portes, Haller, and Guarnizo 2002, 284). Some have concluded that transnational entrepreneurs represent only a small portion of immigrant communities (Portes, Haller, and Guarnizo 2002). Despite their small numbers, these transnational business owners may represent a significant portion of all immigrant entrepreneurs. Furthermore, recent research indicates that these transnational entrepreneurs are often part of the upper class of their communities both in terms of educational and income levels. They are also more likely to be U.S. citizens and to have resided here longer than other immigrants. At the same time, though, these transnational entrepreneurs are generally drawn from first-generation immigrants (Portes 2001). Within the Cambodian community, it appears that the level of transnational business activity and the demographics of those business owners who engage in transnational practices appear to be consistent with studies of other immigrant groups. The numbers of Cambodian entrepreneurs involved in transnational business activities in Lowell represent approximately 20 to 30 percent of the business community and are concentrated in clothing, entertainment (CDs, videos, and DVDs), and travel. In addition, these business owners have resided here many years, are mostly U.S. citizens, and have above-average income and educational levels within the Cambodian community. While it is clear that transnational economic activities usually provide important financial support to the country of origin, these same immigrants also share their economic resources, time, and loyalty with their host country (R. Robinson 2004).

Transnational Political Activity and its Impact on Community Development

Above we focused on *economic* transnationalism; here we focus on *political* transnationalism. Political transnationalism differs from economic transnationalism in focus; nonetheless, it may also have an important impact on community development. Existing literature indicates that only a minority of immigrants (perhaps on the order of one in five) are regularly involved in political transnational action (Ostergaard-Nielsen 2003; Portes 2001). Despite their small numbers, these individuals often play important leadership roles in immigrant communities. The types of transnational political activities vary. One framework for understanding transnational political action, for example, divides political practice into two levels: "narrow" activities such as membership in a political party or civic association in the homeland; and "broad" activities such as involvement in meetings and events related to homeland politics (Ostergaard-Nielsen 2003). Immigrants can become engaged in transnational politics in a variety of ways, but in the local Southeast Asian community they generally involve either supporting or opposing homeland political parties and/or governments. In Lowell, it appears that the number of Southeast Asians involved in "narrow" activities is low, probably less than 10 percent.

The type and level of transnational political activities can affect local immigrant communities. For example, the City of Lowell, Massachusetts, is home to the second-largest Cambodian population in the United States; as a result, all three major political parties from Cambodia have active party apparatuses within the Lowell community. The party in power, the Cambodian People's Party (CPP) is headed by Prime Minister Hun Sen. The second-largest political group—the Royal Party—is now aligned with the CPP and has been an on-and-off coalition partner with the CPP. The Sam Rainsy Party is currently the opposition party. Although only a minority of Cambodian immigrants in Lowell is active in any of the three parties, these party loyalties continue to loom large and not infrequently have led to conflict that has negatively impacted community development within Lowell. These party activists hold influence within the community and their distrust of each other often prevents collaboration on important community initiatives. As this example suggests, political conflict from the homeland can polarize and retard community development efforts among immigrant communities within host communities. The ability of Lowell's Cambodian Mutual Assistance Association (CMAA) to work in the community was compromised by CMAA collaboration with the Cambodian government on some high-profile community events: ultimately, perceived transnationalism may have been a contributing factor in the ouster of the CMAA executive director. In 2001, the CMAA hosted a reception within the Cambodian community with the ambassador to the United States from the government of Hun Sen as the main guest. In addition, the CMAA accepted two traditional racing boats from the Cambodian government for the Southeast Asian Water Festival (at the time, the CMAA was the main organizer) and publicly praised Hun Sen for these gifts. At the time, both the board president and executive director were perceived by some members in the community as controlled by the Cambodian Peoples Party and the country's prime minister. Consequently, members of the community refused to support efforts and programs of the CMAA seen as reflecting the CPP influence. Fortunately, leaders in the various parties in Lowell have come to recognize that past conflicts have created negative consequences for the local Cambodian community. Consequently, these leaders have decided not to allow political disagreements in the homeland to create divisions detrimental to the local Cambodian community.

Issues of transnationalism have also made themselves felt within Lowell's Laotian community. Here the divisive issue concerned which of two Laotian flags would be seen as legitimate and therefore should be supported by the community. Some members of Lowell's Laotian community support the recognition of the current Laos flag, the same flag that has received official recognition from the United States and the United Nations. A minority of the community supports the flag of the royal government that was supported by the United States during the 1970s prior to the Pathet Lao communist government coming to power. Obviously, intertwined with this issue is the support or opposition to the existing Lao government. As in most SEA communities, Laotians arrived in the United States in the late 1970s and early 1980s as political refugees of and opponents to the Pathet Lao communist government. Because at the time all Lao refugees arrived in opposition to this communist government, there was political unity within the community and this unity was conducive to building cohesiveness and community development. Within the last decade, things have changed. The current Laotian government, although still maintaining a one-party state, has begun to open the economy and has allowed political refugees who fled the communist takeover to return home and visit families. These changing circumstances are now creating a rift within Lowell's Lao community. The majority accepted this development as a positive change and they have begun to visit family and friends as well as accept the current government. A vocal minority, on the other hand, continues to hold the view that the flag of the former royal government remains the only authentic flag and they continue to oppose the existing regime. As a result, divisions have emerged within the Lao refugee community that are now preventing collaborating to address local needs and issues within Lowell.

Clashes in Models of Community Economic Development Emerge between Immigrants and Nonimmigrants.

What is intriguing in the infrastructure development just described is how embedded these activities appear to be. To some degree this should come as no surprise: such embeddedness is consistent with social capital ideas and the practices they seemingly promote. Despite their embedddedness, however, these practices are at odds with some of the ongoing practices in the "mainstream" economic development infrastructure in Lowell; they thus encounter unexpected contradictions when the assumption is made that introducing a communal, social capital approach would be straight-forward. This section will illustrate in some detail the contradictions and complications as seen in the development of the Asian American Business Association (AABA) and other infrastructures intended as alternatives to a chamber of commerce and other mainstream models.

Consider the traditional chamber model. Within such a model, a diversified group of businesses and corporations join a local chamber and pursue common interests. Because of the long history and acceptance of the concept of chambers of commerce in the United States, nonimmigrant individuals who choose to join understand why it is in their interest to join and what their involvement is likely to gain. For example, in Lowell the chamber focuses on professional development, networking, information exchanging, and advocacy on large issues (for example, the expansion of a local highway, creating a more favorable business climate, support for large economic develop project).

The AABA was organized originally because at the time the local chamber had demonstrated little interest in reaching out to Asian businesses and addressing their particular needs. As a result, immigrant business owners had not joined the chamber in any sizable numbers. The need for an association of Asian business owners was clear; most were struggling to succeed and grow. Many newcomer business owners had experience in business in their native country, but they lacked the understanding of what was necessary to succeed here. For example, a few entrepreneurs purchased buildings in Lowell with the intent to relocate and expand their businesses. Those decisions, however, were made without familiarity with building codes and zoning issues. Subsequently, these business owners unknowingly made decisions that created major problems for the creation and expansion of the planned businesses. In addition, many business owners lacked an understanding of the need for record-keeping and tax filing in accord with U.S. laws.[1]

The traditional chamber model differs significantly from models that are likely to be familiar to the Southeast Asian newcomer community. Those outside the Cambodian business community often regard the Cambodian business community as very communal. Thus people often assume that the process of organizing an Asian business association along communal lines could be done with ease. In reality, the challenges are significant. Many business owners resisted efforts to join together. A number of reasons for this resistance have become apparent over time: a lack of understanding and experience with a business association; a lack of vision of how joining and participating in an association would be in their interests; suspicions and fears of exchanging information with competitors; and experience of Khmer Rouge collectivism and its impact on their willingness to participate in collective activities in the United States.

The founders of the AABA wanted to focus on educating and advocating for the Asian businesses. This approach was consistent with the concept that economic opportunity develops through a process of learning, empowerment, and organizational building (such as the creation of networks and informal relationships) (Okagaki 1998). Accordingly, the first public session organized by the AABA included a certified public accountant and the building commissioner of Lowell to help educate business owners about recordkeeping and tax filing issues, local building codes, and zoning requirements. The AABA also saw as one of their goals assisting Asian businesses to expand their customer base beyond the Southeast Asian community. An example of this took place when the AABA president invited the executive from a local hospital to a network session. At this AABA event, a board member who owns a wholesale business that supplies import products to Southeast Asian markets provided a variety of complimentary fruit drinks. During a conversation between this wholesaler and the hospital executives, it was suggested that the hospital should consider selling these drinks in their cafeteria because of the large Cambodian community that frequents the hospital. As a result, the Asian wholesaler is now a supplier to the hospital cafeteria. The intention of the AABA was to assist more Asian business owners to secure contracts to provide services and products to both private and public sector institutions. In this role, the AABA planned to be an advocate for Asian businesses, creating opportunity for their inclusion as vendors to major businesses and governmental entities.

Despite these laudable goals of the AABA, it struggled for many reasons. One important barrier was the lack of start-up capital for the organization. A second barrier was the surprisingly strong resistance among Asian business owners to joining a communal organization. In addition, perceptions that the first executive director was inexperienced also became a barrier. The first executive director and president were both under thirty years of age; although successful at developing relationships with local government and nonminority business leaders, they failed to satisfy many board members and Asian business owners. The president and executive director believed that developing relationships outside the community was primary, whereas others on the board and within the Asian community saw the development of relationships within the community as key. The other leaders in the AABA became disillusioned by a lack of organizing and organizational development within the Asian business community.

After the attempt to organize the AABA, the leadership at the local chamber of commerce changed. Under the new leadership, the local chamber made a concerted effort to reach out to Asian and other immigrant business owners. This outreach initiative organized focus groups and meetings in local Asian restaurants to (1) begin a dialogue; (2) determine what were the needs and issues of Asian businesses; (3) explain how the chamber might be of assistance in their business development; and (4) invite Asian entrepreneurs to become members and join the board of directors. Interestingly, the chamber's efforts were to no avail: Asian business owners again failed to become members or to fill the board vacancies reserved for them. This unsuccessful attempt to attract Asian entrepreneurs probably failed for the same reasons as did the attempt of the Asian American Business Association. In addition, it appears that many Asian business owners still see the chamber as a nonimmigrant organization. In particular, the main activities of the chamber—such as organizing business mixers and networking sessions—are probably not considered useful business opportunities by Asian entrepreneurs.

Another reason that many felt a need for an Asian American Business Association at the time was that most existing business development programs failed to connect and assist the newcomer community; they expected the Asian business community to fit into and feel comfortable with a traditional approach. Many Asian business owners complained that business loan programs within the city failed to help them. They considered the process to be bureaucratic, confusing, inflexible, and time-consuming. A recent experience of the Lowell Small Business Assistance Center with its Technical Assistance Program (TAP) is instructive of this disconnect between traditional business development programs and the Asian business community. TAP, funded by the City of Lowell, required all businesses receiving technical assistance to provide copies of their tax returns.[2] Many Asian entrepreneurs initially expressed an interest in receiving technical assistance until they were informed that copies of tax returns were needed to receive services under this program. There appears to be a cultural gap that affects this disconnect.

A further explanation was offered at a meeting of the Lowell Small Business Assistance Center, when a member of the AABA board tried to explain why most Asian business owners would not feel comfortable entering the Small Business Assistance Center or using its services. He tried to explain the underlying cultural issues. Because the center was located in a newly renovated building in the downtown area on the third floor, it would intimidate the community. This board member went on to explain that the difference between an Asian market and Market Basket Supermarket is that the latter supermarket is bright, new, well organized, and clean in appearance. The Asian market was very different in appearance and the Cambodian business community would only feel comfortable in an environment that appeared Asian.

Many governmental and traditional business loan programs also clash with the realities of the newcomer community. To evaluate the viability of newcomer businesses, traditional finance programs typically use certain ratios and criteria that actually undervalue the strengths of these enterprises. Thus many newcomer businesses cannot qualify for traditional financing. Michael Swack, the dean of the School of Community Economic Development at Southern New Hampshire University recalled an instance when a very successful and profitable restaurant run by an immigrant family was rejected for a loan to expand their business. Afterward, Michael Swack approached the bank to understand why this profitable restaurant had been denied financing. The banker explained that the ratio of food costs to gross sales was much higher than typically found in the restaurant industry. Consequently, Swack approached the restaurant owner about this issue. The owner explained that he had a large family that basically lived at and was fed at the restaurant. In addition, he described how he often helped local families in need by feeding them for free in his restaurant. It was obvious that these factors would not be seen in a traditional restaurant and contributed to his food costs within the business. Swack and the restaurant owner later met with the bank and educated the loan officer about these untraditional considerations. As a result, the bank eventually approved the loan. The above examples are indicative of how traditional approaches to business and economic development can clash with the realities of what is needed for successful development in newcomer communities.

Recently, within the Asian business community some practices have begun to change. The method of raising business capital among family and friends informally is a little less common: a few instances of individuals who left the area without paying back business loans have occurred. In addition, younger immigrant entrepreneurs are adopting conventional business practices by utilizing more traditional financing avenues and options. In addition, younger Southeast Asian business owners are beginning to expand into nonimmigrant markets. For example, an Asian-owned real estate firm has an office in Lowell staffed by Asian salespersons that caters to the immigrants and another office in a nearby town staffed by nonimmigrant sales reps that serve the nonimmigrant market. Furthermore, some loan programs are now more flexible and younger immigrant entrepreneurs have become more accepting of traditional lending institutions. Moreover, the number of Asian entrepreneurs receiving assistance from the Lowell Small Business Assistance Center has increased to approximately 16 percent.

Clashes In Developmental Approaches

To understand how local governmental policies highlight these clashes, it is useful to look at the two predominant basic models of local economic development (Blakely and Bradshaw 2002; C.J. Robinson 1989). The *corporate center approach* places the emphasis on real estate development, and attracting commercial and industrial properties. The *alternative approach* focuses on economic development activities and goals in economically disadvantaged communities. Both of these approaches are entrepreneurial and involve some form of partnerships with the private sector.

Under the corporate center approach, the private sector predominates; the public sector role is largely to create an economic climate conducive to private investment (usually outside investment). The local planning process typically has the objective of general economic growth and tax expansion and is often inaccessible to immigrants, refugees, and other minority and low-income groups. Public sector resources are usually focused on serving the needs of private industries. Local government commonly spends a great deal of effort in attracting outside investors and companies. Generally, local officials will work to attract what are perceived to be high-growth sectors, such as tourism, high-end services, and high technology. The public sector will target companies who are considering moving headquarters or branch operations into the city. And local government will concentrate development in the downtown area, particularly on larger real estate development projects. Most job creation activities will focus on highly skilled and white-collar workers. A more recent variation of this approach is the conversion of unused downtown commercial and industrial space to high-end condos and apartments to attract a higher-income residential sector that will require a restaurant and service sector for their needs and desires.

Under the alternative approach, the public sector attempts to guide and influence those private sector investment decisions that will benefit the broad community. In particular, public sector planning objectives usually are accessible to and benefit low-income and newer immigrant and refugee groups. Local government will provide resources conditionally to the private sector to ensure support of desired economic development options. These public sector interventions will usually benefit low-income and ethnic minorities directly (for example, ESL programs, retraining of displaced workers, transportation, and child care). In addition, city officials will target those sectors that meet important local economic needs. The public sector will target the development and expansion of locally owned businesses, placing less emphasis on attracting outside establishments. Locations of development projects are usually decentralized: the focus is on a broader array of local labor needs, particularly on blue-collar, unskilled, and underemployed workers.

In many ways the latter model—the focus of which is the development and expansion of local businesses—is more consistent with the approach emerging in the immigrant communities. Yet the city of Lowell has pursued a "Destination City" strategy that falls to a large degree under the corporate center approach (but does involve a few aspects of the alternative approach). The city has invested considerable resources in large projects within the downtown area that they hope will attract tourists and local residents; two such projects are the Tsongas Arena and the LeLacheur Park. They have focused on attracting outside developers, businesses, restaurants, and specialty shops as part of this strategy. Indeed, the City of Lowell has in recent years pursued a strategy to attract nonimmigrant artists to the downtown area. Policymakers believe that a visible artist community in the downtown will make their "Destination City" strategy more successful by attracting more tourists. While a serious shortage of affordable housing exists within the newcomer community, the city is investing considerable resources to build artist housing.

By pursuing a more corporate center approach, the City of Lowell has overlooked how newcomer communities contribute to local economies. Newcomer communities bring assets, for example, that could support tourism or "Destination City" strategies, yet many of these assets have not been fully incorporated into the economic development strategies employed by local communities. For example, the successful marketing of newcomer restaurants and specialty shops has the potential to pump considerable dollars into a local economy. Many large cities have demonstrated the value of this approach, having successfully marketed ethnic neighborhoods such as "Chinatown" and "Little Italy," as important pillars of local tourism campaigns. In addition, the marketing of newcomer culture can generate sizable income. The presentation of cultural festivals, ethnic artistic performances, and arts and crafts exhibitions have also generated considerable revenue on the local level.

The City of Lowell has not entirely neglected policies that fit more firmly within the alternative approach. In 1994, the city received a federal grant to become an Enterprise Community (EC). Under this grant, the neighborhoods in the city with the lowest incomes and highest concentration of newcomer groups were designated an Enterprise Community Zone. As a requirement of the grant, a board of directors was elected within these neighborhoods to oversee the project's implementation.

The majority of Enterprise Community board members were elected from newcomer groups. Unlike the City of Lowell's tourism-driven "Destination City" strategy, the Enterprise Community was directed by and focused on the immigrant community. Consequently, the newcomer community was viewed as an asset and activities were oriented to their needs rather than those of Lowell's wealthier neighborhoods. The EC board funded a study to assess the skills, interests, and needs of residents within these communities. Based on this assessment, the EC established a Request for Proposal (RFP) process to fund organizations that would provide services and programs to expand small business development, educational enhancement and ESL proficiency, job readiness and technical skills training, and child care. The EC invested in the human and social infrastructure of immigrant and low-income communities.

As the examples in this section suggest, the City of Lowell's decisions about economic development have broad implications for the future of Lowell and its newcomer residents. If the city were to adopt the alternative approach to their "Destination City" strategy, they would focus more on assets and needs that currently exist in Lowell. Instead of investing considerable resources in attracting outside restaurants and specialty shops, they might look at the assets within the immigrant and refugee community that could attract tourists to Lowell. There are opportunities to develop markets and develop the ethnic businesses that are likely to attract tourists. The successes in the North End and Chinatown in Boston as tourist attractions *and* economic development successes represent instructive examples of such an approach. Furthermore, the potential growth of newcomer businesses is limited when the businesses are unable to sell goods and services to markets outside of their community (Bates 1984–85).

Conclusion

These initiatives have helped us explore three questions: (1) What innovative infrastructure developments in the newcomer community have taken place in the Merrimack Valley? (2) What strengths of the newcomer community typically go unrecognized by traditional approaches to community economic development? and (3) What clashes in models of community economic development emerge between immigrants and planners engaging in traditional planning practices? We have highlighted some novel infrastructure developments within the Southeast Asian community that have made important contributions to overall community development. Many of these are clearly embedded within the cultural experiences of these immigrants and refugees, such as the development of the Southeast Asian Water Festival, community-based organizations, informal lending methods, and transnational and locally based ethnic businesses. Unfortunately, incorporated into these innovative infrastructures are the very assets of these newcomer communities that are unrecognized by the traditional community economic development players. The informal mechanisms and social networks that propel the start-up and expansion of numerous Southeast Asian businesses and help ensure the long-term success of these enterprises are just a few of the strengths that have been undervalued by local government and nonimmigrant civic and business leaders. In addition, the existence of transnational entrepreneurs in Lowell who depend on regular commercial activity with Cambodia for their economic prosperity is consistent with the experiences of other established immigrant communities in the United States. Nonetheless, the clashes of models of community economic development between immigrants and nonimmigrants are quite evident within Lowell. This disconnect is certainly hindering the ability of the Southeast Asian community to achieve its potential for community development. Furthermore, these clashes of models are preventing the assets within the Asian community from being utilized most effectively. Unfortunately, unrealized community economic development assets within the Southeast Asian community have negative consequences within both the immigrant and nonimmigrant communities. Our hope is that our discussion of these issues will contribute to a better understanding of how the immigrant and nonimmigrant communities can collaborate more effectively in order to enhance overall community development.

Notes

1. A local CPA shared an experience with us about a client who came to see him for help to resolve an issue with the Massachusetts Department of Revenue (DOR). Apparently, this individual owned a restaurant and was sending more sales tax than his business was required to pay. His motive to do this was based on his experience in his native country. If he sent more money than required, this would ensure that he would never have problems with DOR.

2. The City of Lowell recently discontinued funding for this program.

References

Basch, L. G., N. Schiller, and C. Blanc-Szanton. 1994. Nation Unbound: Transnational Projects, Postcolonial Predicaments, and Deterritorialized Nation-States. Langhorne, PA: Gordon and Breach.

Bates, T. 1984–85. Urban Economics Transformation and Minority Business Opportunity. *Reviews of the Black Political Economy* (winter): 21–36.

Bendick, M. Jr., and M. Egan. 1991. *Business Development in the Inner-City: Enterprise with Community Links.* New York: Community Development Research Center, Graduate School of Management and Urban Planning, New York School for Social Research.

Blakely, J. E., and K. T. Bradshaw. 2002. *Planning Local Economic Development Theory and Practice.* London: Sage Publications.

Briggs, X. 1997. Social Capital and the Cities: Advice to Change Agents. *National Civic Review* 86, no. 2:111–17.

Callahan, S. 1996. The Capital that Counts. *Commonwealth* 123, no. 20:7–8.

Chang, H. N. 1997. Democracy, Diversity, and Social Capital. *National Civic Review* 86, no. 2:141–47.

Flora, C., and J. Flora. 1993. Entrepreneurial Social Infrastructure: A Necessary Ingredient. *Annual of the American Academy* 529:48–58.

Gardner, C. 1996. Building Social Capital: The Case of Mineral County, Nevada. *Economic Development Review* 14, no. 2:60.

Guarnizo, L. E. 1992. One Country in Two: Dominican-Owned Firms in the United States and the Dominican Republic. Ph.D. diss., Johns Hopkins University.

———. 2003. The Economics of Transnational Living. *Center for Migration Studies, New York, Inc.* 37, no. 3:666–700.

Harrison, B. 1974 Ghetto Economic Development: A Survey. *Journal of Economic Literature* 12 (March):1–37.

Irwin, M., and I. Sharkova. 1998. Social Capital of Local Communities. *Metroscope,* 13–19.

Kawachi, I., B. Kennedy, and K. Lochner. 1997. Social Capital, Income Inequality, and Mortality. *American Journal of Public Health* 87, no. 9:1491–98.

Kingsley, G., J. McNeely, and J. Gibson. 1997. *Community Building Coming of Age.* Retrieved March 12, 2007, from http://www/urban.org/UploadedPDF/COM BLDG.PDF.

Laws, G. 1997. Globalization, Immigration, and Changing Social Relations in U.S Cities. *The Annals of the American Academy of Political and Social Science* 551 (May):89–104.

Messer, J. 1998. Agency, Communion, and the Formation of Social Capital. *Nonprofit and Voluntary Sector Quarterly* 21, no. 1:5–12.

Miller, R. 1997. Healthy Boston and Social Capital: Application, Dynamics and Limitations. *National Civic Review* 86, no. 2:157–65.

Okagaki, A. 1998. Strengthening Rural Economies: Programs that Target Promising Sectors of a Local Economy. Washington, DC: Center for Community Change. Available at http://communitychange.org/default.asp.

Ostergaard-Nielsen, E. 2003. International Migration Review. *Center for Migration Studies of New York, Inc.* 37, no. 3:760–87.

Porter, M. E. 1995. The University and the Regional Development Process. *Harvard Business Review* (May–June):55–71.

Portes, A. 2001. Introduction: The Debates and Significance of Immigrant Trans-nationalism. *Global Networks* 1, no. 3:181–93.

———, W. Haller, and L. E. Guarnizo. 2002. Transnational Entrepreneurs: An Alternative Form of Immigrant Economic Adaptation. *American Sociology Review* 67:278–98.

———, and M. Zhou. 1992. Gaining the Upper Hand: Economic Mobility among Immigrant and Domestic Minorities. *Ethnic and Racial Studies* 15, no. 4:491–522.

Putnam, R. D. 2000. *Bowling Alone: The Collapse and Revival of American Community.* New York: Simon and Schuster.

Robinson, C. J. 1989. Municipal Approaches to Economic Growth and Distribution Policy. *Journal of the American Planning Association* 55:283–95.

Robinson, R. 2004. Globalization, Immigrants' Transnational Agency and Economic Development in their Homelands. *Focal,* 1–12.

Wilson, K., and A. Martin. 1982. Ethnic Enclaves: A Comparison of the Cuban and Black Economies in Miami. *American Journal of Sociology* 88:135–60.

Zhou, M., and C. L. Bankston III. 1994. Social Capital and the Adaptation of Second Generation: The Case of Vietnamese Youth in New Orleans East. *International Migration Review* 28, no. 4:775–99.

5 *Tuyet-Lan Pho*

Family Education and Academic Performance among Southeast Asian Students

My Mom always tells me that she had to quit school when she was very young,
because her mother was very poor, so she had to go to work to help her mother
support the two younger boys. She said that if we were still in Cambodia now,
she probably wouldn't have enough money to send me to school. She said to
thank God that we are here and that I can go to school; to be grateful, study
hard, and not waste my time. My Mom says we, her daughters, should get our
education first, before we even think about getting married. She says that if you
have an education, the man will respect you more and won't try to boss you
around so much.

        —Interview with Chenda, female Cambodian student

I started at the high school in this city in the ninth grade, when I was sixteen
years old. I passed all my courses, but I did not have enough credits to move
into tenth grade, so they held me back. I did very well in tenth grade, so they let
me skip eleventh grade, and go to twelfth, and I still did well. In those days at
high school, I would spend about four or five hours a day to do my homework.
I studied by myself, sometimes in my car. I had a car to go to work in, and to
come back in. I would come home from school, then I would go to work, then I
would come back home and study. It's hard to study when you're so very tired.
Sometimes, I would fall asleep, and then the next day, when we had a test, I
would just pass.

        —Interview with Kham, male Lao student

I also found that what we learned in school sometimes was different from what
we were taught at home, because some of the Vietnamese values were different
from the American values, and our behavior as a result of the traditional Viet-
namese values and parents' teachings make us different from other students; and
most teachers do not understand that. While our teachers wanted us to talk in

class and to be independent, our parents wanted us to be quiet and respect older people. Our parents also did not want us to go to school far away from home, and they told us what to study, while they did not know much about the fields of study and the many opportunities in college education. I tried to explain to my parents, but was not very successful.

—Interview with Phong, male Vietnamese student

The "Indochina Conflict" and the "Vietnam War" that lasted for half a century have changed the fate of millions of people from Vietnam, Laos, and Cambodia. The end of the war in April 1975 also marked the beginning of a continuing flow of refugees from these three countries to the United States. Thirty years later there are approximately 1.8 million Vietnamese, Lao, and Cambodians resettled in large cities across the fifty states, and are known to the American people as Southeast Asian (U.S. Census Bureau 2003).

Southeast Asians, like other immigrants who came before them, brought their own cultural values and ways of educating children from their home country to the new land. The tasks that most Southeast Asian parents newly resettled in the United States must face are numerous and complex; one would think that education for their children would be the last thing on their mind. However, most parents were determined to marshal their traditions, learn to adjust their cultural preferences and to accommodate their children's acculturated behavior, support their children's education, and prepare them for a better life in a new society. Some students reached a high level of academic performance, but many others fell through the cracks. Even those who succeeded had to pay for their achievement with long hours of hard work, isolation, self-doubt, and anxiety. Their stories need to be told, and their voices need to be heard through educational researchers who are willing to examine the adaptation of these newcomers to American life. Only with such study shall we truly understand the complex, challenging, and often conflicting lives of Southeast Asian children in American public schools.

In this essay I describe the foundation upon which Southeast Asian parents formulate their family education, explore how cultural values and family life may have influenced the academic performance of their children, and examine the nature of parents and school relationship. The study that I conducted from 1993 to 2005 is composed of a survey of 102 Southeast Asian high school students and a case study of six families, two Cambodian, two Lao, and two Vietnamese, who have resided in Lowell, Massachusetts, since the early 1980s.[1] The survey was conducted in 1993 and data from the case study were collected between 1994 and 2005. Findings from the survey and the case study are presented in four parts: the first gives an overview of the study and its limitations; the second discusses the survey and its findings; the third describes the case study and its findings; and the fourth provides a summary of the findings and recommendations.

An Overview of the Study and its Limitations

Numerous studies have assessed the impact of family education on the academic performance of children from different ethnic and racial backgrounds (Genova 1981; Hess et al. 1987; Haines 1989; Hidalgo 1992; Mizokawa and Ryckman 1990; Gibson and Ogbu 1991; Swap and Krasnow 1992; Kibria 1993; Perry 1993; Kiang and Kaplan 1994; Walker-Moffat 1995; Verna and Campbell 1998; Smith-Hefner 1999; Zhou and Bankston 1999; Chan 2004; Hein 1995 and 2006); few, however, investigated the formation of family education and the change in parental relationship among Southeast Asians since their resettlement in the United States. Two of the notable studies on the education of Southeast Asian children were quantitatively oriented and lacked a comprehensive explanation of why some students perform well in school while others fail. One study was conducted in 1983 by the University of Michigan Institute for Social Research (Caplan, Whitmore, and Choy 1989); the other is the National Education Longitudinal Study of 1988 (National Center for Education Statistics 1992). Among nonfiction books and biographies, it is worth mentioning the work of James Higgins and Joan Ross in two photo journals that open a window into family life of several Cambodian, Lao, and Vietnamese refugees who arrived in Lowell in the early 1980s (Higgins and Ross 1986). The authors followed these families and their children with their camera and recording machine for more than ten years and provided an intimate account of the struggles and joys of these recent immigrants (Higgins and Ross 1997). On the other side of the continent, Linda Himelblau (2005) drew a composite picture of students she taught and young soccer players she coached at San Diego's Central Elementary School for fifteen years; she creates a believable and unforgettable refugee family trying to fit into a new land.

When I reviewed a personal collection of more than one hundred essays written by Southeast Asian students attending a college preparatory program between 1988 and 2002 (New Horizons Anthologies 1992–2002), I recognized that the voices emerging from these short stories and poems were more compelling than any available statistical reports. They reveal the challenges and opportunities these students face at home and in school. Their voices also call for a better understanding from their parents and their teachers. Every single essay in the collection reflects the uncertainty of growing up in two different worlds: between the rigidity of traditional values and the fluidity of the American culture. I realized that the answer to my inquiry could be found among the different voices and perspectives of the students, their parents, and their teachers.

I started this study in 1993 with a survey of 102 Cambodian, Lao, and Vietnamese students attending Lowell High School. In 1994 I developed an interview protocol, using findings from the survey, and conducted a case study of six Southeast Asian families residing in Lowell. I also held several follow-up conversations with the case subjects; the last conversation took place in 2005. The task sequence included a review of the literature on family education, the development of a survey questionnaire, the establishment of interview schedules, and the formulation of the observation protocol for the case study. I also asked a Cambodian and a Lao bilingual teacher to assist me with the review of cultural values among their ethnic communities and with the interviews of parents who do not speak English fluently. Other resource persons who assisted me with this study include a high school teacher, a student counselor, and a social worker.

A theoretical framework was developed and used as guidelines for data collection from the survey and the case study. This framework was based on the different "capitals" that Bourdieu (1977), Coleman (1988), Marjoribanks (1991), Lareau (1987), and Gibson and Ogbu (1991) identified in their studies as factors that may have contributed to or hindered the academic achievement of the children. According to these researchers, the family provides human, social, educational and cultural capitals that are associated with children's development and achievement. In combination, they may either work together or cancel each other out (Pho 1994, 22–31). Throughout the data collection phase of this study, I kept in mind the types of capitals suggested by these authors. I observed and explored resources that I found to exist in each family: parents' educational attainment; the relationship they share with their children; the level of socialization and the educational aspirations they have for their children; and the cultural experiences they provide their children at home.

In addition to this theoretical framework, I reviewed with the assistance of the Cambodian and Lao teachers, the twenty-six family values that Caplan, Choy, and Whitmore (1991) used in their study of the academic performance of the children of the boat people. Together as a team we selected twenty-two values (presented in table 5.1) as a guideline for our survey questionnaire and our interview schedules. Nineteen values represent the traditional perspectives that are observed by many Southeast Asians in their homeland and in the United States. Three values (italicized) are considered more Westernized or Americanized.

Table 5.1

Contributing Factors to Academic Achievement of the Boat People

1. Cultural Foundation	2. Family-based Achievement
• respect authority • perpetuate ancestral lineage • seek salvation • harmony with the land • traditional customs	• education and achievement • a cohesive family • respect for family members • cooperative and harmonious family • family loyalty
3. Hard Work	**4. The Family in Society**
• hard work • sacrifice present for future • carry out obligations • restraint and discipline	• family status in community • *seek new experience* • morality and ethics
5. Self-Reliance and Pride	**6. Coping and Integration**
• respect for elders • ashamed of welfare	• past is as important as present • *balance of work and play* • *seek fun and excitement*

Source: Caplan, Choy, and Whitmore, 1991.

The research method used in this study was subject to a number of limitations. While the lives of these case subjects are continuing to unfold as they live and learn, the investigator is no more than a photographer who came in with a zoom-lens camera to take what she perceived as meaningful snapshots of their learning experience. Therefore, the description is informative and useful, but not complete. The findings are comprehensive, but do not provide definite answers or causal relationship solutions to the phenomena being studied. The benefits of sharing the same ethnic background as their subjects enabled the investigator and her team to probe more deeply into the cultural background and the living and learning experience of their case subjects. But that shared background may also lead to a lack of objectivity, even though this study was carefully designed and conducted to ensure internal and external validity. In an effort to acquire comparable information on each case, the criteria used to select case subjects have posed another limitation to this study: I only investigated the situation of families with both parents. I have left out families with single parents, students with dysfunctional behavior, and students who live in group homes as unaccompanied minors. The Southeast Asian refugee population includes a large number of families with single parents, as well as children who live with extended family members. This investigation only covers relatively stable and functional family life, and did not focus upon disenfranchised families and dysfunctional student behavior. Because the study focuses on a small group of Southeast Asian families living in one geographical location and involves the children attending neighborhood high schools, the findings describe a selected and unique situation that cannot be used to generalize about the larger population of more than a million Southeast Asians residing in the United States.

The study took place in Lowell, an urban city located in Massachusetts. In 1993, the Lowell population was estimated at 103,000 people from different ethnic backgrounds. About 20 percent of the city's population was newcomers from Cambodia, Laos, and Vietnam who have resettled in the city since 1985 (Massachusetts Office for Refugees and Immigrants 1997). The concentration of Southeast Asians in this midsized city has created a cultural setting conducive to naturalistic research. This setting includes an intricate housing pattern, ethnic-owned and -operated shops and stores, service-providing agencies, and religious temples that nested the Southeast Asian community and isolated it from mainstream U.S. culture. Altogether, these establishments have sustained the preservation of cultural heritage and created business opportunities for the newcomers as well as the city residents. The influx of Southeast Asians in Lowell had also fostered a high level of tension in the integration process of the Cambodian, Lao, and Vietnamese (Pho 1997).

Numerous antirefugee incidents occurred between 1975 and 1990 in cities and states with large concentrations of Southeast Asian refugees. These conflicts included protests aimed at new arrivals, property destruction, jobs and social services disputes, harassment and altercations, assault, arson to homes, and incidents that resulted in death for either refugees or natives (Hein 1995). At the peak of the influx of Southeast Asian refugees into Lowell between 1985 and 1988, their children represented more than 25 percent of the school population and posed many difficulties to the city and the school district. The presence of these students was one of the major reasons for a push toward the school desegregation movement and led the residents to pass a referendum to declare English the official language of Lowell. Although the turmoil of neighborhood school versus central enrollment (busing), and English Only versus English Plus has subsided, the uncertainty related to teaching and learning among Southeast Asian students lingered (Pho and Mulvey 2003).

Survey Questionnaire and Its Findings

A survey questionnaire was developed and administered to 180 Southeast Asians enrolled in a college preparatory program for economically disadvantaged students at Lowell High School and other high schools in the Greater Lowell area. One hundred and two, or 57 percent, of the surveyed students completed and returned the questionnaire. Data collected from this survey provided background information about the students and their parents, including ethnic category, age, gender, grade level, year of entry to the United States, English comprehension level, grade-point average, home situations (that is, living with one or both parents or older relatives, number of siblings), parents' education and their economic status as measured by annual income. The survey also identified the cultural values that parents taught their children at home, and how important these values were to the students personally. Student respondents described the support their parents gave them in relation to their schooling; explained the way that they related to their parents at home; and assessed their parents' aspirations for them versus their own educational and career goals.

General Findings from the Survey

Students who responded to the survey came from three different ethnic backgrounds: 40 percent Cambodian, 22 percent Lao, and 38 percent Vietnamese. Their age ranged from 14 to 22 with an average age of 18. The breakdown between genders was 51 percent males and 49 percent females. More than half (53 percent) of the respondents lived with both parents; the rest were with one parent or older relatives. Their length of stay in the United States varied from 1 to 13 years and a majority arrived between 1985 and 1993. More than 62 percent of the respondents came from a large family with 3 to 6 children. Some 42 percent of the respondents' fathers and 68 percent of their mothers had less than a high school education, while approximately 12 percent of parents had some college education. Almost 50 percent of the parents were unemployed and 20 percent were both working at the time of the survey.[2] Their average annual income was reported at less than $20,000 for an average family of six. Some 22 percent of the families were making less than $15,000 per year and only 7 percent earned more than $30,000 annually. By American living standards, a majority of these families lived below the poverty line.[3] Only one-fourth of the students were fluent in English when they entered high school, more than one-third had acquired an average level of English comprehension, and the rest had little or no English capability.

There was a small difference concerning the academic performance across gender; 66 percent of female students reported a GPA between A and B; 58 percent of male students were at the same level. The survey also found academic performance differences among students of different ethnic backgrounds: 79 percent of the Vietnamese students reported a GPA at the A and B level, while 51 percent of the Cambodian and 45 percent of the Lao achieved similar academic performance. Similar findings were found in previous studies (Caplan et al. 1991; Mitrsomwang 1992; Ima and Rumbaut 1989).

Overall, the majority of the respondents achieved an average to above-average academic performance and they did better in math and science than in English and social studies. These results were similar to the findings obtained in the University of Michigan Institute for Social Research's study of 536 children of the boat people in 1983 (Caplan et al. 1991).

Summary of Findings from the Survey

Given the low English proficiency, the traumatic experience with war and displacement, and living in or on the borderline of poverty, a majority of the respondents were remarkably successful in striving for excellence in school (61 percent of students reported their GPA in the range of A, A–B or C.) Two cultural factors, "family loyalty" and "a cooperative and harmonious family" and two types of parent/child relationships, "parents who were very interested in their children's school work" and "parents who told their children of the importance of getting a good education" have a strong statistical relationship with the children's grade-point average. Aspects of the home environment that seemed to be conducive to learning included (1) children who experienced a satisfactory or positive relationship with their parents at home; and (2) parents and children who set a career goal that required a college education (Pho 1994, 70–81).

The Case Study and Its Findings

The evidence that emerged from the survey provided some exploratory explanation about the successful academic experience of this group of Southeast Asian students. Although the evidence was not sufficient to explain why some students succeeded in school and others failed, it provided a good framework for the case study that investigated the impact of cultural values, examined the role that parents played in their children's education and future career, and identified what needs to be done between home and school to improve the learning experience of Southeast Asian students. The case study was conducted with six students selected from respondents of the survey and at the recommendations of teachers and counselors from Lowell High School.

Each case is a unit of analysis and is composed of one student and two parents. Other informants who provided additional information about the case subjects included one or two teachers and a school counselor who either taught or gave academic advice to the student, and an informant from the Southeast Asian community who was knowledgeable about the student's cultural background and family life. The case study data sources included transcriptions of interviews with students, parents, teachers, counselors, and other informants; field notes of home observations; transcription of focus group discussions; and school records.

The interview protocol is composed of three schedules designed for parent, student, and teacher individually. Each schedule helped the interviewer to (1) explore the cultural values that the students feel are important to their family; (2) describe the role parents play in marriage and raising children; (3) measure the level of control parents feel they may have over their children's education; and (4) assess the subjects' knowledge about the learning environment at Lowell High School.

Each structured interview lasted one to two hours, and took place at Lowell High School, the student's home, or the interviewer's home. Two observations were conducted in the home of each of the six families. Interviews with students and parents were in Khmer, Lao, Vietnamese, or English, depending on the ethnic background of the interviewees and their English comprehension level. Two bilingual teachers, a counselor, a parent liaison person, and I conducted a total of forty-four interviews, two with each of the six students, six parents, seven teachers and counselors, and three informants. All interviews were audiotaped. The total interview time for each case ranged from ten to twelve hours and yielded approximately six to nine hours of audiotapes. All tapes were transcribed; some of the transcriptions were forwarded to the interviewees for their review and comments. Field notes of observations were written up following Geertz's thick description framework (1973), and were included in the case database. Three separate focus discussion sessions with teachers and counselors from Lowell High School and an independent moderator were organized for the families of each ethnic group. I joined the sessions as a participant observer or interpreter. All discussions were taped and transcribed; exchanges between parents and teachers, teachers and students, and students and parents were coded and used as a foundation for the discussion of relevant findings that emerged from this study.

Academic records of each student in the case study, and his/her written works that were published in the school anthology or as part of a summer school journal, were reviewed with particular attention to the student's attendance records, grade report cards, standardized test scores, progress through the school years, and thoughts and reflections about his/her learning experience at Lowell High School. The teacher's written remarks about each student were collected as part of the case database.

After all initial fieldwork was completed in 1994 I conducted three follow-up meetings with six families participating in the case study in 1998, four in 2002, and three in 2005. The first two follow-up meetings lasted for one to two hours and took place in the home of the case subjects. I met with each student and his or her parents and listened to their recollection of changes that had taken place in the family since the last time we met. I asked parents about their children's academic performance, their perception of their children's school, and their relationship with their ethnic community. I also discussed with the students the school they attended at that time and the program they studied; I listened to stories about their friends, their social life, and their prospects for future career and marriage. The last follow-up meeting in 2005 with each case subject lasted for three hours and took place at the University of Lowell library. I selected different sections of the Interview Protocol for Students that was developed in 1994 and discussed each section with the students. The objective of the discussion is to identify changes in their perception of traditional values, family life with their parents, and the way they wish to bring up or have brought up their own children. In between the follow-up meetings I maintained close contact with four out of six case subjects through telephone calls and e-mail messages.

As I sorted through the case database, it is evident that three common threads could be pulled together using Yin's (1984) approach to cross-case analysis: (1) the traditional values that members of each family tried to maintain and the American values they wish to adopt; (2) the roles that parents play in raising children and influencing their attitudes toward marriage; and (3) educational goals and career aspirations that students, parents, and teachers set for students, together with their perception of the school learning environment (Pho 1994, 82–85). The discussion of each of these three strands is presented in the following section.

Maintaining Traditional Values and Adaptating to the American Culture

Two questions that set the framework for the study of cultural values and their impact on home life and the learning experience of the students are (1) What are the traditional values that parents and students chose to maintain, and their preferences toward the adoption of American goals? and (2) What impact might these values have on the academic performance of the students?

The review of the traditional values that parents chose to maintain and the American values that they wished to adopt indicates that parents wished to retain their cultural heritage and to bring up their children in their traditional values. The parents' present and past socioeconomic status, their educational background, and their length of stay in the United States did not appear to influence their choice to hold on to most of the traditional values. On the contrary, five of the six students tried to maintain a balance between keeping the traditional values taught by their parents and the Western values suggested by their American friends and their teachers. During the interviews and the focus discussions, these students consistently shifted their preference between "respect authority" and "speak your mind"; "maintain harmony in the family" and "exercise your individual rights"; or "restraint and discipline" and "seek new experience." A Lao female student is the only person who expressed clearly in her school essays the determination to depart from her family culture and to embrace the American lifestyle.

All parents and children in the case study clearly wanted to take advantage of the educational opportunities that were available to them. Nonetheless, parents and children approached their educational goals in different ways. While parents thought that "respect for authority," "being responsible about carrying out obligations," and "being restrained and disciplined" would be necessary to do well in school, their children believed that "seeking out new experiences," "freedom of expression," and "being articulate and assertive" were ingredients for school success.

Although some teachers and counselors have acquired a good knowledge of the Southeast Asian cultures, they did not fully understand the struggle their students experienced in their search for an identity, nor the fear that plagued every parent's mind: losing their children to a strange culture. In their earnest efforts to have their Southeast Asian students adapt to the school-learning environment, the teachers have also widened the cultural gap between the parents and their children by encouraging the children to adopt American values that are not congruent with their traditional culture. I wondered how harmful this practice would be to the academic performance of the students when it was viewed within the context of Gibson and Ogbu's (1991) cultural model; that is, children would not do well in school when school authority that represents the dominant culture negates the family values and teachings.

The Roles Parents Play in Raising Children and Influencing Attitudes toward Marriage

In general, the foundation of family education among Southeast Asians is based on their cultural values and religious beliefs. The process they used to transmit their cultural heritage to their children was role modeling and close supervision. It is important to understand the roles parents play and the decisions they make in bringing up their children. Information about parental role-playing and supervision was collected through observations and interviews with husband, wife, and their children in each family. The evidence that emerged from these observations and interviews provided some answers to the following questions: (1) Have the roles parents played within the family changed since they resettled in the United States? and (2) If children experience a positive or satisfying relationship with their parents, can they benefit from the family education more and learn better in school?

The roles that parents in this case study actually played remained fairly consistent with the home-life tradition among Southeast Asians. There was evidence of minor role modification in response to the economic condition that required both parents to work, full-time in some families and part-time in others. The preferential treatment of boys over girls is also prominent. The parents in all six families were asked if there were only enough money to send one child to college, whom would they select. The answers were unanimous: their oldest son would go to college so that he might take care of his brothers and sisters. Similar evidence emerged from the survey. All students in the survey recognized the gender differences in their family: 37 percent agreed and 36 percent disagreed with the ways their parents treated boys over girls.

All six students in the case study indicated that the pressure that their parents—especially their fathers—placed on them to succeed in school was at times overbearing. They wished that their parents knew more about the school system and available career opportunities in the United States, and would allow them to make decisions concerning their education and their personal life. The students were willing to accept their parents' authority, but they also asked for more flexibility and understanding. They appreciated the sacrifice that their parents had made for them in terms of financial and moral support. They also recognized their parents' limited ability to help them with homework or to get involved with school activities. A Vietnamese male student occasionally cast doubt upon the benefits of his father's decision about his college choice, and a Lao female student found that her father did not understand the benefits of school sports. In general, however, all students believed that their culture and their home life were part of their school success.

The students described the example their parents set in their education as that of nurturing, sacrificing, hard work, perseverance, and determination. They did not think, however, that their parents were capable of helping them with their schoolwork or giving them sound advice regarding education goals or career choices. Although the students questioned the influence their parents claimed to have on their educational attainment, the expectations they set for themselves were not different from their parents' expectations; and four out of six students agreed with the career choices their parents made for them.

The teachers were very critical of the Southeast Asian parent-child relationship, the preferential treatment of boys over girls, and the negative reinforcement methods that parents used to get their children to do better in school. The teachers' recommendations to parents reflected their frustration over the lack of parental participation in school activities and their impatience with parents who were not eager to accept the American school culture. Findings from interviews with parents and teachers reveal that the notion of parental participation in school was very different between parents and teachers. While teachers complained that parents rarely came to school open houses or attended teacher-parent conferences, parents thought they participated sufficiently in their children's school education by reminding their children to do homework and teaching them the value of education.

Parents believed that they must teach their children traditional values, shelter the children from the "bad" influence of their friends, and save them from the "strange" American culture. These parents might not have been aware that the tug-of-war they had with their children might also involve their children's teachers. The difference between family education and the school's teaching was more evident during the focus discussions with students, teachers, and parents. These discussions took place in the home of each family and provided unique opportunities for the teachers to observe the way their students live and how they related to their parents. There were tense moments at some focus sessions, but most participants were eager to state their expectations, express their concerns, and justify the methods they used to ensure a better education for the students. Several teachers who participated in the focus discussion indicated that it was the first time they had met with parents in their homes and that the experience was rewarding.

Educational Goals, Career Aspirations, and the School Learning Environment

"Educational goals, career aspirations, and the learning environment at Lowell High School" is one of the three major sections in the structured interview with parents, students, and teachers. In order to obtain compatible information from three different perspectives, the interview instrument was formulated around two questions: (1) How did each of these individuals perceive the learning environment at Lowell High

School? and (2) Did goal-directedness in terms of education and career have any impact on academic performance?

The learning environment at Lowell High School received a mixed rating from students, parents, and teachers alike. Parents and students were impressed with the opportunities for education and the way school prepared students for college and employment; most parents believed, however, that the school disciplinary system could be improved, as could the instruction in math, science, and reading. All students wished they could have more understanding teachers and more friendly classmates. Students and parents believed that the school environment was safe but not trusting. Students reported that racial slurs and skirmishes occurred occasionally in the hallway and the parking lot. When teachers described the learning environment at Lowell High School, they did not respond to the concerns raised by the parents and students. They did, however, recommend that students take advantage of available academic support programs, establish rapport with teachers, network with other students, and become more engaged with the rest of the school population.

The educational goals that students selected were very close to the expectations that their parents had for them. All parents expected their children to have sixteen years of education or the completion of a college degree; even so, they differed somewhat from their children in terms of career choices. Some parents were aware of the cost of higher education and selected jobs that required only some college education; others chose the traditional prestigious professions that were available in their home country, such as engineer, physician, or lawyer. The students were more specific in their job selection: for example, pediatric nurse, computer scientist, police officer, or teacher. The two main concerns that parents and children had in reaching their career aspirations were the cost of college education in the United States and the level of English proficiency that college education requires. All parents said that English-language proficiency was "extremely important" for their children to succeed in school.

Students and their parents were clear in their expectations and set achievable educational and career goals. They were confident that they could achieve their goals through sacrifice, hard work, determination, and perseverance. The students' academic records indicated that they performed in the top 50 percent of their class (with the exception of one Cambodian male student who was ranked in the top 70 percent of his class). It appears that the goal-directedness they learned from their parents, their personal efforts, and their parents' positive outlook on life in the United States are important contributors to their academic performance. Teachers and counselors believed that all six students would be able to reach their educational goals and career expectations; although three students might require more academic counseling and support services than the others.

Ten years after this case study started, two of the participating families moved out of Lowell and left no forwarding address. All six students in the case study finished high school; one dropped out of college; one finished his education at a community college; and four went on to finish their college education. Three students are working in professional fields and one is completing a Ph.D. program at a prestigious university in California. Three students were married and two have children of their own. One student has a mental health problem and had to resign from her position as a chemist in a pharmaceutical lab. There is no formal follow-up with students who participated in the survey. Nonetheless, available school records indicate that most of them graduated from high schools and approximately 80 percent were admitted to higher education institutions; some were accepted to Harvard, MIT, Brandeis, Brown, Boston College, and other prestigious institutions. Several participants continue to live with their families in Lowell. On several occasions I caught news about these participants from the local newspaper; I learned that many female students entered interracial marriages, one became a Buddhist nun, one was killed by her husband in a domestic violence situation, a male student was incarcerated for murder, and two were killed in automobile accidents.

Summary of Findings and Recommendations

In general, the students who participated in the survey as well as the case study have performed successfully in school, in spite of numerous barriers, including culture, language, socioeconomic status, unfamiliarity with the school system, lack of formal education in some cases, and being subject to racism and prejudices.

The statistical analysis of the survey's responses did not find strong evidence indicating there is a causal relationship between academic performance and cultural values and home life. The frequency counts and chi-square contingency table analysis did show, however, that students who observed traditional values (such as valuing education and family loyalty, cooperation, and harmony) and who said that they believed in the value of hard work, restraint, discipline, and carrying out obligations, reported their GPAs in the top half of the range (that is, A, A–B, and B).

Two important findings that emerged from the survey questionnaire and the case analysis were consistent with each other: (1) some common cultural values and aspects of home life existed in the families of students whose academic performance was in the upper half of the GPA scale, and (2) students who agreed with their parents' teachings achieved a higher level of academic performance than those who did not. The teachings were built on (1) cultural foundation values such as "respect for authority" and "maintenance of traditional customs and rituals"; (2) family-based achievement values that cover "education and achievement," "a cohesive, cooperative, and harmonious family," "respect for family members," and "family loyalty"; and (3) values associated with the work ethic including "a belief in hard work," "sacrifice the present for the future," "responsibility about carrying out obligations," and "restraint and discipline." In addition, findings from both the survey and case study indicated that parents and children who set a high educational goal and professional career aspirations appeared to perform better in school than those who did not.

While the survey findings showed evidence that children who experienced a satisfactory or positive relationship with their parents performed better in school, the patterns that emerged from the case study were more complex. A careful review of the case database indicated that only three students had a very close relationship with their parents; their cumulative class ranks, however, were 12 percent, 20 percent, and 48 percent respectively. Other factors that were not associated with the parent/child relationship may have influenced the student's school performances; for example, lack of formal education or a physical condition that may interfere with one's learning (Pho 1994, 173–78).

The findings that emerged from this study along with the discussion of their implications open a window into the family life of a small number of Southeast Asian refugees and the learning experience of their children. Most of the findings from the survey concur with findings from previous studies of the academic performance among Southeast Asian students. Nonetheless, the case study presents a more intricate picture of family life and a more complex relationship between family education and school achievement of the six case subjects. The values of families as educators could have both favorable and adverse effects on school learning and parental school involvement.

As this body of evidence emerged from the survey and the case study, it raised a number of issues that need to be addressed: What changes have taken place in Southeast Asians' family education since their resettlement in the United States? and How can parents, students, and teachers work together to improve family education and school learning? I recommend that further research be focused on this population. Findings from future studies could offer teacher education a better understanding of cultural differences, help sustain strong family tradition, and improve school practices for all students. Such research might also dispel the myth about Asian Americans as a "model minority" that the media and politicians have used in the absence of well-founded evidence.

Notes

1. All names of individuals used in this paper are pseudonyms to protect the privacy of the subjects. Case study data was following the procedure of and approved by the Institutional Review Board at the University of Massachusetts Lowell. Chenda lived in Lowell with her parents and three other siblings for twelve years when the study started. Her class rank is in the top 20 percent of 494 students. Kham came from Laos with his parents and seven other siblings and lived in Lowell for five years before I interviewed him as a case subject. His class rank is in the top 48 percent of 474 students. Phong came from Vietnam with his parents and five other siblings and lived in Lowell three years before he joined this study. His class rank is in the top 16 percent of 454 students.

2. The survey was conducted at the time Lowell experienced an unemployment rate of 10.4 percent; this rate was more than twice as high among unskilled minority workers (Massachusetts Department of Employment and Training [now under Department of Workforce Development], Lowell Fact Sheet, 1993).

3. According to the U.S. Department of Health and Human Services, poverty income for a family of six is set at $19,270 in the Northeast (as of April 12, 1993).

References

Bourdieu, Pierre. 1977. Cultural Reproduction and Social Reproduction. In *Power and Ideology in Education,* edited by Jerome Karabel and A. H. Halsey, 487–511. New York: Oxford University Press.

Caplan, Nathan, Marcella H. Choy, and John K. Whitmore. 1981. *The Children of the Boat People: A Study of Educational Success.* Ann Arbor: University of Michigan Press.

———. 1992. Indochinese Refugee Families and Academic Achievement. *Scientific American* 266, no. 2:36–42.

Caplan, Nathan, John K. Whitmore, and Marcella H. Choy. 1989. *The Boat People and Achievement in America: A Study of Economic and Educational Success.* Ann Arbor: University of Michigan Press.

Chan, Sucheng. 2004. *Survivors: Cambodian Refugees In The United States.* Champaign, IL: University of Illinois Press.

Coleman, James S. 1988. Social Capital in the Creation of Human Capital. *American Journal of Sociology* 94:S95–S120.

Geertz, C. 1973. *The Interpretation of Cultures.* New York: Basic Books.

Genova, W. 1981. *A Study of Interaction Effects of School and Home Environments on Students of Varying Race/Ethnicity, Class, and Gender. Vol. 1, Summary and Conclusions. Vol. 2, Ethnographies of Five Racial/Ethnic Groups. Vol. 3, A Practitioner's Guide for Achieving Equity in Multicultural Schools.* Newton, MA: TDR Associates. (Now available as EDRS documents: UD 022 515–518.)

Gibson, Margaret A., and John U. Ogbu. 1991. *Minority Status and Schooling: A Comparative Study of Immigrant and Involuntary Minorities.* New York: Garland.

Haines, David W., ed. 1989. Introduction to *Refugees as Immigrants: Cambodians, Laotians, and Vietnamese in America.* Totowa, NJ: Rowman and Littlefield. Pp. 1–23.

Hein, Jeremy. 1995. *From Vietnam, Laos, and Cambodia: A Refugee Experience in the United States.* New York: Twayne.

———. 2006. *Ethnic Origins: The Adaptation of Cambodian and Hmong Refugees in Four American Cities.* New York: Russell Sage Foundation Publications.

Hess, Robert D., Chang Chih-Mei, and Teresa M. McDevitt. 1987. Cultural Variations in Family Beliefs about Children's Performance in Mathematics: Comparisons among People's Republic of China, Chinese-American, and Caucasian-American Families. *Journal of Educational Psychology* 79, no. 9: 179–88.

Hidalgo, N. 1992. "I Saw Puerto Rico Once": A Review of the Literature on Puerto Rican Families in the United States. Boston: Center on Families, Communities, Schools, and Children's Learning, Boston University.

Higgins, James, and J. Ross. 1986. *Southeast Asians, A New Beginning in Lowell.* Lowell, MA: Mill Town Graphics.

———. 1997. *Fractured Identities: Cambodia's Children of War.* Lowell, MA: Loom Press.

Himelblau, Linda. 2005. *The Trouble Begins.* New York: Delacorte Books.

Ima, K., and R. G. Rumbaut. 1989. Southeast Asian Refugees in American Schools: A Comparison of Fluent English Proficiency and Limited Proficiency Students. *Topics in Language Disorders* 9:54–57.

Kiang, Peter N., and Jenny Kaplan. 1994. "Where Do We Stand?" Views of Racial Conflict by Vietnamese American High-School Students in a Black-and-White Context, *Urban Review* 26, no 2:95–119.

Kibria, Nazli. 1993. *Family Tightrope: The Changing Lives of Vietnamese Americans.* Princeton, NJ: Princeton University Press.

Lareau, Annette. 1987. Social Class Differences in Family-School Relationships: The Importance of Cultural Capital. *Sociology of Education* 60:73–85.

Marjoribanks, Kevin. 1991. Family Environment and Cognitive Correlates of Young Adults' Social Status Attainment: Ethnic Group Differences. *Journal of Biosocial Sciences,* 23:491–98.

Massachusetts Department of Employment and Training (now under Department of Workforce Development), Lowell Fact Sheet 1993.

Massachusetts Office for Refugees and Immigrants. 1997. *Demographic Update: Refugees and Immigrants in Massachusetts.*

Mitrsomwang, Suparvadee S. 1992. Family Values and Behaviors in the Academic Performance of Indochinese Refugee Students. Ph.D. diss., Vanderbilt University.

Mizokawa, Donald T., and David B. Ryckman. 1990. Attributions of Academic Success and Failure: A Comparison of Six Asian-American Ethnic Groups. *Journal of Cross-Cultural Psychology* 21, no. 4:434–51.

National Center for Education Statistics. 1992. *Language Characteristics and Academic Achievement: A Look at Asian and Hispanic Eighth Graders in the National Education Longitudinal Study of 1988 (NELS: 88)* (U.S. Department of Education, Office of Educational Research and Improvement). Washington, DC: U.S. Government Printing Office.

New Horizons Program Students. 1992–2002. *New Horizons Anthologies* (personal collection). Lowell, MA: author.

Perry, Theresa. 1993. *Toward a Theory of African-American School Achievement.* Center on Families, Communities, Schools, and Children's Learning Report no. 16. Baltimore, MD: Johns Hopkins University Press.

Pho, Tuyet-Lan. 1994. Family Education and Academic Performance among Southeast Asian Students. Ph.D. diss., University of Massachusetts, Lowell.

———. 1997. Introduction to *Fractured Identities, Cambodia's Children of War* by James Higgins and Joan Ross, 9–16. Lowell, MA: Loom Press.

———, and Anne Mulvey. 2003. Southeast Asian Women in Lowell: Family Relations, Gender Roles, and Community Concerns. *Frontiers, A Journal of Women Studies* 24, no. 1:101–29.

Smith-Hefner, Nancy J. 1999. *Khmer American: Identity and Moral Education in a Diasporic Community.* Berkeley and Los Angeles: University of California Press.

Swap, Susan McAllister, and Jean Krasnow. 1992. *A Saga of Irish-American Achievement: Constructing a Positive Identity.* Center on Families, Communities, Schools and Children's Learning Report no. 2. Baltimore, MD: Johns Hopkins University Press.

U.S. Census Bureau. 2003. Census 2000 Summary File 1 (SF1) and Summary File 2 (SF2) 100-Percent Data and 2000 Census Summary File 4 (SF4) Sample Data; American Fact Finder; http://factfinder.census.gov/servlet/DatasetMain PageServlet?_program=DEC&_lang=en&_ts= (accessed October 7, 2003).

Verna, Marilyn Ann, and James Reed Campbell. 1998. The Differential Effects of Family Processes and SES on Academic Self-Concepts and Achievement of Gifted Asian American and Gifted Caucasian High School Students. ERIC # ED419025.

Walker-Moffat, Wendy. 1995. *The Other Side of the Asian American Success Story.* San Francisco, CA: Jossey-Bass.

Yin, Robert. 1984. *Case Study Research, Design and Methods.* Beverly Hills, CA: Sage.

Zhou, Min, and Carl L. Bankston III. 1999. *Growing Up American: How Vietnamese Children Adapt to Life in the United States.* New York: Russell Sage Foundation.

6   *Khin Mai Aung and Nancy Yu*

Does the System Work for Cambodian American Students?

The Educational Experiences and Demographics of Cambodians in Lowell, Massachusetts

This essay explores various interconnected factors impacting the educational experience of Cambodian youth in Lowell, Massachusetts. Refugees from Southeast Asia—primarily Cambodia—began settling in Lowell in the 1980s, through government refugee resettlement programs as well as secondary migration by refugees initially resettled elsewhere. As a result, the city has been reeling from rapid demographic and socio-economic changes; nonetheless, it has a growing social service and organizing infrastructure, and a reasonably progressive and reform-minded school district and police department.

This project began as an outgrowth of the Asian American Legal Defense and Education Fund's (AALDEF) emerging work concerning educational equity and youth rights issues impacting Cambodian refugees and immigrants in Lowell.[1] AALDEF, founded in 1974, is the first organization on the East Coast to protect and promote the civil rights of Asian Americans through litigation, legal advocacy, and community education. Realizing that education is the road to a better life for immigrants from all countries, AALDEF has provided legal assistance in Lowell to parents and students since the fall of 2003, asserting their rights to equal educational opportunities.

From collaborations with local youth organizing groups and community members, we learned that many Cambodian students were falling through the cracks of an overcrowded and underresourced public school system—leading many students to be truant or drop out. We also received reports of tensions between merchants and working-class youth in the newly revitalized and increasingly gentrifying downtown Lowell, often leading to police intervention and actions that could be characterized as racial profiling. We knew that out-of-school youth were more likely to become involved in the criminal justice system, and we became concerned about the creation of a school-to-prison track for Lowell's Cambodian youth, as well as for other youth of color.

Because of the lack of disaggregated data and the failure of studies regarding education and juvenile justice to address the experiences of Cambodian youth, we decided to embark upon a case study to document these issues through evidence supplied by individuals and grassroots organizations, with supporting data from the U.S. Census 2000.[2] Through interviews with various community stakeholders in Lowell, we solicited comments on issues raised in Lowell's data profile to explain the social dynamics behind the numbers. In selecting stakeholders, we sought individuals who had direct contact with Cambodian youth and families, and we attempted to get representation from both within and outside the school and juvenile justice systems.

As such, we shall provide an overview of Lowell's Cambodian population and the public education system, examine challenges and root causes contributing to the high dropout rate of Cambodian youth, discuss the impact and potential consequences of this problem, and point the way toward some initial solutions. This essay is our effort to highlight the social and political background against which our work in Lowell occurs, and identify new opportunities to foster community development through collaborations among social service agencies, advocacy groups, and city institutions.

Overview of Lowell's Cambodian Population

The influx and resettlement of Cambodian refugees in Lowell was fueled by the high-technology boom of the early 1980s, which led to the proliferation of low-wage computer assembly jobs in Lowell. These low-wage jobs did not require technical skills or English facility, and were filled predominantly by Southeast Asian refugees and other immigrants. Churches and other charitable associations, as well as government agencies like the Massachusetts Office of Refugees and Immigrants, also provided resources to aid the refugees (Gerson n.d.).[3]

Today, Lowell boasts the nation's second-largest Cambodian community.[4] According to Census 2000 figures, some 9,850 Cambodians reside in Lowell, constituting just under 10 percent of Lowell's total population of 105,167.[5] In addition, Census 2000 reported Lowell's total Asian population as 17,371, with 2,424 Asian Indians, 1,598 Vietnamese, and 1,541 Lao. Lowell's population also includes 14,734 Latinos (14 percent),

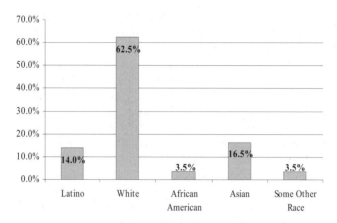

Figure 6.1: Population by Race in Lowell *Source: U.S. Census Bureau, Summary File 1*

3,644 African Americans (3.5 percent), and 65,760 non-Hispanic Whites (62.5 percent).[6] Figures 6.1 and 6.2 depict, respectively, the racial and Asian subgroup breakdown in Lowell.

Cambodian community leaders in Lowell believe their community is actually much larger than 10 percent of Lowell's population, citing a range of factors that could create discrepancies in Census data, such as language and cultural barriers (CA3 2004; Ros 2004), fear of immigration consequences and general fear of government due to Khmer Rouge atrocities (CA3 2004; Liang 2004; Ros 2004), and lack of outreach and insufficient translation (CA3 2004). While it is difficult to verify these estimates, community leaders believe Lowell's total Cambodian population ranges from 25,000 to 35,000 (CA3 2004; Liang 2004; Mam 2004; Ros 2004; Theam 2004).

Enrollment and Outcome of Public Education in Lowell

In the 2002–2003 school year, there were a total of 15,479 students enrolled in kindergarten through twelfth grade within Lowell's public school system (MA DOE 2004b). Of these, 4,635 were Asian or Pacific Islander, constituting almost one-third (29.9 percent) of the total (MA DOE 2004b). The Lowell School Department does not distribute disaggregated enrollment data by specific Asian ethnicity.[7] Census data, however, showed that in Lowell, more than two-thirds (67.4 percent) of the Asian population aged seventeen and under are Cambodian. Aside from two small charter schools (MA DOE 2004a),[8] Lowell High School is the only public high school in Lowell, with an enrollment of approximately

3,795 in the 2002–2003 school year (MA DOE 2004b). Asian and Pacific Islander students constituted 35.8 percent of Lowell High School's population, while 41.7 percent were White, 16.8 percent were Latino, and 5.3 percent were African American (MA DOE 2004b). Despite the high representation of Asian students among Lowell High School's student body, an alarmingly high percentage of Cambodian young adults in Lowell have not graduated from high school. Census 2000 data reported that 36.3 percent of Cambodian women aged 18–24 in Lowell have not graduated from high school, nor have 38.1 percent of Cambodian men. Across adult age groups, more than half (55.6 percent) of all Cambodians have not graduated from high school, compared to 27.9 percent of the overall population.

As table 6.1 demonstrates, a high percentage (46.3 percent) of Lowell's adult Latino population have also failed to complete high school, while their White and African American counterparts are more likely to have obtained a high school degree. Other data on graduation rates in Lowell has shown that only 35 percent of Asians and 18 percent of Latinos have completed high school with a regular diploma within a four-year period, compared to 43 percent of African Americans and 50 percent of Whites. The overall completion rate for Lowell is 38 percent, compared to the statewide rate of 71 percent (Swanson 2004, 64).[9]

According to dropout statistics from the Massachusetts Department of Education and the Lowell School Department, Lowell's overall dropout rate—and that of each racial group in Lowell—is steadily declining. These numbers indicate that Lowell's overall dropout rate has dropped from 11.6 percent in 1999–2000 to 4.4 percent in 2002–2003. In the same period, official statistics reflect that Lowell's Asian dropout rate has

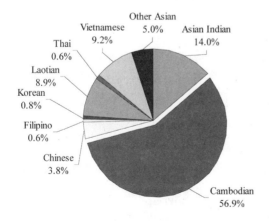

Figure 6.2: Population by Asian Subgroup *Source: U.S. Census Bureau, SF 2; PCT1.*

Table 6.1

Educational Attainment for the Population 18 Years and Over in Lowell

Population Group	% Without a High School Degree
Total population	27.9%
Cambodian	55.6%
Hispanic or Latino (of any race)	46.3%
Non-Hispanic White	22.1%
Non-Hispanic Black or African American	15.9%
Non-Hispanic Asian	42.3%

Source: U.S. Census Bureau, Summary File 4; PCT 65.

gone from 12.4 percent to 3.9 percent, the Latino dropout rate from 21.4 percent to 6.1 percent, the African American dropout rate from 4.4 percent to 2.3 percent, and the White dropout rate from 8.2 percent to 3.3 percent (Rurak 2004; MA DOE 2004a). This places Lowell's Asian dropout rate for both years below that of Latinos, but above that of Whites and African Americans.

Such a rapid and dramatic decline in just four years leads one to wonder whether reporting practices and formulas might actually account for this drop. Researchers have documented serious flaws with the method by which state education departments calculate their dropout rates—including, significantly, the failure to count "missing" students whose whereabouts are unknown, inaccurately classifying missing students as "transfers" to another school district, and failing to follow up with students who transfer to GED programs to ascertain that they in fact attend and eventually graduate (see Orfield, Losen, Wald, and Swanson 2004).

Even using the official data, which tends to underestimate dropout rates, Lowell's overall dropout rate and its Asian dropout rate are still higher than corresponding statewide rates. Lowell's overall dropout rate of 4.4 percent in 2002–2003 is still high compared to the statewide dropout rate of 3.3 percent, and Lowell's Asian dropout rate is 3.9 percent in contrast to the statewide Asian dropout rate of 2.5 percent. Lowell's Asian dropout rate is also still higher than the overall state dropout rate (see figure 6.3) (Rurak 2004; MA DOE 2004a).

Factors Contributing to High Dropout Rates of Cambodians

The community stakeholders that we interviewed reported a diverse range of reasons that may cause Cambodian students to drop out in Lowell, including a lack of representative and diverse faculty (Chea 2004; Long 2004; Rivera 2004), cultural differences between parents and school staff (Chea 2004; Long 2004; Rivera 2004), lack of and insufficient capacity at support programs (Ros 2004), interethnic tensions at schools (Long 2004), students' fear of standardized tests (Chhan 2004; Chea 2004; Meehan 2004), students' financial needs, requiring employment (Chhan 2004; Chea 2004; Ros 2004), lack of transportation[10] (Rivera 2004; FLT 2004) and students' lack of self-esteem or motivation (Chhan 2004).

Cultural and Linguistic Barriers

Because many Cambodian parents lack formal education themselves and/ or do not understand how to maneuver within the American education system, many Cambodian youth fall between the cracks of Lowell's overtaxed school system. According to Dr. Phala Chea (2004), the coordinator of the Lowell School Department's Parent Information Center, many "Cambodian parents cannot assist [their children] because they don't have the language [skills] and many of them don't have the educational background [to do so]." According to one youth advocate who wished to remain anonymous, "some parents themselves never even graduated from middle school, so they don't push their children at all. . . . Even though they value education, it's like their dream and reality is a different story" (CA3 2004). Indeed, Census 2000 data reported that the percentage of

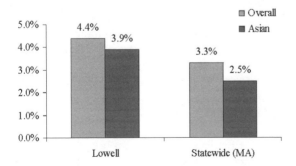

Figure 6.3: Comparison of Statewide and Lowell Dropout Rates *Source: Massachusetts Department of Education.*

Table 6.2

Ability to Speak English by Age

Cambodian Population	*5–17 years*	*18–64 years*	*65+ years*
% Speak English well	22.8%	25.4%	10.3%
% Do not speak English well	7.9%	29.8%	53.1%
% Do not speak English at all	0.7%	9.0%	25.6%
Total % with limited English proficiency	31.4%	64.2%	89.0%

Source: U.S. Census Bureau, Summary File 4; PCT 38.

Cambodians in Lowell with less than a ninth-grade education (31.7 percent) is almost three times that of the overall population (11.2 percent), and 64.2 percent of Lowell's Cambodian population aged 18 to 64 has limited English proficiency[11] (see table 6.2). Juan Carlos Rivera, a street-worker supervisor with the nonprofit youth development organization United Teen Equity Center, maintained that "strengthening communication between parents and the school system is key." He noted, however, that budget cuts have made it difficult for the Lowell School Department to deal with these and other challenges of serving a large and diverse student body (Rivera 2004).

Differences in the perception of the respective roles of parents and schools in Cambodia and the United States also account for part of the problem. "In Cambodia, it's clear that teachers are the authority. It's very different from the White parents who come in and demand [what they want]. A lot of the Asian parents don't do that," reports Mr. Rivera (2004). Further, streetworker Sakieth Long (2004)—also from United Teen Equity Center—reported that many Cambodian parents believe "the school is supposed to take care of [their] kids when they're in school, and [the parents' own] job is to discipline the kids." Because of these cultural barriers, as well as linguistic and educational challenges, many Cambodian parents in Lowell are unable to advocate effectively for their children in the public education system.

Language Ability and English-Language Learners

The high percentage of limited English proficient adults in the community explains the high percentage of English Language Learners (ELL)[12] among children and youth in Lowell's Cambodian population. Census 2000 data revealed that 31.4 percent of the elementary and secondary

school–aged population (ages 5 through 17) are limited English proficient. Furthermore, 85.8 percent of Cambodians in Lowell aged 5 and
over live in a household where *all* members speak a non-English language, and 14.1 percent live in a household where some members speak
English but others do not. These statistics indicate a high level of linguistic isolation in Lowell's Cambodian community.[13]

Several interviewees also emphasized the distinction between academic
English and "slang" English, and indicated that while many students may
easily converse in English, their grammar and writing may still fall far
short of standard academic English (Meehan 2004; Rivera 2004; Theam
2004). Michelle Meehan, executive director of Boys and Girls Club of
Greater Lowell, observed that many of the Cambodian youth attending
her organization's programs *spoke* English quite proficiently—albeit with
a higher than average incidence of grammatical errors. Many of them also
did not have good written English skills (Meehan 2004).

Whether the public school system classifies most of these students as
English-proficient or ELL is unclear, but one thing we do know is that
many ELL students are, in fact, American-born and have some English
ability. Most interviewees seemed to agree that many older teens classi-
fied as ELL came to the United States at an early stage, but younger ELL
students—especially those born after 1990 are predominantly American-
born (Mam 2004; Rivera 2004; Theam 2004). These findings indicate
that a clear distinction between ELL and English-proficient students does
not exist in Lowell's Cambodian community.

Effect of High-Stakes Testing

The ramifications that result from these varying levels of spoken and
written English ability are that Cambodian ELL students experience
greater difficulties in generally keeping up, as well as performing on high-
stakes tests like the Massachusetts Comprehensive Assessment System
(MCAS). Several interviewees pointed out the effect of the MCAS test requirement (Chhan 2004; Chea 2004; Meehan 2004). Under this testing
scheme, students must pass English and math MCAS subject matter tests
to graduate from high school, in addition to subject matter assessments in
a variety of subjects throughout elementary and secondary school (Boston Public Schools 2004). Ms. Meehan (2004) noted that the MCAS has
become "a little bit of a barrier" to graduation, and others also pointed
out that some students—even before they actually take the test—are in-
timidated by the MCAS tests. According to Sophia Chhan (2004), outreach coordinator at the Boys and Girls Club of Greater Lowell, "Some
[students] believe they can't pass MCAS—why go to school for four years

and not get a certificate? They think that they will get the GED later, but they probably don't, [and they] drop out at ninth grade."

When asked whether youth who drop out later return to finish high school or eventually obtain a General Education Development (GED) certificate, interviewees' responses were mixed. Some observed that students later go back for a GED when they are unable to find sustainable employment (Long 2004; FLT 2004), while others observed that many dropouts—especially women—start having families and have to take whatever work is available to support their children (Long 2004; Soeun 2004).

As such, it appears the school system is currently unable to address the needs of this particular group of students fully. Many Cambodian ELL students may be at a real, or at least perceived, disadvantage because of their limited English proficiency and poor verbal and reading ability. Consequently, regardless of whether they are actually able to pass MCAS or not, many believe that they will fail. Hence they feel it is not worth taking the tests and they drop out.

Discontinuation of Lowell's Bilingual Education Program

The language barriers that Cambodian students experience and the effect of high-stakes testing are further compounded by the passage in November 2002 of a statewide Massachusetts initiative that effectively ended bilingual education, replacing it with English-immersion classes. This initiative—referred to as "Question 2" by its ballot number—requires all ELL students to be mainstreamed after only one year of intense English immersion, subject only to a narrow waiver procedure.[14] Question 2 was implemented in the 2003–2004 school year. Although it is too early to examine its impact in broad statistical terms, research shows that most ELL students take anywhere from four to seven years of English study before being able to use English in academic subjects and perform at a similar level as native English peers (Hakuta 2000; see also Thomas and Collier 2003).

Our interviewees also provided anecdotal evidence of Question 2's impact. Their responses were mixed on the long-term efficacy of bilingual education itself—ranging from believing the end of bilingual education to be a significant loss of resources (CA3 2004), to questioning its helpfulness for students who have been in the United States more than a few years (Mam 2004). They also provided insight on other related effects of the new law.

Some interviewees cited the usefulness of bilingual education as a tool for Khmer language and culture retention. Sidney Liang (2004), program director at the Lowell Community Health Center and host of the Cambodian language radio show *Voice of Cambodian Children,* observed:

"When you teach language, you're teaching the culture and history, too. So when you limit the language . . . everything Cambodian is lost or faded away." Although the Lowell School Department does offer Khmer foreign language classes, enrollment in those classes has declined in recent years (FLT 2004) and the phasing out of bilingual education will likely eliminate an additional resource for Cambodian cultural maintenance.

According to Dr. Chea of the Lowell School Department's Parent Information Center, before Question 2, most Cambodian parents opted for their children to be in bilingual education if test results designated them as a candidate for the program. She reported that "less than 5 percent" opted for English-only over bilingual education where available (Chea 2004). Thus, although opinions may differ as to the efficacy of bilingual education and Question 2's merits, it is fairly clear that Question 2 will have a significant impact on ELL Cambodian students in Lowell, given the overwhelming rate at which Cambodian parents chose bilingual education over mainstream programs.

Interestingly, although the percentage of ELLs in Lowell's elementary and secondary school–aged Cambodian population (at almost one-third) is alarmingly high, it is considerably *lower* than the rate of ELLs in comparably-aged populations in some other Southeast Asian enclaves.[15] Census 2000 reported the percentage of ELLs for Hmong in Saint Paul, Minnesota, as 54.4 percent. For Vietnamese in Westminster, California, it is 44.9 percent. For the Iu Mien and Lao in Sacramento, California, it is 44.3 percent, and for Cambodians in Long Beach, California, it is 39.6 percent.

One possible explanation for Lowell's comparatively lower rate of ELLs could, in fact, be the early establishment of its Khmer language bilingual program and Khmer language support. Lowell's Khmer language bilingual program was created in the early 1980s, and expanded significantly in 1985 to meet the needs of its rapidly growing Cambodian student population (Duch 2004). By contrast, schools in Saint Paul began to implement a select number of Hmong literacy programs just five to six years ago (Vang 2004), Westminster implemented a Vietnamese language support program (but not bilingual education per se) for ELLs from 1993 through 1999 (Dallison 2004). Long Beach had a Cambodian bilingual program that began in 1993, but disbanded after Proposition 227 passed in 1998 (Khoun 2005). To date Sacramento has never had either a Lao or Iu Mien bilingual program or language support (Gilman-Ponce 2004).

Further study is certainly needed to measure the actual effect of discontinuing Lowell's bilingual education program. In the absence of these data, we felt it was important to make note of Question 2 and its potential to impact the dropout rate of Cambodian students in Lowell.

Lack of Representative and Diverse Faculty

The lack of Cambodian faculty in Lowell public schools appears to be another contributing factor preventing the school system from fully meeting students' needs. Although Lowell's superintendent and Lowell School Department have the reputation of being progressive and generally student-oriented (Rivera 2004; CA3 2004), Lowell High School's enormous size is a barrier to providing sufficient personal and academic support for students. According to Sayon Soeun (2004), the executive director of the youth service agency Light of Cambodian Children, "The guidance counselors can't even handle the seniors. They're not equipped to provide resources to all students because there's only one high school in Lowell. The school will serve those who are aggressively seeking assistance." Since our interviews, the Lowell School Department has created a stand-alone Freshman Academy in an effort to encourage incoming freshmen to stay in school. We hope this program can indeed provide new freshmen with more attention and services to help them remain in school.

Several interviewees also agreed that the lack of Cambodian faculty in Lowell public schools—particularly at the high school level—hindered the schools' ability to serve Cambodian students (Chea 2004; CA3 2004; Rivera 2004). According to Dr. Chea (2004): "At Lowell High, we have close to 3,500 kids—and we have a huge population of Asians. And there's one housemaster who's Cambodian. There's one guidance counselor I know of who's Cambodian. Maybe two or three teachers who teach Khmer language. There are no Cambodian teachers in the mainstream classroom to give them guidance or support."

In addition, Question 2 included a clause requiring all teachers to be fluent in English. In Lowell, a number of long-term, tenured teachers—including a number who attended college and even graduate school in the United States—were terminated for failure to pass a standardized English exam. AALDEF represented seven former bilingual teachers[16] dismissed pursuant to Question 2.[17] We challenged the Lowell School District's failure to assess fluency through classroom observation before resorting to testing, as well as the fact that the fluency test Lowell School District used (and recommended by the Massachusetts Department of Education) has never been calibrated for high-stakes use and does not diagnose the level of English ability needed for effective teaching. In spring 2006, AALDEF and pro bono co-counsel Weil, Gotshal, and Manges won reinstatement with full back pay and benefits for three of these teachers; this judgment, however, has not been enforced owing to a pending appeal. Of the original seven complainants, two were previously reinstated, and another two settled for temporary nonteaching jobs. The loss of Cambodian teachers due to Question 2 fluency testing appears to have exacerbated a preexisting problem in teacher resources.

Question 2 unfavorably impacts the number of Cambodian teachers and role models within the school system. In turn, the loss of connection to Cambodian staff may yield a cultural gap: if Cambodian students feel disengaged and isolated at school, they may seek support from their peers or elsewhere.

Dropout Policies and Administrative Barriers

Many of the staff and teachers within the Lowell School Department work actively to help students succeed in the system; nonetheless, there are certain school policies and administrative obstacles that are set up in such a way that students are either, explicitly or implicitly, encouraged to drop out. Under Lowell's truancy policy, school officials must take progressive corrective measures as a student accrues successive unexcused absences. At the time our research was conducted, such measures included a letter to parents after five absences, a review hearing after ten, and—assuming the student is permitted to return after the review hearing—automatic removal after fifteen consecutive absences (Lowell High School 2003). Similar measures remain in place, but the number of absences required before each intervention has been shortened (Lowell High School 2006).[18]

Advocates reported to us that often no meaningful review hearing actually occurs, leading to students *automatically* being dropped after accruing the requisite absences, *without* a meaningful opportunity to present their cases.[19] We also learned that students short of the required threshold of consecutive absences were sometimes dropped from the rolls.[20]

One advocate who declined to be named informed us of a case wherein a student was suspended for a week for wearing the color blue (a common gang color) and, although a suspension hearing of some sort was held, because of administrative difficulties the school did not actually meet with the student's parents for two weeks (CA3 2004). An employee of the Middlesex County Juvenile Court Department who did not wish to be named added, "I think that the school needs to actively communicate with the parents when their kids start missing school. Instead, school officials wait until the kids have missed 15 or 20 days of school before they inform parents" (LJC1 2004).

As a result, the student was eventually allowed back, but was told he had missed so much class that he was now failing; eventually he dropped out (CA2 2004). At the time of our interviews, school policy allowed students to receive a No Credit grade for class—even when they are in a class in which they are passing, but they have reached their tenth absence—essentially leaving them little incentive to stay in class.[21] The policy is even stricter now, allowing students only five unexcused absences per semester (Lowell High School 2006, 44).

Additionally, Mr. Rivera (2004) of United Teen Equity Center informed us that "at the age of sixteen, you actually get the option [to drop out]." Indeed, a student over 16 years of age may withdraw voluntarily for personal reasons, but only after a discussion with a guidance counselor, provided documented attempts were made to keep the student in school (Lowell High School 2003, xviii). But in one distressing case reported to AALDEF, a 15-year-old Cambodian student was wrongly mistaken for another older student that was suspected of being involved in gang activity. Because the two students shared the same name, the school consequently dropped the 15-year-old from the rolls.

The Lowell School Department and superintendent have worked with AALDEF and local community advocates to ameliorate some of these inequities in the system.[22] Mr. Rivera (2004) reported back that "the [Lowell] School Department has been incredibly open to developing new programs and ideas that best fit the diversity of this district. The Superintendent has been progressive since we first established our partnership." Despite such efforts, however, AALDEF and its community partners continue to encounter and must advocate on behalf of students who have been dropped from the rolls pursuant to these procedures.

Financial Constraints

Lastly, other personal issues seem to contribute to the high dropout rate among Cambodian students, such as the need to work, lack of convenient transportation, or a lack of awareness of available resources (FLT 2004; CA1 2004; CA2 2004). Census 2000 data revealed that Cambodians have the lowest median household income of any Asian group in Lowell. At $37,328, the median household income for Cambodians is comparable to that of African Americans ($37,941), and squarely between that of Latinos ($25,963) and Whites ($51,386). However, an even bleaker story emerges when we examined per capita income. The per capita income for Cambodians in Lowell is the *lowest* across all racial and ethnic groups (as well as other Asians) at $9,727—compared to $10,595 for Latinos, $16,025 for African Americans, and $20,771 for Whites (see fig. 6.4). This discrepancy indicates that Lowell's Cambodian households are larger than other racial and ethnic groups, accounting for the greater total family income compared with a lower per capita

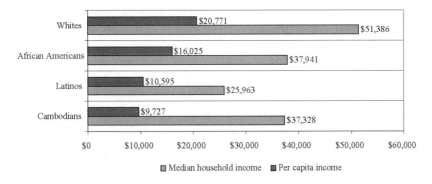

Figure 6.4: Income in 1999 by Race in Lowell *Source: U.S. Census Bureau, Summary File 4; PCT 122 and PCT 130.*

income. Further, 13.8 percent of Lowell's Cambodian children and youth under 18 live in poverty.[23]

Our interviewees provided insight as to why the median income for Lowell's Cambodian community is so low. One youth advocate and community activist hypothesized: "Cambodian experiences are probably more similar to that of Latinos—they don't have the advantage of a networking structure—old boy's network—to help obtain employment opportunities." He further observed, "Cambodians came here during wartime as refugees, without preparation, financial resources, or connections or support from any other family members or foundation or community base" (CA3 2004).

Samnang Mam (2004), a paralegal at Merrimack Valley Legal Services who runs the organization's Cambodian Outreach Unit, said, "Back in Cambodia, many [members of Lowell's Cambodian community] were farmers, so they don't have any transferable skills. And many of them came here when they were older, so it is hard for them to go back to school." Other interviewees also cited language difficulties and lack of employment skills and education as contributing factors for the low income rate of Lowell's Cambodian population (CA3 2004; Mam 2004; Ros 2004).

As a result, Cambodian youth in Lowell face challenges due to low socioeconomic circumstances. According to Mr. Ros (2004) of the Cambodian Mutual Assistance Association, "When you don't have resources, you don't have the support. Parents are trying to make ends meet. And the kids are left to fend for themselves." Michelle Meehan, executive director of the Boys and Girls Club of Greater Lowell, also stressed that financial needs may cause youths to drop out to work: "I don't think students necessarily drop out for negative reasons," she observed. "It could be for positive reasons, such as helping the family out financially" (Meehan 2004).

Implications of Dropping Out or Being Pushed Out of School

Because of the high dropout rate in Lowell's Cambodian community, one key concern was what youth do with their time after dropping out. Thus, we asked the interviewees a series of questions concerning young people's experiences outside of the school environment, as well as how those experiences impact their ability or incentive to continue their education. Many young Cambodians, according to interviewees, stay home for the time being or spend time with peers on the street (often to prevent parents from discovering they had dropped out) (LJC2 2004; Chhan 2004; Soeun 2004). Others find low-skill jobs such as factory jobs or landscaping. Often, youth take "under the table" jobs if they are unable to find or are not of age for legal employment (Chhan 2004; Rivera 2004). Mr. Rivera (2004) of United Teen Equity Center pointed out that his organization tries to encourage dropouts to instead attend GED or job training programs.

Gang Involvement and Interfacing the Juvenile Justice System

According to Dr. Chea (2004), coordinator of the Lowell School Department's Parent Information Center, Cambodian students often "don't know how to seek assistance from their teachers, don't think the teachers understand them, and sometimes they seek outside help (friends or gangs, or other kids of support that may not be positive)." Michelle Meehan (2004), expressed concern that youth sometimes become gang-involved in response to failures or frustration dealing with the school system, especially if their parents are not engaged in their education and an older sibling is already involved with a gang—offering the "instant gratification" of needed support and belonging.

Other interviewees agreed that youth who spend a lot of time "on the streets" (dropouts, as well as youth who are still enrolled in school but are truant) are more likely to get involved in criminal or gang activity, or at least be profiled as such. Judge Jay Blitzman (2004), associate justice of the Middlesex County Juvenile Court (sitting in Lowell) said, "Kids who are truant are close to 50 percent more likely to be involved in delinquent or criminal behavior. That's been reported in CHINS (Children in Need of Services) studies. . . . There's a clear public safety concern or connection between kids out of school and kids who appear in court." Thus, we must keep this in mind as a potential secondary consequence of Lowell's high dropout rate, and as one key way that education policy can produce outcomes in the juvenile justice system.

When asked whether Cambodian youth are overrepresented in Lowell's juvenile justice system, Judge Blitzman (2004) pointed out a lack of sufficient disaggregated data to show such trends. He stated that although the Massachusetts Department of Youth Services keeps racially disaggregated data of youth who are confined in secure facilities, a comprehensive racially disaggregated data profile covering all court-involved youth, including youth in probation or diversion programs, simply does not exist.

Without access to supporting data, the judge was forced to conclude, "Based on anecdotal evidence it appears that there are a high percentage of cases involving Cambodian youth. It may be that the number of cases reflects the demographic reality of the community, but it is in our collective interest to ascertain the facts" (Blitzman 2004).

Gang and Racial Profiling of Cambodian Youth

Furthermore, at times Cambodian or Southeast Asian youth may be profiled as being in a gang, whether they actually are or not. According to a youth advocate who declined to be named, "There's also definitely gang profiling—a youth just hanging out with a group of Cambodians or Southeast Asians will be labeled. And then there are some who actually do get involved in criminal activity" (CA1 2004). Interviewees also observed that youth who are truant—and thus on the streets in daytime, especially downtown—are more likely to be labeled as gang members and consequently get into trouble. They further observed that youth who dressed in hip-hop style clothing were more likely to be viewed as gang members (CA3 2004; Long 2004; Rivera 2004).

Other interviewees, however, did not feel that Cambodian or other Southeast Asian youth were necessarily profiled by police. Rather, they observed that youth sometimes get into trouble because they are in the wrong place at the wrong time, or because matters escalate at valid police inquiries because youth are impolite or "talk back" to officers (LJC1 2004; Soeun 2004). These certainly may be contributing factors, and most agreed that the Lowell Police Department is not monolithic. United Teen Equity Center's Mr. Long (2004) pointed out that "there are definitely police officers in the schools who get to know the kids [and help them out]. Some officers are the teens' best advocates. It depends on the officer and their own style."

Additionally, AALDEF has received reports from the Cambodian community of police taking pictures of youth for a gang pictures book or database. According to these reports, at times—in particular during warm weather when youth are more likely to be outside—police will stop groups of Cambodian youth downtown after school hours or in Cambodian neighborhoods and take their pictures for a "known gang member" album or database. Although such youth are not charged with any crime, we are told that these pictures will be placed in police records for later use such as in identification lineups.[24]

Such a practice, if it exists, runs an extremely high risk of labeling innocent youth as gang members. Because youth could be photographed without being charged with a crime, it can sweep within its reach a young person who is simply in a public place spending time with a person who is gang-affiliated—or worse, merely Cambodian and hence suspected of gang membership.

Suspension or Expulsion from School

Finally, youth who are involved with the criminal justice system run the additional risk of being suspended or expelled from school *as a result of* such involvement—even if they are still enrolled in school. Under Massachusetts law, a juvenile or criminal justice adjudication can in some circumstances lead to punitive action through school disciplinary procedures. A student who is merely *accused* (and not yet convicted) of felonies may be suspended pending adjudication if that student's continuing presence at the school will, in his or her principal's opinion, have a "substantial detrimental effect" on the school's "general welfare."[25] Students accused or convicted of nonfelony crimes—while not explicitly covered by this provision—are also subject to suspension or other discipline under general school disciplinary provisions.[26] Needless to say, this law provides principals with significant discretion to remove students perceived as troublemakers even though they have not yet been found guilty of any crime. Such students may later be expelled if they are found—or plead—guilty.[27]

While the legislature's concern with protecting schools from potentially violent youth is understandable, these provisions create a dangerous causal loop. Being barred from school through suspension or expulsion will in turn further increase the risk of additional criminal justice involvement.

Risk of Deportation

It is worthwhile noting that noncitizen youth and young adults in Lowell's Cambodian community are particularly vulnerable to the additional risk of criminal deportation. According to Census 2000 figures, 13.8 percent of Cambodian youth under the age of 18 in Lowell are noncitizens, compared to 8.2 percent of the overall youth population. But more than two-thirds (70.7 percent) of Cambodians aged 18 years old and over are noncitizens, compared to 37.5 percent of African Americans, 20.4 percent of Latinos, and only 4.4 percent of Whites. Owing to more vigilant enforcement of criminal deportation laws after September 11 and a recent agreement with the government of Cambodia to allow repatriation of deportable Cambodian nationals from the United States, a noncitizen Cambodian in Lowell stands to be deported to Cambodia for conviction of certain enumerated crimes, including some as minor as receipt of stolen property and some theft offenses.[28] This substantially increases the degree of risks and scope of harm that could flow to a young Cambodian in Lowell who is gang-involved or criminally active, or profiled as such. Thus, the risk of deportation is another potential consequence of the challenges Cambodian youth face within the education system.

Addressing the Unmet Needs of Cambodian Students

Appropriate support and intervention, as well as a sense of belonging, are key in determining whether a struggling student stays in school or drops out.[29] A number of community-based youth programs in Lowell exist to provide a positive environment and community for Cambodian youth (Rivera 2004). There is even a dropout prevention program within the school system called Student Connections. Each in its own limited capacity helps keep youth off the streets—whether through summer camp, mentorship, or drop-in after school programs for writing, sports, and so forth.

Unfortunately, due to inadequate or restricted funding and resources, such programs do not seem to be fully meeting the community's needs (Long 2004; CA3 2004). The Student Connections program, for example, started in September 2002, and collectively served more than five hundred students a year, as well as their parents and relatives. In addition to the program director and administrative assistant, four case managers were originally hired by the Lowell School Department to support students and parents. In addition to an English-speaking counselor who served the general population, a bilingual Khmer counselor served Cambodians and other Asian students, a bilingual Spanish counselor served

Latino students, and a bilingual Portuguese counselor served the growing Brazilian student population. But the Student Connections program has since been largely defunded, and only able to maintain a part-time Spanish-speaking counselor in the 2006–2007 school year.

Several interviewees also pointed out the need for parent support programs, both to engage parents in their children's education, and to keep youth out of the juvenile justice system (Mam 2004; Meehan 2004; Soeun 2004). Cambodian parents are often unaware of support programs both within the school system and in the local community. Furthermore, one youth advocate who preferred to remain anonymous stated, "[A] majority [of Cambodian parents] do support such programs because they're concerned with the safety of their children and such programs provide a reliable haven, but some prefer their children to be at home where it is not only safe but also less exposed to by some of what they perceive as negative values of Americans (e.g., dating, teen pregnancy)" (CA3 2004). This variance shows conflicting cultural values at play. Effective interventions to get parents more involved are needed to take this into account.

Greater outreach and diversity efforts by the Lowell School Department for both its academic and extracurricular and sports programs should be developed. An employee of the Lowell juvenile courts who declined to be identified felt that there should be student mentorship programs with adult Southeast Asian role models (LJC2 2004). Another piece of the solution seems to be additional capacity-building resources, like job training, community organizing, or further development of community-based organizations. Such initiatives would serve the dual role of engaging young people in their community and provide them with the skills, discipline, and confidence to succeed in school as well.

Intervention programs for youth already deeply involved in gangs, though desperately needed, are few and far between (Chhan 2004). Judge Blitzman (2004) went on to expound upon specific unmet needs and necessary supports for Lowell's court system:

I think there are some stressors impacting the Cambodian population that are different from other immigrant populations. Going through a holocaust has created unique transitional problems. The native culture is intact in other populations. . . . [In the Cambodian community,] I see a reverse parentification process. I see kids who are leading their parents through a court system. Court interpreters doing the best they can. There are only 2 or 3 [Khmer] interpreters, statewide. . . . And many of the parents are illiterate in Khmer.

The issues the judge raises—low English fluency, insufficient language access, low native-language literacy, cultural stressors associated with the Khmer Rouge experience,[30] and the difficulties Lowell faces in meeting

these challenges as a predominantly working-class city—demonstrate where additional funding and resources are needed.

Lastly, our interviewees pointed out that adult English literacy programs do exist in Lowell (CA3 2004; Soeun 2004), but may be difficult to prioritize for working-class parents struggling to make ends meet. Thus, allocating additional resources for Khmer language interpretation would go a long way toward opening a stronger line of communication with parents of Cambodian youth in the schools—as well as those in the juvenile courts.

Judge Blitzman (2004) aptly summarized the many challenges and opportunities Lowell faces with his observation that the city "should be applauded and celebrated for its unique diversity and willingness to accept the challenges posed by attempting to help out a large, high needs immigrant community in a relatively short period of time. The demographic composition of the inner city has changed radically in a relatively short period of time and the city's tax base and resources have been stretched dramatically. There is a need to work collectively and constructively to address the complexity of these issues." United Teen Equity Center's Mr. Rivera agreed with the judge that many of the challenges pointed out are severely exacerbated or caused by the limitations in the city's resources and tax base, despite the good intentions and efforts of many individuals within city government and the School Department (Rivera 2004; Blitzman 2004).

In this essay, we have explored various interconnected factors impacting the educational experience of Cambodian youth in Lowell, as well as a number of resulting effects. We examined challenges faced by low-income students in completing their education owing to a shortage of resources and infrastructure or a need to work to support their families. We looked at difficulties faced by Lowell's overcrowded public high school in trying to meet student needs—difficulties exacerbated for Cambodian youth because of a lack of representative faculty and parental lack of capacity to advocate owing to cultural, educational, and linguistic barriers. We also considered the impact of high-stakes testing and students being tracked, or subtly encouraged, to pursue a GED instead of a high school degree.

We further examined the additional challenges posed by the high proportion of ELLs among Lowell's Cambodian youth—even among those who are American-born—and considered the distinction between social and academic English ability. Finally, we considered the impact of the ending of bilingual education in Massachusetts and its related impact on Khmer cultural and linguistic retention.

We sought to link these educational issues with some potential effects of the high dropout rate in Lowell's Cambodian community, especially the increased likelihood of criminal justice involvement (which, for non-citizens, carries the risk of deportation). We also uncovered community concerns about racial profiling by both school authorities and law enforcement—which, if founded, could hasten youths' path from educational difficulties, to dropping out, to involvement with the juvenile and criminal justice system, and even potentially deportation.

This essay provides a backdrop for AALDEF's own work with the Cambodian community in Lowell. By documenting the above issues and solutions, our intention is to explore an area about which comparatively little research has been completed, as well as to create a rough blueprint for our future work in collaboration with community members and local community-based organizations to address these challenges.

Notes

1. We are extremely indebted to Ivy Oracion Suriyopas for her countless hours conducting tireless research and thorough interviews, to Samuel S. Kang for assisting with data analysis, to Lisa Khandhar for her research assistance, and to the many community stakeholders in Lowell who took time from their busy schedules to speak to us for this project. We owe them many thanks for their efforts and interest.

2. U.S. Census Bureau; Census 2000 Summary File 1 (SF1) and Summary File 2 (SF2) 100-Percent Data and 2000 Census Summary File 4 (SF4) Sample Data; generated by Nancy Yu; using American Fact Finder; <http://factfinder.census.gov/servlet/DatasetMainPageServlet?_program=DEC&_lang=en&_ts=>; (October 7, 2003).

3. See Hai Pho's account in this volume (chapter 2).

4. The nation's largest Cambodian community is in Long Beach, California (population 17,396).

5. The data reported in this article reflects single-race responses. These numbers should, therefore, be considered the minimum population size as we do not account for multiracial individuals in our analysis.

6. The data reported in this article refer to the non-Hispanic or Latino race, Hispanic or Latino origin (or any race), or ancestry of a population or household.

7. The high dropout rates in Lowell's Cambodian community will invariably also impact enrollment rates.

8. Lowell has two small charter schools, which had a total enrollment of 453 for the 2002–2003 school year.

9. This data uses the Cumulative Promotion Index to estimate and measure high school graduation rates.

10. There is no busing whatsoever for high school students. There are distance cutoffs for elementary (0.75 mile) and middle school students (1.75 miles).

11. Limited English proficiency is defined by advocates as the ability to speak English less than "very well" (McCully 2005; Tenoso 2005).

12. An English Language Learner (ELL) is defined as a person who is in the process of acquiring English and has a first language other than English (LAB 2004).

13. The U.S. Census Bureau defines a linguistically isolated household as one in which no member fourteen years old and over speaks only English, or speaks a non-English language and speaks English "very well." In other words, all members fourteen years old and over in a household have at least some difficulty with English.

14. Question 2: English Language Education in Public Schools, Massachusetts General Laws, §71A (2002).

15. The authors chose four cities as comparison groups to Lowell's Cambodian community because of their distinct and substantially sized Southeast Asian refugee populations. According to Census 2000 data, there are 24,389 Hmong in St. Paul, Minnesota; 27,109 Vietnamese live in Westminster, California; 5,924 Laotians (a designation that includes the Iu Mien, Khmu, and Thaidam, in addition to ethnic Lao) reside in Sacramento, California. The nation's largest Cambodian community is in Long Beach, California (17,396).

16. Four of these teachers are Cambodian, two are Latino, and one is Lao.

17. Duch et al. v. Lowell School Committee (arbitration began on September 29, 2004) (Boulanger, Arb.).

18. Now a letter must be issued after three consecutive absences, a hearing after seven absences, and a student may be removed after only ten consecutive absences (Lowell High School 2006).

19. AALDEF received this information through confidential reports from community members and advocates in Lowell on March 29, 2004, and May 17, 2004.

20. It is unclear why this is the case, although it could be because language barriers prevent parents from deciphering the letter issued after five absences, or perhaps administrative burdens on the overcrowded school district prevent officials from following up thoroughly with absentee students.

21. When a student reaches his tenth absence in a class in which he is passing, the teacher is required to submit a Grade Disposition Form (U Form) to the housemaster, who reviews the student's file to determine if documentation of absences is sufficient. If the documentation is insufficient, the U grade will not be cleared and the student receives a No Credit grade five school days after the semester ends (Lowell High School 2003, 3–18).

22. A university-government-community effort of note is Gear-Up (Gaining Early Awareness and Readiness for Undergraduate Programs) a project of the federal Department of Education and the Massachusetts Board of Higher Education. One of its goals is to identify middle and high school students with attendance and retention issues and to increase the likelihood of more children pursuing postsecondary education. The University of Massachusetts Lowell's Center for Family, Work, and Community and Middlesex Community College have participated in the program since 2000. Retrieved on January 22, 2007 from http://www.gearup.mass.edu/Default.aspx.

23. Cambodians fall squarely between Latinos (18.2 percent, the highest percentage of youth living in poverty) and African Americans (6.4 percent), with Whites trailing below (2.6 percent).

24. AALDEF received this information through confidential reports from youth and advocates in Lowell on March 29, 2004.

25. 71 Massachusetts General Laws §37H 1/2 (1993).

26. See, for example, 71 Massachusetts General Laws §37H (1993), et al.

27. Under both federal and Massachusetts law, students must have some sort of hearing before being expelled. At the hearing, they must be given a chance to give their side of the story, and have the right to representation. Students can appeal negative decisions to the superintendent. See, for example, 71 Massachusetts General Laws §37H (1993), et al.

28. 8 U.S.C. §1101(a)(43), §1227(a)(2)(A)(iii) (1996). These provisions are part of the Illegal Immigration Reform and Immigrant Responsibility Act of 1996.

29. See Tuyet-Lan Pho's essay in this volume (chapter 5) for a discussion of how cultural values and family life may have influenced the academic performance of their children and the nature of the parent-school relationship.

30. See Leakhena Nou's essay in this volume (chapter 10), which examines the psychosocial adjustment of Khmer refugees in Massachusetts from an insider's perspective.

References

Blitzman, J. July 22, 2004. Personal communication.

Boston Public Schools. (2004). *MCAS . . . It Counts! A Guide for Parents of the Boston Public Schools*. Retrieved June 22, 2004, from http://boston.k12 .ma.us/teach/mcas.asp.

Chea, P. August 3, 2004. Personal communication.

Chhan, S. July 20, 2004. Personal communication.

Community Advocate 1 (CA1). July 15, 2004. Personal communication.

Community Advocate 2 (CA2). July 27, 2004. Personal communication.

Community Advocate 3 (CA3). July 15, 2004. Personal communication.

Dallison, S. October 8, 2004. Personal communication.

Duch, V. November 22, 2004. Personal communication.

Former Lowell School District Teacher (FLT). August 5, 2004. Personal communication.

Gerson, J. N.d. The Cambodian-Americans of Lowell, Massachusetts: A Cautionary Tale of New Immigrant and Refugee Political Incorporation. Unpublished manuscript.

Gilman-Ponce, S. November 17, 2004. Personal communication.

Hakuta, K. 2000. How Long Does It Take English Learners to Attain Proficiency? *University of California Linguistic Minority Research Institute. Policy Reports*. Retrieved November 16, 2004, from http://repositories.cdlib.org /lmri/ pr/hakuta.

Khoun, O. August 4, 2005. Personal communication.

Liang, S. July 26, 2004. Personal communication.

Long, S. July 27, 2004. Personal communication.

Lowell High School. 2003. *Parent & Student Handbook, 2003-2004*. Lowell, MA.

———. 2006. *Parent & Student Handbook, 2006-2007*. Lowell, MA.

Lowell Juvenile Courts Employee 1 (LJC1). August 6, 2004. Personal communication.

Lowell Juvenile Courts Employee 2 (LJC2). July 20, 2004. Personal communication.

Mam, S. July 18, 2004. Personal communication.

Massachusetts Department of Education. 2004a. *Dropout Rates in Massachu-setts Public Schools: 2002–2003*. Retrieved June 17, 2004, from http://www.doe.mass.edu/infoservices/reports/dropout/0203/.
———. 2004b. *Enrollment by District/Grade/Race, School Year 2002–2003*. Retrieved November 17, 2004, from http://www.doe.mass.edu/infoservices/reports/enroll/default.html.
McCully, C. June 24, 2005. Personal communication.
Meehan, M. August 3, 2004. Personal communication.
Orfield, G., D. Losen, J. Wald, and C. Swanson. 2004. *Losing Our Future: How Minority Youth are Being Left Behind by the Graduation Rate Crisis*. Cambridge, MA: Civil Rights Project at Harvard University. Contributors: Advocates for Children of New York, The Civil Society Institute.
Rivera, J. C. July 26, 2004. Personal communication.
Ros, V. July 23, 2004. Personal communication.
Rurak, T. August 10, 2004. Personal communication.
Soeun, S. July 20, 2004. Personal communication.
Swanson, C. B. 2004. *Who Graduates? Who Doesn't? A Statistical Portrait of Public High School Graduation, Class of 2001*. Washington, DC: Urban Institute Education Policy Center. Retrieved July 11, 2005, from http://www.urban.org/UploadedPDF/410934_WhoGraduates.pdf.
Northeast and Islands Regional Educational Laboratory (LAB). N.d. *Teaching Diverse Learners*. Retrieved September 10, 2004, from http://www.alliance.brown.edu/tdl/.
Tenoso, G. June 24, 2005. Personal communication.
Theam, S. July 19, 2004. Personal communication.
Thomas, W., and V. Collier. (2003). Reform of Education Policies for Bilingual/Bicultural Students: Research Evidence from U.S. Schools and the Astounding Effectiveness of Two-Way Bilingual Enrichment for All. *El Noticiero* 27, no, 3.
Vang, M. October 8, 2004. Personal communication.

Susan Thomson

Along the Path to *Nibbana*

Civic Engagement, Community Partnerships, and Lowell's Southeast Asian Buddhist Temples

Watlao Mixayaram, a Lao Buddhist temple, sits in a quiet residential neighborhood in South Lowell, Massachusetts, just off Interstate 495. As you enter the gated temple compound, the monks' residence is to the left; to the right is the main temple hall, just three years old, painted soft yellow with intricate green and red designs bordering the eaves. It is mid-October, and as my son and I go through the temple doorway, we pause to remove our shoes. We enter the front hallway and see our friend to the left, helping other Lao women prepare the monks' food and arrange it on large, circular bamboo trays for their daily meal. Looking further into the hall, we find her mother and six-month-old daughter, who is quietly observing the scene from her baby carrier. We sit beside them on the matted floor, unpacking the bananas, snacks, and other offerings we have brought for the monks. Because this is a special celebration to mark the end of the monks' retreat during the rainy season, many people have gathered: women and children are sitting in the back of the room, and men and older boys are in the front, just behind a row of six monks, who are facing the group. Behind them, a large golden Buddha sits on an elevated altar, surrounded by vases of colorful flowers. Elaborate, original paintings from Laos encircle the hall with the story of Buddha's life. Across the ceiling, just before the altar, is a red, white, and blue garland, reminiscent of those decorating New England towns on the Fourth of July and other patriotic holidays. Just in front of the Buddha, propped on a tower of artfully folded dollar bills, is a small American flag.

Back in downtown Lowell, the hexagonal main building of Middlesex Community College's city campus—formerly a training center for Wang Laboratories—sits astride the Pawtucket Canal and the Concord River, waters that once powered Lowell's textile mills. The newly restored Federal

Building, now serving as the college's library, is just across the street. In front of both buildings, the American flag and the Massachusetts state flag fly high. As with most community colleges, the majority of the students come from the surrounding area; for the Lowell campus, this is the multicultural community of greater Lowell, including first- and second-generation immigrants from more than fifty different countries. The college also hosts a considerable number of international students each year. As you pass by groups of students on a weekday morning, you are as likely to hear conversations in Spanish, Portuguese, or Khmer as in English.

At the Middlesex graduation ceremony in 2002, a former international student from Cambodia—Tooch Van—was invited to give the commencement speech. A graduate of both Middlesex Community College and Tufts University's Fletcher School of Diplomacy, he offered the following advice: "I really believe that the beauty of human beings is when we have a chance to help each other out, when we have a chance to give back to the community. May you use what you know to help make the world a little bit better place each day" (cited in McMahon 2002).

Van's words resonate with Middlesex Community College's own commitment to civic responsibility and service as an outcome of education. With campuses in suburban Bedford and downtown Lowell, Middlesex includes active civic engagement as one of six pillars expressing its primary values, goals, and mission, thereby emphasizing participation with both local and global community institutions as well as its extensive service-learning program. In 2003, Middlesex Community College partnered with Lowell National Historical Park to launch an ambitious three-year project: the Lowell Civic Collaborative, aimed at increasing civic engagement opportunities in the curriculum and through community partnerships. Yet, as the college works to engage a broader range of students in civic awareness and participation, questions as to how to accomplish this loom large. The Lowell campus, in particular, has a high percentage of students from many of the city's newer immigrant groups: Southeast Asian, African, Brazilian, South Asian, and Latino, communities that have historically been politically marginalized and demonstrated low levels of participation in Lowell's civic arena.[1] To encourage involvement of these students in the Lowell Civic Collaborative and other community initiatives, a key question is, what does civic engagement mean within these diverse cultural frameworks?

In the Lowell context, this question is illuminated by a focus group study conducted by the One Lowell Coalition in 2001,[2] revealing that for recent immigrants in the city, attending church and/or temple is by far the most common way to participate in community life (Fahlberg 2001). This connection between religious institutions and civic engagement in American democracy is underscored in Robert Putnam's seminal work

Bowling Alone (2000), wherein he writes: "Faith communities in which people worship together are arguably the single most important repository of social capital in America." He adds that churches, in particular, "provide an important incubator for civic skills, civic norms, community interests, and civic recruitment" (66).

And yet, the extent to which religious institutions should be directly involved in American public life and its secular institutions has been the source of much debate, especially during the past twenty years. Certainly many citizens are increasingly uncomfortable with the efforts of religious groups to pass legislation supporting their own particular moral views on such issues as abortion and gay marriage, or to promote their own political candidates and judicial appointments. But as the religious scholars Robert Wuthnow and John H. Evans (2002) point out, "Not only is there a close relationship in American culture between conceptions of conscience and understandings of citizenship; there is also a well-established tradition of grassroots participation in public life through the activities of local churches and synagogues" (2).

Considering this strong association between religious organizations and civic engagement leads one to ask, Does Tooch Van's plea for service and engagement, voiced in a secular educational context, correspond to the religious grounding of most Southeast Asian immigrants in Theravada Buddhism?[3] And if a common ground is found, could it be a catalyst to spark the involvement of Southeast Asian community college students in civic service and public life, and to form partnerships among Southeast Asian temples and Middlesex Community College, Lowell National Historical Park, and other Lowell public institutions?

To address these questions, I shall provide the following: an identification of three key approaches to civic engagement and community life within the context of Theravada Buddhism; a description of how Lowell's Lao and Cambodian temples exemplify these approaches through two contrasting temple-community activities fostering civic engagement; and a concluding reflection on how these three types of engagement underlie growing connections between Lowell's Buddhist temples and the public life of the city as a whole.

Community, Civic Engagement and Theravada Buddhism

All of Buddhist thought dates back to the insight of Gotama Buddha (c. 525 centuries BCE), and in that sense Buddhism may be seen as one religion. After Buddha's death, however, contrasting opinions and migrations of people led to the growth of separate branches. Although many Cambodians in Lowell refer to their religion simply as *sasana boran*, or the original teachings of Buddha (J. Massey, personal communication, September 24, 2006), Theravada (the way or tradition of the elders) is the formal term for the school of Buddhism most prevalent in Southeast Asia and Sri Lanka, with an estimated 100 million Theravada Buddhists worldwide. It is historically older and distinct from the second main branch of Buddhism, Mahayana Buddhism (the Greater Vehicle), currently found throughout China, Tibet, Japan, and Korea. A third branch of Buddhism, Vajrayana (the Diamond Vehicle) also exists, and is especially influential in Tibetan Buddhism. Alongside of these established schools, the contemporary emergence of "engaged Buddhism," a term first introduced by the Vietnamese monk and social activist Thich Nhat Hanh in the 1960s, is felt by Western scholars such as Christopher Queen (2000) to be "unprecedented, and thus tantamount to a new chapter in the tradition" (1). Engaged Buddhism's deep imperative for social action alongside of mindfulness is revealed not only by Thich Nhat Hanh's work in Vietnam, but also by a host of other liberation movements, including the Dalai Lama's efforts to preserve Tibetan culture. In the West, however, this particular school tends to be more associated with organizations of Western converts to Buddhism rather than with practices of temples composed mainly of Asian immigrants.

When we turn specifically to the overall notion of community in Theravada Buddhism, we see an immediate connection with the Pali word *sangha*.[4] As explained by Paul David Numrich (1998), "*sangha* literally means 'comprising,' that is, an 'assembly' of some kind" (148). In sacred texts, this word is often combined with others to specify the particular type of assembly: for example, *savaka-sangha* (assembly of hearers or disciples) and *bhikkhu-sangha* (assembly of monks). Numrich further clarifies that traditional Theravada Buddhism "functionally narrowed the usage of the general term *sangha* to refer exclusively to the *bhikkhu-sangha,* or order of monks" (148). This separation is usually maintained by immigrant Theravada interpretations in America. Yet, as Wendy Cadge (2005) notes in her comparison of Wat Phila in Philadelphia, Pennsylvania, and the Cambridge Insight Meditation Center in Cambridge, Massachusetts, in temples or meditation centers serving mainly Western converts, and also in the ideal sense initiated by Buddha himself, the concept of *sangha* may extend to include the wider community of monks and laypeople (122–25).

When I spoke with Venerable Sao Khon, senior monk at the Lowell-area Trairatanaram Temple, and asked him about ideas of community in Buddhism, he spoke first of *sangha,* defining it as a group of Buddhist monks and novices. He noted that in Theravada Buddhism the order of nuns (*bhikkuni*) had mostly died out, although occasionally a nun is ordained. To distinguish the community of laypeople, he used two different terms: *upasaka* for men, and *upasaki* for women. When I asked if there was any term that included both monks and laypeople, he mentioned *sahacom,* meaning large society (implying also an association of Buddhists), and *samacom* for small society. When I inquired further if there was any mention in Buddhism about a person's responsibility to this community, Sao Khon explained that the monks are the teachers and spiritual counselors of the whole community—and also that for laypeople, Buddhism stresses the responsibilities of wife to husband, husband to wife, and parents to children (S. Khon, personal communication, March 4, 2004).

Through their roles as spiritual counselors and teachers, monks also serve as role models for the lay community. On the website of Wat Buddhabhavana, a Lao temple in Westford, Massachusetts, just outside of Lowell, Ajahn David Chutiko (n.d.) notes the significance of the alms round (*tak bat*), when the monk appears in public, walking from house to house to collect his daily food through donations from community members. In his words: "The act of begging for food keeps the community together in a bond of mutual dependency. The monk on the one hand receives material support from the laity and in return makes himself accessible for spiritual comfort as well as counsel. The monk is given the opportunity to practice humility and gratitude and the lay person his or her generosity. And generosity is considered one of the highest perfections required for the foundation of our basic morality and construction of our civic responsibility and good citizenship."

Wendy Cadge (2005) further explains that "merit is the glue that holds the community together through religious ceremonies based in exchange between the monks and lay people" (138). In addition to providing food for monks on the alms round in the community, lay people make merit (*bun*) through a wide variety of donations they make at the temple: food, housing, clothing, cooking, cleaning, money, and other necessities. By acting virtuously in this way, they accumulate good *kamma* (consequences of actions), which will help them and their ancestors to be happier both in the present and any future lives, ultimately reaching *nibbana* (release from suffering; enlightenment).

This concept of community life as revolving around relationships between monks and laypeople is readily evident in a very instructive book for children entitled *Buddhism for Young Students* (Phangcham 1993) written by a monk at a Thai Theravada Buddhist temple in Chicago (Wat Dhammaram), and given to me when I visited Watlao Mixayaram in South Lowell. In the chapter "Relationship between Temple and Community," it is explained that in Thailand, the temple was always the center of the community. Included within the temple compound was not only the residence for the monks, but a main *Dhamma* hall that provided shelter for travelers and students and also served as a public meeting hall and/or school. In addition, the temple operated as "an information center, a community and recreation center, and refuge for the mentally distressed and aged people" (64). The temple grounds were used for cultural programs and for polling centers for elections, and monks often did voluntary work in the wider community, including construction work in rural areas. In this way, the temple functioned as an educational, spiritual, and community resource.

Confirming the key role many monks play in life outside the temple, even where the surrounding community is predominantly non-Buddhist, substantial research on the civic activities of Theravada monks in the United States has begun to emerge over the last few years. For an excellent example of these activities, Wendy Cadge and Sidhorn Sangdhanoo (2002) conducted interviews with Thai monks and laypeople at all the Thai Theravada Buddhist organizations in the United States. Through these interviews, they found that temples and monks are involved with their local communities in a wide variety of ways, from teaching in prisons to donating food to homeless shelters (17).

In support of these findings, when I spoke with Sao Khon at the Trairatanaram Temple, he mentioned work at prisons and hospitals; at my first visit to Watlao Mixayaram, collections were under way for the Red Cross following the devastation of 9/11. Recently, Ajahn Mangkone Sananikone, with the help of other monks at Wat Buddhabhavana, started a Lao radio program at 91.5 FM, the University of Massachusetts Lowell's radio station. This program combines traditional and contemporary Laotian music with Buddhist teachings and community announcements, and is appreciated by a wide variety of listeners, including prisoners at nearby Fort Devens. Monks from Wat Buddhabhavana also teach the prisoners—most of whom are Americans not of Southeast Asian descent, but also including a few Laotian, Thai, and Cambodian prisoners—at this correctional facility. Since August 2005, Ajahn Mangkone has also served on the board of directors of the Lowell Community Health Center.

Yet the extent to which Theravada monks should be involved in the world outside the temple, and whether they should concentrate their efforts on American society or their Southeast Asian homeland, remains controversial and has at times led to temple schisms. Nancy Smith-Hefner (1998) describes the two factions in this controversy: "The first . . . openly admits that it is more concerned with helping rebuild Buddhism in Cambodia than with the future of Buddhism in the United States. . . . The second . . . [is] deeply concerned with social and educational issues. They argue that it is important for the temple to help youth in this country learn about Buddhism in an innovative and relevant way" (pp. 64–65). Precisely such a conflict is at the root of a current schism in the Lowell-area Trairatanaram

Temple, one that has resulted in the temple's being literally split into an up-stairs group and a downstairs group, each with its own monks, laypeople, and organizational structure. This situation is exacerbated by the particular predicament of the temple and the monks as being caught between two worlds: their homeland and America, and not being fully integrated in either cultural context.[5]

To unravel the complexities involved here, looking at the historical and political role of Buddhist temples in Southeast Asia is instructive. Historically, Buddhism became the state religion of those Southeast Asian countries where it flourished; thus to understand the traditional role of monks in the wider society one must see it within the context of the whole polity and, in particular, the role of the king. This tension is explored at length in Stanley Tambiah's work, *World Conqueror and World Renouncer* (1976). Examining the Buddhist genesis myth found in the *Aggañña Suttanta,* Tambiah explains: "according to the Buddhist scheme of things, relating to the world, there are two foremost or superior beings, the *bhikkhu* (monk) and the king. . . . The king is the fountainhead of society; the *bhikkhu* is of that society and transcends it" (14–15). Yet, as discussed in the contemporary examples given above, the monk also had an expected role in the wider world: "to be a field of merit and to reciprocate and give spiritual and humanitarian service to the laymen . . . while remaining detached and renouncing the fruits of action" (518).

In addition to the active participation of monks in community service, another link between Buddhism and Western secular notions of civic engagement are the basic doctrines of Buddhism itself: the Four Noble Truths and the Eightfold Path. The first of these truths is that all existence is *dukkha,* or suffering; the second that *dukkha* arises from a desire for permanence in the midst of a changing world; the third is the cessation of *dukkha,* and this is *nibbana;* and the fourth that *nibbana* can be reached by following the Eightfold Path. The Eightfold Path includes right action, right speech, and right livelihood (morals); right effort, right mindfulness, and right concentration (concentration); and right view and right intention (wisdom). Morals are seen as a precursor to concentration (for example, someone who has committed a crime will not be able to concentrate effectively), and concentration is seen as a precursor to the development of wisdom. Included within the Eightfold Path are five basic precepts frequently taken by laypeople and by all monks: (1) do not kill, (2) do not steal, (3) do not commit adultery, (4) do not gossip or slander, and (5) do not partake of intoxicating substances or drugs.

Furthermore, Buddhist teachings (*dhamma*) emphasize responsibility to six different categories of people in society: parents, teachers, wife and children, friends and kin, colleagues and employees, and monks and nuns. In *Buddhism for Young Students* specific guidelines for meeting these responsibilities are outlined, including such statements as "Good friends guide their friends to avoid harmful drugs, smoking and intoxicating drinks" and "Be sincere in all endeavors, constantly strive to improve work, and praise, honor and remain loyal to employers" (Phangcham 1993, 72–73). The four divine abodes (*brahma viharas*) of loving-kindness (*metta*), compassion (*karuna*), joy in others' happiness (*mudita*) and serenity (*upekkha*) are also presented to children and adults alike as states of mind that can help deal with difficulties in life, leading to "beauty and perfection in our humanity"(Sumedho 1998, 27).

By providing such an individual system of morality, Buddhist teachings go far toward strengthening social relationships, laying the groundwork for happiness and productivity in the wider society. To connect with secular notions of engagement, in the words of Robert Wuthnow (2004): "Civil Society is about social relationships. Its strength lies in the quality of those relationships; whether they are enduring and supportive, whether they provide assistance when assistance is needed, and whether they make it possible for people to mobilize to achieve their values" (4).

My final point concerning notions of community in Theravada Buddhism refers to the temple activities themselves. Far from concentrating solely on individual meditative or merit-making practices, temples typically feature a whole calendar of communal rituals, ranging from festivals such as New Year's and *Vesak* to regular monthly gatherings on important days according to the lunar calendar. During the festivals, in particular, large gatherings of people of all ages are present. After merit-making activities (such as feeding the monks), a communal meal is shared by laypeople, offering ample time for informal conversations and meetings. All of this shared activity helps to build friendships, thus allowing laypeople and monks to be more connected and involved members of society at large. As Gillian Cohen (1994) discovered in her study of the political socialization of Southeast Asian refugees in Lowell, temples are where people tend to meet each other, and form "an important social network within the community" (80).

In light of the above discussion, characteristics of community life and civic engagement in the Theravada Buddhist context include: the *sangha*, traditionally limited to the order of monks, and including monks who function as spiritual counselors, role models, and/or community activists; the ethical teachings of Buddhism, which develop a sense of responsibility, loving-kindness, and compassion toward others; and the intergenerational connections between laypeople, which foster social networks both within and without the immediate temple community. To examine these civic values and activities of Theravada Buddhism within a particular American landscape, let us now turn to the Cambodian and Lao Buddhist temples in Lowell, looking closely at two ways these temples participate in civic life: a partnership between the Lowell Police Department and monks at the Trairatanaram Temple to help runaway youth, and the New Year's celebration at Watlao Mixayaram.

Runaway Teens and the Sangha: Operation Middle Path at Trairatanaram Temple

Two Cambodian temples, both founded in the 1980's, are located in the greater Lowell area: Trairatanaram Temple in North Chelmsford, and Glory Buddhist Temple in the Lower Highlands neighborhood of Lowell itself. When I met with Venerable Sao Khon at Trairatanaram Temple for an extensive interview in March 2004, he characterized his main role as one of spiritual teacher, leader, and counselor. Earlier, by way of an article in the *Lowell Sun* entitled "Serenity Now: Monks Will Help Police Combat Teen Violence" (Minch 2003) I had learned of a program started by Captain Robert DeMoura of the Lowell Police Department and Venerable Sao Khon to help troubled Southeast Asian youth and stem gang violence in the city. This program, dubbed Operation Middle Path, was begun in the spring of 2003, initially funded through the Weed and Seed program (a U.S. Department of Justice program to promote both community policing and neighborhood restoration) but later receiving a grant specifically targeted for runaway youth. After this funding terminated in summer 2004, the program took a hiatus of several months, but plans were under way to reinstate it under Project Safe Neighborhood (R. DeMoura, personal communication, January 2005; as of January 2007, however, such has not occurred.)

In addition to Venerable Sao Khon and Captain DeMoura, a key player in Operation Middle Path was Jendhamuni Sos, a young Cambodian college student who has a close connection with Venerable Sao Khon and who was also a project assistant with the Weed and Seed program. During 2003–2004, she was a Youth Violence Projection program analyst with the Lowell Police Department, the program that included Operation Middle Path. She personally credits Venerable Sao Khon with convincing her parents to allow her to pursue a college education, and thus is a testimony to his influence in the Cambodian community (J. Sos, personal communication, February 26, 2004).

In May 2003, Operation Middle Path began by meeting with ten runaway Southeast Asian youth to evaluate their background knowledge of Buddhism and meditation skills. After that, these youth—including both boys and girls—went to the temple twice a week for after-school training sessions by the monks. Captain DeMoura noted that, unfortunately, if a strong leader is present, ten kids run the risk of becoming a gang itself, and many of these kids already have experience with gangs. Other difficulties experienced included recruiting youth and getting them to the temple; even when taxis were offered, many were reluctant to come. Thus by March 2004, only three youths were participating in the twice-weekly sessions at the temple; when I checked back three months later, no youths were participating. This decline was exacerbated by the lack of funding mentioned above (R. DeMoura, personal communication, March and June 2004).

Trisha Camire, coordinator for Weed and Seed and the Youth Violence Prevention program head attributed the lack of participating youth to difficulties in working with the families and lack of full-time project staff to provide adequate outreach and follow-up. She stressed that personal relationships are key to working successfully with the Southeast Asian community; such relationships, however, involve considerable time and commitment on the part of the project staff involved. Overall, she commended Venerable Sao Khon's work with these troubled kids, but also noted that he can only help once the youth are participating in the program (T. Camire, personal communication, June 28, 2004). Venerable Sao Khon also has many other commitments that limit his involvement: as the head of an association of seventy-five Buddhist temples in the United States, he travels very frequently, and has additional responsibilities with regard to the construction of a new temple in South Carolina.

Yet it is clear that Venerable Sao Khon has been concerned about youth programs for quite some time. As he explained, this project in partnership with the Lowell Police Department has a much longer history: As a monk, he has always worked with troubled youth. Earlier, in the late 1980s and early 1990s, he was associated with then Middlesex District Attorney Tom Reilly (current Massachusetts attorney general) and worked with runaway youth in Middlesex County to teach training, respect, chanting, and meditation. At that time, rather than twice-weekly one-hour programs, the kids used to stay at the temple and were ordained as monks with the full consent and sponsorship of their parents.

Ordaining teenagers and young men as monks for a short period of time is common in Southeast Asia, and many see it as a prerequisite for marriage. Sometimes the period of time as a monk is very short; at the Trairatanaram Temple, the shortest time was just forty-five minutes. As John Massey, an American of German heritage who was a monk at this temple for three years, explained, "He just wanted to send some photos back to Cambodia—you can become a monk in America, look at me. Other times kids will just do a 24 hour walk around the temple and then disrobe." He further suggested that many different reasons for becoming a monk exist: "Some people get ordained because it's part of the culture, to go through adolescence; some get ordained when one of their parents die; some, just because they want to be monks" (J. Massey, personal communication, March 4, 2004).

When I asked Sao Khon whether ordaining the youth as monks made any difference, and if so, why, he said: "after one to two years many kids did change—they knew about bad and good, bad way, good way, middle way; it was successful." He especially felt that one very positive aspect of this experience was that every day one of the parents would come to offer food to their child for their daily meal. He felt that seeing their parents take care of them made a big impression on the kids, and helped to change their attitude. The parents also respected their children more for their ability to stay at the temple and live the life of a monk. Sao Khon emphasized that this role of the temple in helping families is practiced in his homeland, too: "In Cambodia, if a father-mother has a problem with their kids, they bring the kid to go to the temple. If the kid runs away from school, then he goes to the temple—the temple will fix that kid, that's the system in Cambodia" (S.Khon, personal communication, March 4, 2004).

One obstacle faced by the Operation Middle Path program, was that because of liability issues, runaway youth could not be kept overnight at the temple. Venerable Sao Khon felt that this restriction jeopardized the program; without an extended stay that removes kids from their habitual environment and friends, they lapse too easily back into gangs and violence. As John Massey explains, "if you ordain them then you even remove them further from their identity because they have a shaven head, eyebrows and they wear a monk's robe" (J. Massey, personal communication, March 4, 2004).

Lacking the option of ordainment and an extended stay, Sao Khon instructed the kids in the after-school program through Buddhist teachings and stories. Most important, he told them the story of his own life, including some experiences in Cambodia and Thailand, some in the United States. This sharing is especially meaningful to children whose parents suffered under Pol Pot's regime, but are not able to speak with them about it. To help these kids, Sao Khon also sometimes spoke directly with the parents. As he explained, "Oh, I want to have freedom, I hate my mother, I hate my father—kids say this. . . . I ask them why, tell me why? Sometimes I need to talk with the parents, so I ask them, why does your daughter hate you? I want to know both sides—I'm the middle path" (S. Khon, personal communication, March 4, 2004).

Over the years, some of these kids who stayed as monks at the temple have done very well: "We have three master's degrees of kids who used to be in gangs" (J. Massey, personal communication, March 4, 2004). But failures also exist: another youth who was ordained was arrested for armed robbery and spent eleven years in jail.

Venerable Sao Khon's long-standing practice of helping troubled youth provides an important example of how Buddhist monks may participate in community life and be of service to the larger public good—and in the case of Operation Middle Path, also get involved with Lowell public institutions such as the Lowell Police Department. Let us now look at another type of community activity, this one involving an annual event: the New Year's celebration at Watlao Mixayaram.

A Communal Ritual and a Political Past: The Lao New Year's Celebration

I was first introduced to Watlao Mixayaram by Vanesa Thongkhamvilay, one of my students at Middlesex Community College. At the time of my visit in the fall of 2001, the temple was in a small, one-story brick house purchased by members of the Lao[6] community in 1996. For large celebrations, a tent was set up outside in the one-acre area surrounding the building. Plans were under way to construct a much larger building to permit large indoor gatherings; this building was completed in the summer of 2003, and is now used regularly. The temple decorations and designs are taken from the That Laung temple in Vientiane, Laos.

Watlao Mixayaram does not regularly host events and programs that reach out into the wider Lowell community or provide for cross-cultural connections; even so, members do consider their temple to be open to all—Buddhist and non-Buddhists. At present, the temple's most public event is also its largest fundraiser: a food stall at the Lowell Folk Festival, a renowned citywide cultural event organized by Lowell National Historical Park. At the 2003 festival, the temple made a profit of approximately $9,000 selling traditional Lao food prepared by temple members.

Earlier, Watlao Mixayaram also participated in the Southeast Asian Water Festival—the largest and most public festival in Lowell celebrating Southeast Asian cultural traditions. Yet, despite this event's ability to draw vast numbers of Southeast Asians to the city to enjoy song, dance, food, and boat races along the banks of the Merrimack River, it had been plagued with organizational difficulties; at one point separate Lao and Cambodian events were considered. But in 2004, Lao and Cambodian groups collaborated to form the Lowell Southeast Asian Water Festival, Inc., a nonprofit organization including the following groups: Cambodian Mutual Assistance Association of Greater Lowell, Lao Family Mutual Association, Light of Cambodian Children, Wat Buddhabhavana, and the Thai Association of Boston.

Notably, this list includes Wat Buddhabhavana, a Lao temple that originated in Lowell in 1996 but moved to new facilities in nearby Westford in

2005. In contrast to Watlao Mixayaram, this temple is envisioned primarily as a monastery and meditation center, and is located near a bird sanctuary, a brook, and nature trails. While its membership and support comes primarily from the Lao community, it also seeks to include other ethnic groups. To encourage this diverse participation, the name of the temple does not specify any particular ethnicity, and instruction in Buddhist meditation is provided in both English and Lao. Wat Buddhabhavana was responsible for coordinating the Friday-evening Floating Candles Ceremony and the Buddhist tents at the 2005 Southeast Asian Water Festival; because of their outreach, the number of non-Asian participants was considerably larger than in previous years (A. Mangkone, personal communication, August 2005).

Although not so publicly visible as the Southeast Asian Water Festival, the Lao New Year's celebration is an excellent example of how an annual festival celebrates Lao community life in Lowell; at the same time, it suggests avenues for increased participation in the wider civic life of the city. Preparations for this event begin at home, where Lao women prepare traditional steamed buns, rice, and fruits, along with American consumer products such as Capri Sun juice boxes, to place in ornate silver bowls and offer for blessing by the monks. As they are offered, these food items are transferred into the monks' bowls, and then sorted in larger baskets according to perishable and nonperishable items. After the monks have eaten, the perishable items are given back to the people, whereas the nonperishables and money donated are kept at the temple for the monks. In this way, laypeople accumulate merit (bun), to help ensure good luck both in this life and any subsequent lives.

During the New Year's ceremony, laypeople also pour water in various places to increase their chances for a healthy, prosperous New Year. Water is poured from glasses while monks chant blessings, and down a tray that then drips onto a small statue of the Buddha, and also at the bases of trees, signifying that as the tree grows and prospers, so will the person who pours water at its trunk. Along with hoping for prosperity, this pouring of water turns into fun as well: people pour it down one another's backs and teenagers bring large American water guns to squirt at each other. In this way, even disaffected teenage boys enjoy the festivities and, through the use of water pistols, connect to the wider American youth culture.

Other ways prosperity and good luck are offered are by two sand stupas set up on the temple grounds. People write wishes or the names of ancestors who have passed away on small flags, which are then stuck into the sand for good fortune in the coming year. Another feature of the New Year is the tying of strings on each person's wrists while a monk chants a blessing for his/her welfare. As Vanesa Thongkhamvilay explained, this offers protection against bad dreams and omens. For this to work, the strings should be kept on for three days following this ceremony (V. Thongkhamvilay, personal communication, April 2003).

In addition to these practices, a main event of the New Year's ceremony is the presentation of the seven contestants in the Miss New Year Pageant Contest. This contest is held prior to the New Year's celebration, and is based on a Lao folktale. According to this story, a man who has seven daughters loses a bet while gambling; as a result his head is cut off. After this tragedy, one of his daughters volunteers to anoint her father's head.[7] To commemorate this, seven girls are chosen to represent the seven daughters, and one girl (considered the winner) is chosen for the role of anointing her father's head. Contestants are judged by their overall knowledge of Lao culture, including dress and grace while walking. The winner receives a prize (about $300 in gold) and a crown.

During the New Year's ceremony, these teenage girls are present, and the monks chant for them. Then, at the end of the ceremony, a procession parades around the temple several times. In the procession the winner of the contest is shielded by an umbrella, signifying her special role. She holds hay to represent the hair of her father's head. Temple members of all ages join in the parade, carrying both the temple flag and the American flag. When this procession occurs in Laos, it lasts for three days, and local politicians often participate. People take it very seriously; it is a very big parade and show with elaborate decorations (S. Komsonkeo, personal communication, April, 2003).

In her account of the New Year's celebration in Louang Prabang, Laos, anthropologist Ing-Britt Trankell (1999) characterizes the New Year's festival as one of two state rituals in postrevolutionary Laos (191–213). Prior to 1975, this celebration involved performances by the court ballet, but around this same time the beauty contest was introduced. By participating in the parade, being shielded by the umbrella, and pouring water over the statue of the Buddha, the winner of this contest performs duties previously exercised by the king, while simultaneously representing "an idealized national femininity" (204). In the immigrant context of Lowell, the beauty contest functions as a symbolic re-creation of this Lao identity, both for the teenage girls who participate and for the many others who admire their achievements.

Taken overall, the Lao New Year's celebration reveals the dual personal and political nature of Theravada Buddhism. Clearly, most attendees come to receive merit and ensure good luck for the coming year, but the event also reinforces social ties, symbolizes a collective Lao identity, allows youth to participate in ways meaningful to them (beauty pageants for young girls, squirt-gun fights for teenage boys) and celebrates inclusion in American society through the presence of the flag. In this way, it lays the groundwork for further connections into a wider civic life.

Engaging the Wider Public: From Temple Events to Community Partnerships

To return to the question posed at the start of this essay, it is clear that Theravada Buddhist notions of community service and civic engagement—despite the paradox surrounding the monk's involvement in this world—do support monks who choose to help resolve community problems affecting both Buddhist laypeople and the wider non-Buddhist society. This choice is demonstrated most ably in the example of Venerable Sao Khon's work with troubled youth at the Trairatanaram Temple, recently through his partnership with the Lowell Police Department on Operation Middle Path, as well as by his earlier practice of ordaining young boys for short periods as monks. These practices reveal the adaptation of a traditional Buddhist practice for the specific purposes of reframing these young people's personal identities, improving their relationship with their parents, removing them from a destructive environment at school or home, and instructing them in basic Buddhist beliefs and ethical practices that both alleviate their own personal suffering and allow them to be more constructive members of society. The practices are potentially of enormous benefit to the wider society, because youth gangs in Lowell have made several areas of the city unsafe, have been responsible for a considerable amount of violent crime, and have made many parents fear sending their children to the public schools.

Turning to the second example discussed in this paper, the Lao New Year's celebration provides evidence of a temple ceremony that in its traditional expression in Laos symbolized national identity and incorporated political figures—in essence, a state ritual. Yet in its current manifestation at the Lowell temple, this political piece is missing (with the noteworthy exception of the American flag's inclusion during the culminating procession). Similar to the reinvention of the Southeast Asian Water Festival along the Merrimack River in Lowell, the New Year's celebration could be used as a catalyst to encourage the political integration and participation of Lao immigrants (perhaps by inviting local political figures), thus increasing levels of civic knowledge and participation. In this way, Southeast Asian young adults could be encouraged to recognize that by participating in American democracy, they are connecting with their own cultural traditions as well. Yet many in the Southeast Asian community are wary of incorporating local politics into their temples, because of rivals and factions within their own community and because of their experiences in their homeland.

On the other hand, most Southeast Asians are quite comfortable with using art forms, including those traditionally associated with the New

Year's celebration, to encourage knowledge about their cultural heritage. Such a connection has recently been demonstrated by the Cambodian Expressions Film and Arts Festival exhibit at Lowell National Historical Park's Boott Mills Museum—a collaboration between Middlesex Community College, the Cambodian Artist's Association and Lowell National Historical Park—first presented during April and May 2004, and then again during April 2005 and 2006. The 2005 exhibit, which continued through the summer, emphasized the role that art, in particular, plays in community life by illustrating intergenerational themes in the Cambodian community. Accompanying the artwork were very informative biographical sketches of the artists highlighting their connections to the community; many of the artists were interviewed by Middlesex Community College students as part of a civic engagement project in an art appreciation course. As a result of this experience, one student became acquainted with a local Cambodian who was running for city council, and decided to help him with his campaign the following fall (Rack 2006). In this case, knowledge of and interaction around Cambodian art helped forge a political connection.

Continuing the collaboration between Middlesex Community College and Cambodian Expressions, in 2006 students in my introduction to cultural anthropology course interviewed and photographed both the artists and organizers of this event, creating posters that were then displayed as part of the Boott Mills art exhibit. Attending the exhibit with my students, and viewing artwork celebrating contemporary village life in Cambodia as well as the horrors of the Khmer Rouge, provided an opportunity for Cambodian students to explain to classmates about their cultural background and experiences. Other events held during Cambodian Expressions bringing together MCC students and the Cambodian community included a pottery demonstration in the college cafeteria by master artist Yary Livan; showings of the film *The Monkey Dance,* a compelling story about the role of traditional dance both in Cambodia and for Cambodian teenagers in Lowell; and a celebration of art in the Cambodian New Year, which included a fashion show by Cambodian students from the Lowell Charter School and an explanation of the role of art in the New Year celebration by Samkhann Khoeun, local Cambodian activist and leader.

Altogether, the Cambodian Expressions Film and Arts Festival provides an example of how art may be used to encourage civic engagement, an avenue that many Southeast Asians find more celebratory of their cultural traditions than a more politicized approach. In addition, the festival represents a very promising and growing partnership between Middlesex Community College, Lowell National Historical Park, the Cambodian Artists' Association and many other public institutions in Lowell. Together with the Southeast Asian Water Festival, these public events reveal that through community partnerships, activities formerly isolated in the temples and other Cambodian associations are moving into venues where they may be experienced and understood by a much wider public.

Ultimately, fostering civic engagement in American public life among Middlesex Community College's diverse young adult student body requires an equal commitment to encouraging engagement within each student's own cultural heritage. As our discussion has shown, teaching students about conceptions of community and civic engagement in Theravada Buddhism, both in its historical basis in Southeast Asia and contemporary manifestation in Lowell, will bring forth many civic lessons clearly applicable in the American context. By exemplifying three key types of Buddhist engagement—the role of the *sangha*, including the reciprocal relationship between monks and laypeople as well as those monks who choose to be community activists; the ethical teachings of Buddhism, emphasizing the Eightfold Path and the values of loving-kindness and compassion; and intergenerational communal celebrations, illustrating responsibility to others and connections to the wider society—the Lao New Year's festival and Operation Middle Path present points of intersection between Southeast Asian Theravada Buddhism and American civic life. As such, they suggest a myriad of opportunities for collaboration and instruction. The recent launching of the Cambodian Expressions Film and Arts Festival, as well as the more established Southeast Asian Water Festival, are increasingly successful models of such civic partnerships. Like the meeting of two crossroads, finding and developing such points is central to creating two-way, mutual engagement that respects and allows for interchange and free passage along all sides of the road. In this way, everyone involved—college students, Buddhist monks and laypeople, community organizers, and the wider public—will have the best chance to develop the emotional, spiritual, intellectual, and social resources to, in Tooch Van's words, "make the world a little bit better place each day."

Acknowledgments

My deepest thanks go to Vanesa Thongkhamvilay, Sird Komsonkeo, Venerable Sao Khon, Sak Seang, Ajahn Mangkone Sananikone, John Massey, Jendhamuni Sos, Trisha Camire, and Captain Robert DeMoura for their patience and help with all my questions, as well as their review of this essay. Wendy Cadge provided critical insights on the first draft and was very generous in sharing her own research. Sylvia Cowan patiently guided me through the editing process, and Meg Bond offered useful suggestions. I especially thank Jeffrey Gerson for his encouragement and for connecting me with sources and people instrumental to this work. My sincere thanks also goes to Pamela Edington, former dean of social sciences at Middlesex Community College and the Lowell Civic Collaborative project head, for allowing me considerable freedom in the choice and implementation of this research. Finally, I thank the Corporation for National and Community Service for their generous financial support.

Notes

1. In 2005, slightly less than 25 percent of Middlesex Community College's student population, including both its Lowell and Bedford campuses, was composed of minority groups (that is, Asian, Black, Hispanic, Native American, nonresidential alien) with 9 percent identified as Asian. See MCC Student Profile on the MCC website, https://www.middlesex.mass.edu.

2. The One Lowell Coalition was one of three demonstration coalitions selected to be part of the Building the New American Community project, 2001–2003, funded by the Office of Refugee Resettlement.

3. Some Southeast Asian refugees did convert to Christianity, both in the refugee camps in Thailand and after arrival in the United States. However, the majority of Southeast Asian refugees in the Lowell area, and the United States as a whole, continue to identify themselves as Buddhist.

4. Pali is the liturgical language used in Theravada Buddhist canons.

5. See Gerson in this volume (chapter 9) for a fuller discussion of the conflict.

6. The predominant population of present-day Laos is composed of ethnic Lao who live in the lowland regions. But the country as a whole also includes highland minority groups such as the Lua, Hmong, Yao, Dao, and Shan, as well as many others. The term *Laotian* is generally considered to be a political term that is not limited only to ethnic Lao, but includes all citizens of Laos.

7. This folktale was told to me by Sird Komsonkeo in consultation with monks at the Lao temple in Lowell. Alternate, more elaborate versions can be found in Trankell (1999) and Swearer (1995).

References

Cadge, W. 2005. *Heartwood: The First Generation of Theravada Buddhism in America.* Chicago: University of Chicago Press.

———, and S. Sangdhanoo. 2002. Thai Buddhism in America: A Historical and Contemporary Overview. Presented at the Society for the Scientific Study of Religion Meetings, Salt Lake City, Utah.

Chutiko, A. D. N.d. The Importance of a Monk in the Ethnic and General Community. Retrieved October 20, 2006, from www.greatwisdomcenter.org.

Cohen, G. D. 1994. Knowledge of How to Combine: The Political Socialization of Southeast Asian Refugees in Lowell, Massachusetts, 1984–1988. Senior Honors Thesis, Radcliffe College.

Fahlberg, V. 2001. Barriers Faced by Refugees and Immigrants Residing in the City of Lowell, Massachusetts. Retrieved on October 20, 2006, from www.onelowell.net/resources.html.

McMahon, S. 2002.True Survivor Tells MCC Grads to Face Challenges, Never Give Up. *Lowell Sun,* May 30.

Minch, J. 2003. Serenity Now: Monks Will Help Police Combat Teen Violence. *Lowell Sun,* May 23.

Numrich, P. D. 1998. Theravada Buddhism in America: Prospects for the Sangha. In *The Faces of Buddhism in America,* edited by C. S. Prebish and K. K. Tanaka.Berkeley and Los Angeles: University of California Press.

Phangcham, C. 1993. *Buddhism for Young Students.* Warren, MI: Wat Dhammaram Sunday School.

Putnam, R. 2000. *Bowling Alone: The Collapse and Revival of American Community.* New York: Simon and Schuster.

Queen, C. S., ed. 2000. Introduction: A New Buddhism. In *Engaged Buddhism in the West.* Boston: Wisdom Publications.

Rack, M. 2006. Cambodian Expressions: A Civic Engagement Project. In *The Lowell Civic Collaborative: A Guidebook for Projects between Community Colleges and National Parks,* edited by S. Thomson, 6–8. Bedford, MA: Middlesex Community College.

Smith-Hefner, N. J. 1998. Rebuilding the Temple: Buddhism and Identity among Khmer Americans. In *Diasporic Identity,* edited by C. A. Mortland. Selected Papers on Refugees and Immigrants, vol. 6. Arlington, VA: American Anthropological Association.

Sumedho, V. A. 1998. *Gratitude to Parents.* Hertfordshire, Eng.: Amaravati Publications.

Swearer, D. K. 1995. *The Buddhist World of Southeast Asia.* Albany: State University of New York Press.

Tambiah, S. J. 1976. *World Conqueror and World Renouncer: A Study of Buddhism and Polity in Thailand against a Historical Background.* Cambridge: Cambridge University Press.

Trankell, I. 1999. Royal Relics: Ritual and Social Memory in Louang Prabang. In *Laos, Culture and Society,* edited by G. Evans, 191–213. Bangkok: Silkworm Books.

Wuthnow, R. 2004. *Saving America? Faith-Based Services and the Future of Civil Society.* Princeton, ,NJ: Princeton University Press.

——, and J. H. Evans. 2002. *The Quiet Hand of God: Faith-Based Activism and the Public Role of Mainline Protestantism.* Berkeley and Los Angeles: University of California Press.

Lao Refugees in Lowell

Reinterpreting the Past, Finding Meaning in the Present

At the First International Conference on Lao Studies held at Northern Illinois University (NIU) in May 2005 and organized by the Center for Southeast Asian Studies at NIU, more than 350 attendees (scholars, experts, researchers, educators, students, and the general public) from all over the United States, Europe, Asia, and Latin America came together for presentations, celebrations, and discussions of many aspects of the Lao experience. This interdisciplinary exchange included discussions of history, music, language, art, immigration, textiles, political structures, and community organization. The interaction among scholars, government officials, and community representatives revealed a complex interweaving of the past and present. At times the air was ripe with tension, as disparate views clashed—on current development in Laos, on the war and its consequences, on the refugee and immigrant experience, and on Lao communities across the United States and beyond. The discussions were stimulating and provocative, encompassing a wide spectrum of quiet pride, distant memories, painful transitions, successes, and dissenting voices. It is not surprising that different interpretations of history and visions of the future emerged. With more than sixty ethnic groups, Laos is one of the most diverse countries in the world in proportion to its population (Hein 2006). Lowell's Lao community is also a mosaic, as refugees and immigrants of different generations struggle to make sense of the past, leave it behind and live in the present, and keep it alive for their children.

Less numerous and visible than other Southeast Asian groups in Lowell,[1] the experiences of Lao[2] are similar in many ways to those of the other groups. All have faced challenges of language and cultural differences, confronted economic difficulties, sought educational opportunities, addressed social and psychological issues in the community. Lao have attempted to maintain their cultural ties, largely through the temples and cultural events, sometimes shared with other Southeast Asian groups. Yet the Lao have come with a previous history with the United States that is both pivotal and little known (Inui 1998; Legacies of War n.d.). That past and the way it is interpreted affects attitudes and relations among Lao in the United States in the present. With the smallest numbers, Lao lack the "critical mass" to garner significant resources. Nor does the community speak with one voice. Many find themselves between cultures, balancing homeland ties and memories with the realities of present-day life in Lowell. Nevertheless, Lao and Lao Americans have achieved much in educational and economic stability, and have contributed significantly to the City of Lowell with their cultures, energy, perceptions, and understanding of the world.

This essay seeks to surface the little known history of the Lao in the United States and to provide a context for understanding their unique experiences. Together, Lao demonstrate ethnic resilience, form social networks, pursue education, keep alive traditions, and teach the younger generation the customs of their culture. They face challenges of discrimination and barriers in their efforts to re-create their lives in the new land. Individuals adapt to their circumstances and make meaning of their current lives in a variety of ways, especially as they reinterpret connections with the homeland. One example—a controversy over which Lao flag to use—symbolizes how varying interpretations of the past influence identity and actions in the present. Background research, observation of and participation in community events and celebrations, interviews and informal conversations with members of the community and those working with the community—all have brought to this study valuable data and perspectives.[3]

Defining Moments in Lao History

The diversity of Laos is evident both in its history and in current population estimates. Of a total population currently estimated at almost five million, between forty-seven and sixty-eight ethnic groups have been identified (Dao 2005). "At no time has territory designated as Lao been ethnically or culturally homogeneous" (Stuart-Fox 1993, 111).[4] Those who migrated to the United States are generally categorized into two groups: the Hmong and lowland Lao. The Hmong, whose ancestry can be traced back to ancient China, sought mountainous regions; eventually many moved from southern China to Vietnam, Laos, and Thailand. People referred to as lowland Lao had different origins. They lived in valleys and plains, and constituted about 50 percent of the population in the

1970s. They mostly resided in urban areas, and controlled the government. In Laos they had a position of dominance. These two groups differ in many ways, including language, culture, and religion (Hein 2006).

While Laos can be traced back to 1365 or earlier (Stuart-Fox 1993), the history of Laos from the end of the nineteenth century is dominated by international involvement. From 1893 when Lao territories east of the Mekong were ceded to France, until 1954 when Laos became independent, no independent center of Lao power existed (Stuart-Fox 1993). During sixty years of colonization, Laos was dominated by French rule. Three conflicts known as the "Indochina Wars" erupted in the wake of World War II, and were fought in Southeast Asia from 1947 until 1979, between nationalist Vietnamese against French, American, and Chinese forces.[5]

During the period between 1945 and 1953, in the process of the struggle for identity, "a new, specifically Lao, political culture developed which proved sufficiently durable to provide a degree of historical continuity over the subsequent transition from Kingdom to People's Republic in 1975" (Stuart-Fox 1993, 116). In 1975 the Pathet Lao came into power, and the kingdom gave way to the creation of the Lao People's Democratic Republic, which continues today (Stuart-Fox 1993).

In the new government, "strictures against Buddhism struck at the heart of Lao culture, and threatened a deeper discontinuity." (Stuart-Fox and Rod Bucknell, cited in Stuart-Fox 1993, 112). The mass exit of tens of thousands of Lao fleeing imprisonment in reeducation camps and repression resulted in a devastating depopulation, with the loss of 90 percent of the educated class. What carried the country through this period, according to Stuart-Fox, was "the resilience of Lao culture." With the revival of Buddhism, cultural continuities reasserted themselves. "Within ten years, members of the Politburo were attending major Buddhist ceremonies." Stuart-Fox sees the struggle for independence and unity, and a genuinely national Lao political culture, as the basis for contemporary Lao history (Stuart-Fox 1993, 112).

Lao Historical Relationship to the United States

America's role significantly contributed to how events unfolded in Southeast Asia in the 1960s and 1970s. Despite extensive U.S. use of military force to support pro-American governments, communist regimes took charge. South Vietnam fell to North Vietnam communist forces in 1975, and the communist Khmer Rouge took over in Cambodia. In Laos, communist forces took over the government in late 1975. Hein observes that the refugees created by these events had a special relationship to the country whose involvement was pivotal in the region: "The more than one million Indochinese refugees who subsequently resettled in the United States came not for higher wages and modern lifestyles, as do many immigrants, but because the United States has a responsibility for their fate different from that of other refugees who arrived during the cold war" (Hein 1992, quoted in Hein 1995, 2).

While all refugees from Cambodia, Vietnam, and Laos experienced major trauma in their home countries, and faced agony, upheaval, and challenging readjustment in their journeys to the United States, the Lao refugees have been the least noticed of these groups (Souvannarath 2005). Perhaps this emanates at least in part from the well-kept secret history of their particular role in the "American War" (known as the "Vietnam War" in the West). What happened in Laos has become known as the "Secret War" (Inui 1998; Legacies of War n.d.).

The so-called secret war conducted by the Central Intelligence Agency (CIA) had devastating effects particularly for the Hmong. Apart from the fact that the Geneva Accords of 1962 guaranteed Laos neutrality, the CIA utilized Hmong, under the leadership of General Vang Pao, to fight the Pathet Lao. Hmong villagers were recruited to gather intelligence, rescue American pilots shot down over Laos, and fight communist troops in the borderlands between Vietnam and Laos (Inui 1998). As more soldiers were killed, the United States, attempting to interrupt supply routes along the Ho Chi Minh trail through Lao jungles, resorted to air power, and dropped more than two million tons of bombs on Laos—more than the total tonnage dropped on Germany and Japan combined during all of World War II (Chan 1991, 1994; Legacies of War n.d.).

The U.S. involvement in Laos during that time was little known by the American people. These bombing missions were kept secret. With the focus of the American media on Vietnam, few noticed what was happening in the "little-known country of Laos." Chan explains: "It was possible for the U.S. government to hide this war from the American public—indeed from Congress itself—because reporters were forbidden to interview pilots who left on bombing missions over Laos from American airbases in Thailand" (Chan 1994, 42). The same restrictions on reporters did not occur in Vietnam. Only in 1969 did the U.S. Senate Foreign Relations Subcommittee on U.S. Security Agreements and Commitments Abroad hold hearings to investigate what was happening in Laos (Chan 1994). Seven years after the first accounts of the bombings, the Senate acknowledged in a 1971 report that the United States had undertaken a large-scale air war over Laos to destroy the Pathet Lao and interrupt North Vietnamese infiltration (Legacies of War n.d.).

Many historians conclude that the United States brought the Hmong into their war, and, when the United States lost, abandoned them (Chan 1994; Hein 2006, citing Hamilton-Merritt 1993; Quincy 2000; and

Warner 1996). When the United States ended combat operations in Southeast Asia, there were approximately 17,000 Hmong soldiers who had been killed, and 50,000 Hmong civilians who had died from the attacks of Pathet Lao and North Vietnamese (Hein 2006, citing Dommen 2001). In 1975 when Laos came under communist control, the U.S. military only evacuated 2,000 Hmong. In spite of "the promise" that many Hmong believe was made by the United States to protect them in the event that the war was lost, tens of thousands of Hmong were left to face their fate in the hands of the Pathet Lao (Hein 2006).

Many Hmong and lowland Lao fled their country, fearing their fate under the new regime. Many escaped to Thailand, and in refugee camps awaited resettlement, sometimes waiting for years before being accepted into another country. Most did not return to Laos. It is estimated that 10 percent of the inhabitants of Laos (some 350,000) settled in Thailand, the United States, Canada, Australia, France, and other countries. This migration, which most saw as compulsory, lasted more than ten years (Fuentecilla 2005).

Lao Immigration to the United States

The Lao, as among the millions displaced by the Second Indochinese War, were basically political refugees (Fuentecilla 2005). Because their government had historically had a relationship with the United States and many had fought side by side with American soldiers or allies for the American cause, many Lao looked toward the United States as their first choice for asylum. They anticipated that they would be welcomed in the United States. For Lao refugees in Thai camps, 84 percent of the Hmong and 64 percent of the lowland Lao indicated that the United States was their first choice for resettlement (Hein 1995).

It is estimated that between 1975 and 1992, more than 123,000 ethnic Lao were admitted as refugees into the United States. During the same period, 108,400—primarily Hmong, but also Mien, Tai Dam, and Lao Theung—were admitted (Fuentecilla 2005). Like the Hmong, others who left had reason to fear reprisals. Many were officials of the deposed royal government and high-ranking military officers who were easily identified by the Pathet Lao as collaborators with the U.S. government agencies operating in Laos (Fuentecilla 2005).

This history affected attitudes of Lao refugees entering the United States. Hein (2006) notes that "some Hmong attribute their refugee status directly or indirectly to the U.S. state" (72). Many Hmong hold the U.S. government responsible for abandoning them, in spite of Hmong loyalty to the United States during the war (Hein 2006). Some have even

sought some form of redress. The passing of the Hmong Veterans Naturalization Act by Congress in 2000, which modified the requirements for
their obtaining citizenship, symbolically demonstrated responsibility of
the American society to Hmong refugees. In November 2001, the House
passed a resolution proclaiming July 22 as Lao-Hmong Recognition Day
"to honor their sacrifices during the war in Southeast Asia" (U.S. House
of Representatives 2001). These acts—twenty-five years after the first
Hmong refugees entered the United States—reflect solidarity among the
Hmong to organize their communities and lobby for recognition.

While the U.S. resettlement policy for Southeast Asians was national,
the actual resettlement was left more to local and state officials.[6] While
offering a safe haven, the policy also created hardships, especially for
such groups as the Hmong, who consider clan and extended family support essential to their traditional social fabric. In order not to have any
one municipality overburdened, immigration policy specified that the refugees be dispersed throughout the nation. The effect was to split up families and interrupt traditional social ties (Kaufman 2004). Lao refugees resettled in places as distant from one another as Lowell, Massachusetts;
Rockland, Illinois; Milwaukee and Appleton, Wisconsin; Minneapolis–
Saint Paul, Minnesota; Hickory-Morganton, North Carolina; Providence
and Woonsocket, Rhode Island; Bridgeport, Connecticut; Garden Grove
and Anaheim (Orange County), California; and Des Moines, Iowa. In the
beginning they were directed to locations determined by immigration authorities, and to the locations of their sponsors.

While a small number of refugees arrived in Lowell prior to 1979,
between 1979 and 1983 approximately one hundred Cambodian and
Laotian families (about 1,400 people) were resettled in Lowell, as Lowell
had been chosen as one of six clusters across the United States to receive
refugees from these countries.[7] In this group were ordinary villagers, low-
level government workers and soldiers, and a small number of skilled, educated lowland Lao (Fuentecilla 2005). While many of the first wave of
refugees left from fear of political violence and warfare, later migrants
left because of hardships experienced under the new regime, wanting to
reunite with their families, seeking more freedom or economic and educational opportunities, or better climates. Many Lao came to Lowell in the
early 1980s, with large numbers entering in 1981. Secondary migration
brought additional Southeast Asian families to Lowell (mostly Cambodian) between 1984 and 1990.[8]

The U.S. Census 2000 of the Lao population breaks down Lao settlers
into two groups: ethnic lowland Lao (168,707) and Hmong (169,428)
(Fuentecilla 2005).[9] Massachusetts, with 3,797, is fourteenth on the list
of the largest settlement of lowland Lao; California has the highest concentration.[10] In the early influx of Southeast Asian immigrants to Lowell,

Lao were numerous. In 1982 Khmer/Cambodians began coming in larger numbers, and currently constitute the largest population of Southeast Asians in Lowell, whereas Lao are the smallest group.

According to data on refugee arrivals in Massachusetts, there were 1,285 Lao refugees who entered the state between 1986 and 1997 alone.[11] The Massachusetts Department of Education estimates that in 2004 there were 553 Lao speakers whose first language was not English in K–12 schools across the commonwealth. The Lao community in Lowell, Massachusetts, is currently estimated at 1,102.[12] Lao in Lowell are primarily lowland Lao. Most Hmong who came to the state settled in Fitchburg and Leominster; very few Hmong families settled in Lowell.[13]

Adaptation to the United States: Challenges, Support, Barriers, Resilience

The Lao in Lowell faced many challenges, including learning English, finding jobs, earning a living, coping with a very different culture—all in addition to the traumatic experiences of their leaving their homeland and stays in refugee camps. The host community at times was welcoming and supportive; at other times it erected barriers. Perhaps what Stuart-Fox (1993) referred to earlier as "the resilience of the Lao culture" (112) was a factor in the ability of Lao to adapt—both individually and collectively.

Language Barriers and Host Community Support

Language proved to be one of the biggest problems. It was in education that the host community both provided support and presented obstacles. While in 1979 there were but a few Southeast Asian students in the Lowell schools, by 1991, there were 1,880, only 252 of whom were Lao (Lowell School Department statistics, reported in Francis 1994). As the lack of English-language skills was a major barrier for newcomers, the Lowell schools provided assistance. In 1980–1981 an English as a Second Language program (ESL) was established for non-native speakers of English to assist them with their English-language skills (see table 8.1). Transitional bilingual education had been required by the state of Massachusetts since 1971 wherever there existed a sufficient number of students who spoke a language other than English. A bilingual program was begun in 1983 to assist Khmer speakers, and later a program was established at the Rogers Middle School for Lao students. The program provided students opportunities to learn subjects in their own language while learning to speak English. The schools faced the challenge of finding

Table 8.1

Bilingual Education Enrollments in Lowell Public Schools,
Southeast Asians (SEAs)

Year	Southeast Asians and Others		
1979–1980	5		
1980–1981	62		
1981–1982	195		
1982–1983	283		
1983–1984	355		

Year	Southeast Asians		
1984–1985	640		
1985–1986	850		
1986–1987	1,143		

Year	Cambodians	Laotians	Vietnamese
1988–1989	1,492	233	97
1989–1990	1,510	248	95
1990–1991	1,527	252	101
1991–1992	1,399	195	107
1992–1993	1,381	181	133
1993–1994	1,371	173	138

Note: For the first five years of the program, Southeast Asian enrollments were included with other minority groups. From 1984 to 1987, a separate category for Southeast Asians was established. From 1987 on, separate categories were established for Cambodian, Laotian, and Vietnamese enrollments. Also included in the program were Spanish, Portuguese, and Gujarati.

Source: Lowell School Department. Reported in the *Lowell Sun*, April 10, 1994, p. 23. Condensed to include only Southeast Asians. Statistics from subsequent years were not available.

books and curriculum materials in the appropriate language, teachers who were fluent in Lao, Khmer, and Vietnamese, and finding space for the newly arrived students (Francis 1994; Kiang 1994).

The host community and the newcomers worked together in meeting educational challenges. Teachers reported that for a number of years the program in transitional bilingual education helped many students through the difficult adjustment period of acquiring a second language. Bilingual classes, staffed by teachers who knew the language of the students and had experienced similar difficult transitions to the "new country" provided support on many levels. Many classes were taught by a team of an American and a Lao teacher. In the bilingual program there were six Lao teachers, five of whom held teaching certificates along with the B.A. or M.A. degree, and two Lao paraprofessionals. These teachers took great pride in seeing the students, who came with no English skills at all, grow, learn, and graduate. For many the mutual respect among teachers, students, and parents was quite evident. Teachers generally felt strong support from the larger Lao community in Lowell.

For Lao children born in the United States or in refugee camps and brought here at a young age, cultural differences presented challenges between the parents and their more Americanized children. Often parents did not understand the U.S. education system, and the generational differences were great. The bilingual program offered opportunities for parents to learn about the educational system their children had entered and cultural differences. It reached beyond the classroom into the community, providing opportunities for connections among the parents and the larger Lowell community. Cultural and social events encouraged parents to feel a part of the school and community. They brought traditional foods and were able to connect to institutions in their "new community," while celebrating their own heritage. "We were like a family," one teacher remarked (personal communications, November 2005).

Financial support from government sources was crucial to the success of these programs. Other success factors included small class size (allowing focus on students' particular needs); high motivation generated by the relevance of their studies to the "real worlds" they live; and high standards and expectations that respected students' abilities.[14]

Resistance within Host Communities

Not only do immigrants experience enormous change in moving to a new community; the host community itself feels the impact of the influx of large numbers of newcomers. While many welcome the new vitality that immigrants bring, others are resentful that "things just aren't the same." Sometimes tensions arise from the fear that resources will be diverted away from the "native" population to the newcomers.

Many immigrants coming to the United States have experienced some lack of welcome—or even hostility. This is also true for Southeast Asians. One study identified ethnocentrism (an "us-versus-them" mentality) as more important in determining attitudes toward refugees than age, economic status, or education levels (Hein 1995, citing Ruefle et al. 1992). Hein (1995) observes differences between incidents of hostility perpetrated by whites, and those by minorities, and concludes that the conflicts with whites appear to be rooted in more general antagonism, while conflicts with minorities seem rooted in the perceived threat to existing resources and institutions.

One response in Lowell to the influx of a large group of Southeast Asians centered around language. In a movement led by school committeeman George Kouloheras, in 1989 an "English as the Official Language" nonbinding measure was approved by 72 percent of Lowell voters.[15] This issue sparked a major controversy throughout the 1990s, with charges of discrimination against immigrants—and others charging discrimination against mainstream students—along with numerous debates on the effectiveness and necessity of bilingual education. In 1994, about 45,000 Massachusetts students were enrolled across the state in bilingual education courses (Trott 1994). The debates on bilingual education came to a head with a statewide referendum. In November 2002 the regulations calling for bilingual education were overturned, and funding ceased. The new law required that transitional bilingual education classes be replaced by English-immersion classes starting in the 2003 school year. All teachers of such classes were required to be "fluent and literate in English" (Zehr 2003, 22).

Many felt the end of transitional bilingual education and the new law had a severe impact on immigrants—teachers and students—in the city. One result was that in several Massachusetts districts, some teachers—native speakers of a language other than English—were laid off when they were unable to pass the English-fluency tests (Zehr 2003). Lao teachers had been teaching successfully for more than a decade in the Lowell schools. Many did not want to take this exam, as they felt it was an insult—one more barrier placed before them. Some dropped out of teaching altogether. Others took the exam, but did not achieve the results desired. That left only one Lao teacher in the Lowell schools.[16]

Following these changes, Lao students, along with other immigrants, were immersed in the English Language Learners (ELL) program. Small numbers of Lao did not provide the critical mass to influence schools in hiring additional Lao teachers. The Parent Information Center, established to serve all Lowell parents, has bilingual staff and remains the official and primary place of support for parents from Southeast Asia. The one Lao teacher who remains in the Lowell system is not being utilized specifically for the Lao student population, but teaches mainstream students in the high school.

Group Support and Resilience among Lao

Lao have found ways to form social networks and support one another in their transition. A mutual assistance association, the Lao temples, and cultural events have provided practical help and ways of keeping Lao culture alive. Vertovec (2003) cites three concepts from various realms of sociology for understanding group formation and maintenance in the new land: social networks, social capital, and embeddedness. He applies these to migration patterns and transnationalism. Because for migrants, social networks are crucial for finding jobs, housing, services, goods, information, and psychological support, Vertovec notes: "Migration is a process that both depends on, and creates, social networks" (644). Differentials in social power and influence contribute to the "social capital"—defined as connections as resources, and ability to activate these, in networks.[17]

To respond to the many challenges facing them on arrival—adjustment and the disrupted social connections—Lao immigrants, with the help of government funding, founded the Laotian American Organization in 1985. The organization received some assistance from state and local grants. Especially for the purpose of assisting those newly arrived Lao, the association provided health and social services along with English instruction and citizenship classes, job assistance, family counseling, and interpreter/translator services for health appointments. "One of our goals is for the community to acknowledge that we exist as a population," Sommanee Bounphasaysonh, president of the board of directors, affirmed in 1993 (Arnold 1993).

The grants that funded this program expired; the organization ran into financial difficulties and ceased to exist in 1997. In an immigrant–host community–university collaboration, a group of Lao got together and, with the guidance of the CIRCLE (Center for Immigrant Refugee Community Leadership and Empowerment) program at the University of Massachusetts Lowell,[18] formed the Lao Family Association. Initially this organization had no outside funding, and met in the home of one of the founding members. They wanted to continue to provide vital services for the Lao community, such as translating and interpreting for health and hospital visits, an after-school program for children, and other social services. The Lao Family Association raised small amounts of money from the communities and shared, with the Cambodian Mutual Assistance Association, a small grant from the city to provide after-school care for children. The organization has become concerned with promoting Lao culture and educating their children about it. They have participated in events like the Southeast Asian Water Festival with traditional Lao boats (Deely 2000), and have organized other events to keep Lao culture vital in Lowell. With no outside funding currently, the organization runs completely on volunteer labor. As the executive director put it, "We do as much as we can, but cannot do 100 percent to serve the people. However, there is not the need now there was in the beginning. Most people [in the community] already know [their way around]."[19] In addition to this formalized social support, people in the community informally try to help one another. Many, however, are working two jobs and raising children; they find it difficult to devote time to community volunteer activities.

Maintaining Lao traditions and culture serves to foster group identity, primarily through special celebrations and events, traditional foods, and religious practices. As Lao are traditionally Buddhist, many traditions center around the temple. The temple serves as a place to bring together the community in peaceful celebration of time-honored traditions.[20]

Wat Lao Mixayaram of New England, Inc., the largest (though not the only) Lao temple in Lowell,[21] is the primary center for the gathering of Lao and a means for keeping traditions alive in the community and introducing them to the next generation.[22] Located in South Lowell, it serves not only the Lowell Lao community, but also Lao in Rhode Island, Maine, Vermont, and New Hampshire, many of whom drive two hours to participate. Some see the role of the temple as bringing the community together harmoniously. Amidst differences of opinion within the community, the temple is seen as a place of peace.[23] Even many who did not attend the temple regularly in Laos come and participate in the special events. Especially at New Year's people celebrate and parade around the temple.[24] Some of the older generation lament that there are not more young people who are active in the temple and in these celebrations.[25] Though some of the younger generation remark that they don't feel *that* Buddhist, they come to honor their parents and keep their traditions.

Ethnic traditions are celebrated as Lao join with Cambodians for the annual Lowell Southeast Asian Water Festival on the banks of the Merrimack River.[26] This festival is a traditional celebration of the importance of rivers to people in Southeast Asian cultures, and marks the harvest of new rice in the home countries of Laos, Cambodia, and Thailand. Exquisitely painted boats shipped from Laos and Cambodia are rowed over the waters of the Merrimack in friendly competition. Tiny model boats or trays or floats with flowers and candles are launched onto the river with a request for blessings, to receive merit, to release the bad and wish for the good.[27] Through events like this Lao celebrate their ethnic identity and their homeland. The reflection of imported Lao boats on the Merrimack River vividly symbolizes attempts to unite native land and new land.

Identities across Borders

While connected in social networks and by language, customs and traditions, Lao in Lowell do not form a monolithic community bounded by either the Merrimack or the Mekong; rather, the community stretches across both. While immigrant communities can provide vital sources of support through social networking and celebration of traditions, they can also be "sites for intense conflict about the pace and direction of the adaptation process" (Hein 1995, 153). Some have observed three Lao communities in Lowell: those who want to maintain Lao traditions in their new communities while at the same time their lives are definitely focused in Lowell; those who want to go back to the past and revive the Royal Lao; and those who do not really care about political issues in the homeland, and just want to get on with their lives here. While divisions may not be this distinct, there are different ideas of "who we are"—as a group that celebrates and honors traditions, as citizens or residents of the new land, and as peoples caught between two cultures and two histories. The image of immigrants who either assimilate or integrate into, or remain marginal and isolated from their new culture (Berry et al. 1995) does not capture the complexities experienced by Lao in Lowell. Those immigrants embedded in more than one context, location, or social structure often develop complex ways of negotiating their identities. Their experiences must take into account the past and the present, the home country and the current location.

By one definition, "transnational migration is a pattern of migration in which persons, although they move across international borders, settle, and establish relations in a new state, maintain ongoing social connections with the polity from which they originated. In transnational migration people literally live their lives across international borders. Such persons are best identified as 'transmigrants'" (Glick Schiller, and Fouron 1999, 344). Yet the range and variety of transnational activity and perception of migrants is broad. Individually and as a group, there is no solitary way Lao interpret their past and bring it into the present.

One vivid example illustrates different interpretations of the past in the present. The diversity and divisions within the Lao community are revealed in a controversy over the flag. Motivated by the desire to "do something for memory of the history of Laos, life in the past" (G. Sengvongchanh, personal communication, November 28, 2005), in 2004 Gary Sengvongchanh joined with others from Lowell and surrounding communities to petition the Lowell city council to recognize the Royal Lao Heritage and Freedom Flag as the official flag of the Lao-American community in Lowell, "because of its long history as a symbol of resilience, freedom, and democracy, both in Laos itself and the Lao-American community throughout the city of Lowell and elsewhere."[28] On August 10, 2004, the Lowell city council passed a proclamation to this effect.

On August 14, 2005, a group gathered to celebrate the first anniversary of the Lao-American Heritage and Freedom Flag day.[29] The parade of about sixty marched from the Boott Cotton Mills complex to the Lowell city hall, where city councilors spoke about supporting freedom. Proclamations were read honoring the Lao-American community from the State House of Representatives and Senate, the governor and lieutenant governor, and Lowell Congressman Marty Meehan. The national anthem was sung, and the Laotian Royal Heritage and Freedom Flag was flown, alongside the American Flag. Two young Lao-Americans spoke, proclaiming, "It [the flag] is the symbol of our freedom. . . . This is an opportunity to represent ourselves. It's a chance to come out after all these years" (Piro 2005).

The coordinator of the event, Gary Sengvongchanh, and member of the Laotian Heritage Foundation, a group that has coalesced around the flag issue, described the event as a way of bringing two communities together, the larger Lowell community and the Lao-American community. He spoke about the pride of being Lao, and stated that the purpose of the foundation is "to teach the younger generation to know about the history, where we are from, why we are here. We have no chance to go back to the country. We are American citizens, our children are born here. We are educating the children about where they come from." Mr. Sengvongchanh expressed sadness that some people in the Lao community "misunderstand us. We do not want to be in conflict with anybody. We do not want to make controversy. We want to make memory of [our] history" (G. Sengvongchanh, personal communication, November 28, 2005).

In his efforts to educate the larger community on the goals of the Laotian Heritage Foundation, Mr. Sengvongchanh has mounted a Web site to discuss in more detail the purposes of the organization. While many in the community understand his efforts as attempts to "go back to the past" and "revive the Royal Lao," Mr. Sengvongchanh clarifies in his Web site that the recognition of the Laotian Heritage flag does not mean recognizing the former royal government of Laos: "the Royal government of Laos no longer exists and we accept that reality. The recognition of the Laotian Heritage flag is recognition of the dear values held close to the hearts of Laotian American community. We fled communistic Laos to live freely and to be able to openly express ourselves here in the United States" (Laos Democracy, n.d.).

The flag proclamation by the Lowell city council states that "the vast majority of Lao-Americans embrace the red with three-headed white elephant Heritage and Freedom Flag symbol of the Lao-American community."[30]

This claim, however, is disputed by others in the Lao community, for whom this movement represents a small minority. The current government's flag has been recognized by the United Nations and the United States as the official flag of the People's Democratic Republic of Laos. Some groups in the Lowell community are friendly with the current government in Laos, and use the current government's flag. They want it to be safe for people to go back to visit. They recognize changes in the current government's policy and ideas, and that Lao people there have a better life than ten years before. Some Lao in Lowell still have family in Laos; others just want to be able to visit the homeland for a few weeks or a couple of months.[31]

Many Lao express discomfort with the attention the Lao Heritage Foundation has brought to the community. These community members do not want to cause problems; they take the "pragmatic" position that the others should "wake up and smell the coffee," and stop living in the past. They feel the past should be buried to get on with their lives here. They do not want to jeopardize the possibility of traveling back to their homeland or connecting with those currently living in Laos. In addition to these two positions, there are Lao who do not wish to get embroiled in a controversy that divides the community on an issue that lies in the past, far from their present lives. They experience the past as painful and do not wish to revisit it.

The history shared by Lao immigrants has diverse manifestations. How one deals with memories of the past and action in the future reveals complex layers of culture, thought, and motivation. Issues of identity, justice, fear of reprisal, social alliances, passing on legacies to children, and power emerge. Relationship with and perspective on the homeland are prominent in the equation. As Hein points out, no immigrant group is immune from a connection with the past. Embedded in how a person relates to his or her country of origin are the cultures learned early in those lands: "cultures, as well as homeland histories and politics, establish ethnic boundaries and ethnic identities that influence how immigrants respond to new boundaries and identities in the host culture" (Hein 2006, xxi). For some, maintaining harmony and avoiding conflict is primary. For others, reclaiming an identity central to being Lao is crucial. Still others find the nature of this disagreement and conflict within the community itself embarrassing.

Identities are not simply bounded by the geographical space of their homelands or the new community. Immigrants in diasporas also live between worlds, in transnational space. How individuals navigate this space and define their identities varies. Guarnizo et al. (2003) note that "the meaning and scope of transnationalism is not uniform. Although there are common forces bearing on all immigrants, the particular circumstances of each community also affect the extent and character of these activities. For some immigrants, transnational politics is a means to maintain an active presence in their country's centers of power; for others, it is a means to avoid such centers in order to provide direct assistance to their native regions; and for still others, it is a practice to be avoided in order to leave a violent and unsettling past behind" (1237–38).[32]

Some members of the Lao community, while concerned with maintaining Lao culture through customs and traditions, are not interested in devoting time, energy, or resources to influencing others. For immigrants who have left behind a violent past, the memory of violence is an important factor in their participation—or nonparticipation—in transnational activism. Participation in ongoing relationships with relatives and friends, in social networks, and civic engagement of a nongovernmental nature may be much more prevalent than political activity (Guarnizo et al. 2003, 1212). These different stances illustrate various ways memory is interpreted in the present.

The purpose of this project was to bring to light factors that have influenced Lao in migrating to and establishing homes in Lowell, and to explore ways the past is reinterpreted and meaning arrived at in the present. History, personal stories, events, and institutions have provided a glimpse of this population, their struggles and triumphs, their traditions and diversity. Theories of adaptation, transnationalism, trauma, and resilience provided important frames of analysis and useful comparisons. The process was enriching and humbling. The dominant cultural values reveal themselves in the present-day realities of life in Lowell; at the same time they are ever-changing across generations, requiring reevaluation and reinterpretation as the layers of complexity and meaning emerge.

At this writing the Second International Conference on Lao Studies is scheduled for May 2007 in Arizona and a second International Conference on Hmong Studies is planned for 2008. These provide international forums on issues pertinent to the more than 25 million people in the Lao diaspora. Thirty-plus years after the end of the war in their country of origin, Lao in Lowell continue to thrive and to struggle, to raise children, to maintain traditions and customs, to learn new ones, to negotiate boundaries between homeland and the new land, to become a part of the larger community of the city. Many have realized a level of economic stability (although still lower than the level of the general population).[33] Some have attained higher degrees and advanced education. Lao continue to reevaluate their past, make meaning of the present, and re-vision their futures. In doing so, they are a vital part of the fabric of diversity and complexity that is Lowell.

Acknowledgments

There are many people to thank for their openness and willingness to participate in this study. Above all, I am grateful to the Lao community members who talked with me, explained the meaning of traditions, shared their life experiences, described their struggles, triumphs, joys, and the history of their community or organizations in Lowell. I am particularly grateful to Douangmany Malavong-Warren for her invaluable insights, her devoted energy to the telling of experiences, and her kindness extended at every turn. I am also grateful to my coeditors Lan Pho and Jeffrey Gerson, who provided encouragement, practical information, and critiques throughout the research and writing process. Final decisions were my own, and I take full responsibility for these. My hope is that this brief discussion will foster a better understanding of the Lao people and their history, and stimulate the curiosity of readers to continue the much-needed research in exploring the layers and complexity of a people with whom the United States shares a crucial point in history and Lowell shares an important moment in the present.

Notes

1. Chan estimates that in 1991 only 10 percent of all Southeast Asian refugees were from Laos. (1991)
2. While the dominant population of Laos is composed of ethnic Lao living in the lowlands, many ethnic groups populate the country. Those who immigrated to the United States are usually divided into two groups: lowland Lao and Hmong.
3. This research took place over a period of time primarily from September 2003 through January 2007. A prior visit to Laos in 2000 provided a background for understanding the culture, country, and people. Many of those interviewed preferred to remain anonymous, and their comments are cited simply as "personal communication" to protect their identities.
4. Stuart-Fox describes three broad groups of people in Laos: (1) the Lao Loum, or Lao of the valleys, which include ethnic Lao and also upland Tai; (2) the Lao Theung, or Lao of the mountain slopes, who speak Mon-Khmer languages; and (3) the Lao Soung, or Lao of the mountaintops, who speak Tibeto-Burman languages. In terms of population percentages, the Lao Loum constitute approximately 65 percent, the Lao Theung, approximately 25 percent, and the Lao Soung, approximately 10 percent. There are more ethnic Lao living in Thailand than in Laos. (Stuart-Fox 1993)
5. See Chandler and Steinberg (1987) for a comprehensive discussion of this period of Southeast Asian history.
6. See Hai Pho's account in this volume (chapter 2).

7. See Hai Pho's account in this volume (chapter 2). The refugees were settled by the regional chapter of the American Fund for Czechoslovakian Refugees in Lowell.

8. See Pyle's discussion of secondary migration in this volume (chapter 3).

9. The Hmong consider themselves natives not only of Laos but also of China, Myanmar, and Vietnam.

10. In descending order of population numbers of Lao received, between California and Massachusetts on this list are the following states: Texas, Minnesota, Washington, North Carolina, Illinois, Georgia, Wisconsin, Oregon, Tennessee, and Iowa.

11. Data compiled by the Massachusetts Office for Refugees and Immigrants, using Department of Public Health/US Quarantine Service Arrival Data.

12. Based on Lowell Public Schools data for Lao speakers (216) and estimating 5.1 persons for each student's family. Data collected October 2004. Later data aggregated counts for Southeast Asians.

13. About 40 percent of the Hmong refugees resettled in Minnesota initially, although many later moved to the San Joaquin Valley in California (Chan 1991).

14. Resettlement of Southeast Asian Refugees and Immigrants in Massachusetts in Retrospect. Presentation by Douangmany Malavong-Warren at the University of Massachusetts, Lowell, May 29, 2003.

15. Full text of the nonbinding referendum reads: "Shall it be the policy of the people of Lowell that English is the official language of the city of Lowell and that our city governments requests: 1) Our Senators and Congressmen to vote for English as our National Language; 2) Our State Legislators make English our official state language." Critics commented that most of the city's immigrant population was still unable to vote, and those supporting this measure did not fully understand what it meant (Crittenden 1989).

16. Forty Cambodian teachers in Lowell left their jobs after the changes in the transitional bilingual education law. P. Chea, in seminar, Learning from Diverse Voices: Seminar on Southeast Asian Refugees (SEA) in the Mill City: Changing Families, Communities, Institutions, held at the University of Massachusetts, Lowell, June 2, 2005.

17. See discussion of social capital by Turcotte and Silka, this volume (chapter 4).

18. Peter N. Kiang created the CIRCLE program at the University of Massachusetts Boston, Amherst, and Lowell (see Kiang et al. 1997).

19. Blong Xiong, personal communications, November 2005.

20. See also Thomson's and Gerson's articles in this volume, which discuss the importance of the temples (chapters 7 and 9).

21. Just outside of Lowell in Westford is Wat Buddhabhavana of MA, Inc., which also serves the community. In addition there are small groups of people who meet in homes to continue their Buddhist ceremonies and traditions.

22. The temple serves as the principal vehicle for continuing Lao traditions deeply rooted in Buddhism. Even so, one small Christian community is active in maintaining important social ties and language. Some Lao converted to Christianity in the refugee camps, while others were sponsored by Christian organizations or families, and joined the religion of their sponsors.

23. For another perspective on temples, see Jeffrey Gerson's account of conflict in the Cambodian temple (chapter 9).

24. See Susan Thomson's description of New Year's celebration in this volume (chapter 7).

25. See also Susan Thomson's accounts of Wat Mixayaram in this volume (chapter 7).

26. Joining with others has not always been easy, and at one point separate Lao and Cambodian events were considered. However, in 2004 a nonprofit organization was formed to continue the festival with joint efforts of the community.

27. Participant/observation of festival events, August 2004 and 2005.

28. Official Proclamation of Lowell City Council, August 10, 2004.

29. Again in 2006 a group gathered to celebrate this anniversary.

30. Official Proclamation of Lowell City Council, August 10, 2004, p. 1.

31. The flag issue is not unique to the Lao American community. Many Vietnamese Americans have not accepted the "red flag with the yellow star" of communist Vietnam.

32. In addition to considering nationality and the attitudes and context of the receiving country, Guarnizo et al. (2003) compares three groups of Latino migrants and points to the need to examine factors of age, gender, class, education, and race in understanding transnational activity. While they did not specifically investigate race, they indicated that the attitudes of the receiving country were important. Concepts of race might significantly affect how migrants are perceived and treated in the receiving communities.

33. Anecdotal examples of progress are available. The Federal Reserve Bank reports that immigrants who arrived in the United States after 1990 have a median household income of $37,500, compared with $45,210 for immigrants who arrived before 1980. Regardless of when they immigrated, the region's immigrants have household incomes below those of the native-born population. Retrieved from Federal Reserve Bank of Boston, http://www .bos.frb.org/commdev/immigration/caprofileOverview.htm, December 20, 2005. The U.S. Census Bureau (Reeves and Bennett 2004) in a publication on Asians in the United States reported that in 2000 the percentage of occupied housing for Laotian home ownership was 52.4 percent, compared with 38.7 percent for Hmong, 53.2 percent for Vietnamese, and 43.6 percent for Cambodians. Japanese was the Asian group with the highest percentage, at 60.8 percent. All Asian groups were below the U.S. total population at 66.2 percent. The same publication cites the poverty rate in 1999 for Laotians at 18.5 percent, and that for Hmong at 37.8 percent, while the total population is assessed at 12.4 percent. Median family income for Laotian in 1999 was reported at $43,542, for Hmong at $32,384, while for all families it was $50,046.

References

Arnold, David. 1993. City's Laotian-Americans Struggle to Gain Acceptance, Social Services. *Lowell Sun*, December 16, p. 1.

Baubock, Rainer. 2003 Towards a Political Theory of Transnationalism. Center for Migration Studies of New York. *IMR* 37, no. 3:700–723.

Berry, John W., and D. Sam. 1997. Acculturation and Adaptation. In John W. Berry, Marshall H. Segall, and Cigdem Kagitçibasi, editors. *Handbook of Cross-Cultural Psychology*, vol 3, *Social Behavior and Applications*. Boston: Allyn and Bacon.

Castle, Timothy J. 1993. *A War in the Shadow of Vietnam: U.S. Military Aid to the Royal Lao Government, 1955-1975*. New York: Columbia University Press.

Center for Migration Studies of New York, Inc. 1993. *Migration World Magazine* 21, no. 1:24–25.

Chan, Sucheng. 1991. *Asian Americans: An Interpretive History*. Boston: Twayne.

———. ed. 1994 *Hmong Means Free: Life in Laos and America*. Philadelphia: Temple University Press.

———. 2003 *Not Just Victims: Conversations with Cambodian Community Leaders in the United States*. Urbana: University of Illinois Press.

Chandler, David P., et al. 1987. *In Search of Southeast Asia: A Modern History*. Edited by David Joel Steinberg. Honolulu: University of Hawaii Press.

Cole, Ellen, Oliva M. Espin, Esther D. Rothblum. 1992. *Refugee Women and Their Mental Health: Shattered Societies, Shattered Lives*. Binghamton, NY: Harrington Park Press.

Community Development. 2005. Retrieved from Federal Reserve Bank of Boston, http://www.bos.frb.org/commdev/immigration/caprofileOverview.htm, December 20, 2005.

Conway, Kenneth, and James Morrison. 1995. *Shadow War: The CIA's Secret War in Laos*. Boulder, Co.: Paladin.

Crittenden, Jules. 1989. English Referendum Passes nearly 3 to 1. *Lowell Sun*. November 8, pp. 1 and 6.

Dao, Yang. 2005. The Contributions of the Laotian Ethnic Minorities in Building of Laos. Presentation at the 1st International Conference on Lao Studies, Northern Illinois University, DeKalb, Illinois, May 20–22.

Deely, Kathleen. 2000. A Sunny Day to Celebrate Faith, Tradition. *Lowell Sun*, August 20, p. 13.

Dommen, Arthur J. 2001. *The Indochinese Experience of the French and the Americans: Nationalism and Communism in Cambodia, Laos, and Vietnam*. Bloomington: Indiana University Press.

Espiritu, Yen Le. 1992. *Asian American Panethnicity: Bridging Institutions and Identities*. Philadelphia: Temple University Press.

Francis, Dana. 1994. Program Expanded to Handle Unexpected Immigration. *Lowell Sun*, April 10.

Fuentecilla, J. "Pete." 2005. Lessons of Refugee Survival: The Experience of Lao Nurses in the US. Presentation at the 1st International Conference on Lao Studies, Northern Illinois University, DeKalb, Illinois, May 20–22.

Ghosh, Sutama, and Lu Wang. 2003. Transnationalism and Identity: A Tale of Two Faces and Multiple Lives. *Canadian Geographer* 47, no. 3:269–82.

Glick Schiller, Nina, and George E. Fouron. 1999. Terrains of Blood and Nation: Haitian Transnational Social Fields. *Ethnic and Racial Studies* 22, no. 2:340–66.

Guarnizo, Luis Eduardo, Alejandro Portes, and William Haller. 2003. Assimilation and Transnationalism: Determinants of Transnational Political Action among Contemporary Migrants. *American Journal of Sociology* 108, no. 6 (May): 1211–48.

Hamilton-Merritt, Jane. 1993. *Tragic Mountains: The Hmong, the Americans, and the Secret Wars for Laos, 1942-1992*. Bloomington: Indiana University Press.

Hein, Jeremy. 1992. *States and International Migrants: The Incorporation of Indochinese Refugees in the United States and France*. Boulder, Colorado: Westview Press.

———. 1995. *From Vietnam, Laos, and Cambodia: A Refugee Experience in the United States.* New York: Twayne.

———. 2006. *Ethnic Origins: The Adaptation of Cambodian and Hmong Refugees in Four American Cities.* New York: Russell Sage Foundation.

Herman, Judith, M.D. 1997. *Trauma and Recovery: The Aftermath of Violence—from Domestic Abuse to Political Terror.* New York: Basic Books.

Inui, Miki. 1998. Assimilation and Repatriation Conflicts of the Hmong Refugees in a Wisconsin Community: A Qualitative Study of Five Local Groups. *Migration World Magazine* 26, no. 4:26.

Kaufman, Marc. 2004. American Odyssey: They Fled Terror in Laos after Secretly Aiding American Forces in the Vietnam War; Now 200,000 Hmong Prosper—and Struggle—in the United States. *Smithsonian* 35, no. 6:84.

Kiang, Peter N. 1994. When Know-nothings Speak English Only . . . In *The State of Asian America: Activism and Resistance in the 1990s,* edited by Karin Aguilar-San Juan, 125–45. Boston: South End.

———, Jeffrey Gerson, et al. 1997. "New Visions in University-Community Transformation. *Change* (January–February).

Kimball, Virginia. 1994. Refugee's Escape to Freedom Led to New Faith. *Lowell Sun,* December 10.

Laos Democracy. N.d. Retrieved from www.laosdemocracy.com, November 10, 2005.

Legacies of War. N.d. Retrieved from www.legaciesofwar.org, May 22, 2005.

Lowell Public Schools Records for Lao speakers (216). 2004. Data collected October.

Lowell School Department statistics. 1994. Reported in *Lowell Sun,* April 10, p. 23.

Manz, Beatriz. 1988. *Refugees of a Hidden War: The Aftermath of Counterinsurgency in Guatemala.* Albany, NY: State University of New York Press.

Piro, Rebecca. 2005. Laotian Pride Rises with Freedom Flag Day. *Lowell Sun,* August 15.

Public Interest Projects, Legacies of War. N.d. Retrieved from www.legaciesofwar.org, May 22, 2005.

Quincy, Keith. 1998. *Hmong: History of a People.* Cheney: Eastern Washington University Press.

Reeves, Terrance J., and Claudette Bennett. 2004. We the People: Asians in the United States: Census 2000 Special Reports. Cense-17. U.S. Department of Commerce, U.S. Census Bureau.

Ruefle, William, W.H. Ross, and Diana Mandell. 1992. Attitudes toward Southeast Asian Immigrants in a Wisconsin Community. *International Migration Review* 26, no. 3:877–98.

Souvannarath, Vinthany. 2005. Presentation on Narrative Analysis of Six Lao Women Refugees Facing Assimilation Issues, 1st International Conference on Lao Studies, Northern Illinois University, DeKalb, Illinois, May 20–22.

Stuart-Fox, Martin. 1993. On the Writing of Lao History: Continuities and Discontinuities. *Journal of Southeast Asian Studies* (March 24):106–16.

Trott, Robert W. 1994. Legislator Calls State's Bilingual Education Law Discriminatory. *Lowell Sun,* March 17, p. 17.

U.S. House of Representatives. (2001, November 13) *Expressing the Sense of the Congress that the President Should Issue a Proclamation Recognizing a National Lao-Hmong Recognition Day (Tancredo).* 108th Cong., 1st sess. H.Con.Res.88. Retrieved from htp://www.house.gov/burton/RSC on December 5, 2005.

Vertovec, Steve. 2003. Migration and Other Modes of Transnationalism: To-wards Conceptual Cross-Fertilization. Center for Migration Studies of New York. *IMR* 37, no. 4:641–65.

———. 2004. Migrant Transnationalism and Modes of Transformation. Center for Migration Studies of New York. *IMR* 38, no. 3:970–1001.

Warner, Roger. 1996. *Shooting at the Moon: The Story of America's Clandestine War in Laos.* South Royalton, VT: Steerforth Press.

Wolin, Steen J., M.D., and Sybil Wolin, Ph. D. 1994. *The Resilient Self: How Survivors of Troubled Families Rise above Adversity.* New York: Villard Books.

Zehr, Mary Ann. 2003. Mass Teachers Learn a Hard Lesson: Flunk the English Test, Get Fired. *Education Week* 23, no. 1:22.

Jeffrey N. Gerson

The Battle for Control of the Trairatanaram Cambodian Temple

The scene inside the Middlesex Superior Court building in April 2004 was unusual to say the least. The seats on one side of the courtroom gallery were filled with two dozen monks wearing traditional orange robes, with shaven heads. The other half of the courtroom's spectators were Cambodian Americans who were not monks, although a few Buddhist nuns were present. The nonmonk group was there to represent those monks who believe it is not proper for them to attend an American judicial proceeding.[1]

Sitting in front of them, before Judge Paul A. Chernoff, were the attorneys representing both sides in what was then a five-year-old legal battle. On its face the judicial struggle was about who were the rightful owners of two buildings, the Trairatanaram Temple and Parsonage of North Chelmsford, Massachusetts. The Trairatanaram Temple is one of two Cambodian Buddhist temples in the greater Lowell, Massachusetts area, which is home to twenty thousand Southeast Asian immigrants and refugees.

One side, represented by attorney Jocelyn Campbell, claimed that a real estate transaction that transferred the ownership of the temple's two properties from the original executive board that founded the temple in 1986 to the Venerable Sao Khon and his national organization, the Community of Khmer Buddhist Monks, Inc. (CKBM) was illegal. The other group, represented by attorney Rick Brody, claimed its members, including Sao Khon, had been illegally ousted from power at a board meeting that failed to follow the Massachusetts Articles of Organization, the rules and regulations of the nonprofit corporation, and due process. The ouster was the work of the temple's newest monk, Venerable Choun Chek, and his community supporters, according to Brody (Brody 2004; Campbell 2004).

The conflict between the monks in North Chelmsford reached such a pitch (there were threats of violence) that the court ordered both groups to stay away from each other and through a restraining order demanded each group to remain on one floor of the temple. The "upstairs monks" are the Community of Khmer Buddhist Monks, Inc (CKBM) led by Sao Khon; Choun Chek leads the "downstairs monks."

This essay digs below the surface of this legal conflict to examine what broader issues might be involved. The individuals involved claim that there are several factors that underlie the rift between the factions of monks and their supporters. One significant factor is Cambodia homeland politics. Another is differing notions of how power should be structured; that is, centralized versus decentralized (a desire on the part of the CKBM to restructure the American Cambodian temple and re-shape it into a national Vatican-like hierarchy, while the other side favors local control by laypeople in a congregational style organization). Yet a third is differing religious visions, with one group expressly advocating "Engaged Buddhism." The issues in the North Chelmsford temple are similar to those found at Cambodian temples around the United States: charges of misappropriation of funds and improper recordkeeping, deep personality conflicts, rivalries among the monk leadership, and legal attempts to evict monks and their supporters from the temple (Kessler 2005). These charges appear to stem in part from a lack of trust in the integrity of the monks as spiritual leaders following the Cambodian genocide perpetuated by the Khmer Rouge (KR) regime during the middle 1970s. A new questioning of the value of religion itself and the monks as leaders emerged post-KR (Chigas 2005). Many Cambodian immigrants no longer believe their monks are free of corruption and live moral lives.

Methodology

The research for this chapter was conducted in the summer of 2004 and 2005. Approximately a dozen people were interviewed; including lawyers involved in the temple case, the chief monks and their bilingual public spokespersons.[2] Others who have knowledge of the community and history of Cambodian Buddhism were consulted, as well as secondary sources and newspaper articles. I attended two sessions of the Massachusetts Middlesex Superior Court, observing both parties in the conflict. In the summer of 2004 I carried out these interviews with Lewis Rice, a freelance journalist writing a piece on the monks' conflict for *Boston Magazine*. Working together with Rice was an attempt to avoid duplication of interviews, given the possible difficulty of obtaining them; this is an active legal case and we are noncommunity members (L. Rice 2004).

Theoretical Framework

According to Lien, Conway, and Wong (2004) there are four conceptual frameworks that dominate the study of Asian American political incorporation and social adaptation. They are assimilation/acculturation, segmented assimilation, transnationalism, and panethnicization and racial formation. The first is the dominant paradigm and has been changed over time to reflect different rates of incorporation. They write: "success in one adaptation state does not automatically lead to success in another or the natural abandonment of homeland or ethnic ties" (20). In segmented assimilation, "adaptation patterns exhibited by a group will depend in large part on social and residential class context" (21). Transnationalism argues that ties to the country of origin do not fade; political, economic, and social links are maintained, creating multiple identities for immigrants and refugees. Focus on homeland politics may harm the development of interest in American politics. With panethnicization and racial formation, "internalized racial experiences may be transformed into group consciousness and serve as a catalyst for community mobilization" (23).

In this study I seek to find which of these frameworks offers the best way to understand the politics of Cambodian religious organizations and community. I have argued in a previous article on the Cambodian American community of Lowell that homeland politics has emerged in local Cambodian American politics and confirms the transnationalism literature's finding that in most cases homeland politics has widened the divide, rather than increased cooperation and harmony, among Cambodian community organizations (Gerson 2005).

So far temple struggles have received the attention of only regional newspapers and magazines. Most of the research on Asian Americans and religion is conducted by sociologists, anthropologists, theologians, religious studies and comparative ethnic studies researchers, and historians.[3] Political scientists have not addressed or tackled this "varied and complex religious terrain" to see how immigrants and refugees have "transplanted their belief systems in the United States, and moreover, how those systems as well as the immigrants have undergone transformation in the building of new spiritual homes for themselves and successive generations" (Yoo 1999, 4).

The Cambodian Buddhist temple is widely viewed as central to Cambodian American life. Many Cambodians believe it has an important role to play in helping to preserve Cambodian culture and to educate people about their homeland's religious traditions and customs. This may or may not be the case for the second-generation Cambodians born in the United States after resettlement from Southeast Asia starting in 1979.

Southeast Asians and Religion

In *A New Religious America: How a "Christian Country" Has Become the World's Most Religiously Diverse Nation,* Harvard anthropologist Diana Eck (2001), describes how the United States is undergoing a religious change that has no equal in the world: "Immigrants around the world number over 130 million, with about 30 million in the United States, a million arriving each year. The dynamic global image of our times is not the so-called clash of civilizations but the marbling of civilizations and peoples. Just as the end of the Cold War brought about a new geopolitical situation, the global movements of people have brought about a new geo-religious reality" (4).

Well-established religions from other parts of the world have put down roots here. And a growing number of immigrants are practicing Buddhism. The majority of Indo-Chinese refugees and Thai immigrants are Buddhists. Together they constitute 40 percent of the Asian American population. The overall figure went from ten thousand in 1974 to more than three million in 2000 (Min and Kim 2002). In the mid-1990s it became apparent there was little scholarly research on Asian immigrants' religions (Prothero 2004).

A few new books have sought to fill the gap (Yoo 1999; Warner and Wittner 1998; Ebaugh and Chafez 2000; Iwamura and Spickard 2003). While something is known about the new immigrants' origins, patterns of settlement, social networks, and school achievement, little is known about their religious practices, organization, and politics. One thing that *is* documented is the centrality of religion to the immigrant's sense of self, provision of social services, and celebration of ethnic customs and languages.

The History of Buddhism and the Role of Monks in Cambodian Society

Theravada Buddhism is the religion of Cambodia; Sri Lanka, Burma, Laos, and Thailand follow this branch of Buddhism as well. Prior to the Khmer Rouge, Thomas J. Douglas (2003, 162) writes: "Cambodian Buddhism has no formal administrative ties with other Buddhist bodies, although Theravada monks from other countries, especially Thailand, Laos, Burma, and Sri Lanka, may participate in religious ceremonies in order to make up the requisite number of clergy. Cambodian Buddhism is organized nationally in accordance with regulations formulated in 1943 and modified in 1948. During the monarchical period, the king led the Buddhist clergy. Prince Sihanouk continued in this role even after he had abdicated and was governing as head of state. He appointed both the heads of the monastic orders and other high-ranking clergy. After the overthrow of Sihanouk in 1970, the new head of state, Lon Nol, appointed these leaders. The monk traditionally occupied a unique position in the transmission of Khmer culture and values. By his way of life, he provided a living model of the most meritorious behavior a Buddhist could follow. He also provided the laity with many opportunities for gaining merit. For centuries, monks were the only literate people residing in rural communities; they acted as teachers to temple servants, to novices, and to newly ordained monks. Until the 1970s, most literate Cambodian males gained literacy solely through the instruction of the *sangha*" (retrieved August 31, 2005 from www.country-studies.com).

Most commonly, "sangha means the order of ordained Buddhist monks or nuns (that is, there is one sangha of monks and one of nuns). In a stricter sense, sangha can mean the assembly of all beings possessing some degree of enlightenment, such as *arhats* and *bodhisattvas;* this is referred to as the *arya-sangha* or noble sangha. Unlike Cambodia's past, in modern Western countries, sangha is often used much more loosely to refer to any group of Buddhist laypeople, with a meaning similar to 'congregation'" (retrieved August 15, 2005, from http://dictionary.labor lawtalk.com/Sangha).

During its four years in power (1975–1979) the Khmer Rouge destroyed Cambodian Buddhism. It is estimated that fifty thousand monks were killed and temples were abandoned or destroyed. "Today Buddhism is struggling to re-establish itself although the lack of Buddhist scholars and leaders and the continuing political instability is making the task difficult" (retrieved August 10, 2005, from www.buddhanet.net/e-learning/buddhistworld/cambodia-txt.htm).

In the post–Khmer Rouge years, "communities that wanted a wat had to apply to a local front committee for permission.[4] The wat were administered by a committee of the local laity. Private funds paid for the restoration of the wats damaged during the war and the Khmer Rouge era, and they supported the restored wats. Monks were ordained by a hierarchy that has been reconstituted since an initial ordination in September 1979 by a delegation from the Buddhist community in Vietnam. The validity of this ordination continues to be questioned. Two Buddhist superiors, Venerable Long Chhim and Venerable Tep Vong, were both believed to be from Vietnam" (retrieved December 20, 2005, from http://www.country -data.com/cgi-bin/query/r-2136.html).[5]

With the existence of a Buddhist hierarchy in Cambodia that lacks credibility in the eyes of Cambodia refugees living around the world, monks who were able to escape the Khmer Rouge, living in Thailand or border camps, have sought to re-create Buddhism as they saw fit in the

United States, free from directives of the home authority. This independence of Buddhist organization and practice in America is common among Southeast Asian temples in the United States (Ebaugh and Chafetz 2000, chaps. 3 and 4). In addition, as R. Stephen Warner has argued (cited in T. Smith 1978), immigrant congregations are arenas of change, often founded by laypeople and dependent upon the community's wishes for structure, leadership, and liturgy.

Parties in the Conflict

This free-for-all state of Cambodian American Buddhism is just what the Community of Khmer Buddhist Monks, Inc. (CKBM, incorporated in Massachusetts, with organizational variations in other states) see as the current problem facing the Cambodian diaspora. This organization has been involved in several temple conflicts aside from North Chelmsford (Andrade 2005).

In the various conflicts the CKBM are engaged in around the country, they face a local board of directors who founded each temple. The local boards argue that their CKBM monks were invited to the temple to serve the community and can be asked to leave at any time the boards deem it necessary. The local temples do not see Cambodian American community life in a state of crisis, while the CKBM does. In fact, the boards argue that before the current tensions broke out into full-fledged confrontations, the temples were performing a valued service to their local community; they even reached out to Cambodia to build temples, schools, and other public projects there.

"Correct" Role of the Monks in the Temple

Just what role should the monks play in contemporary American society? The Community of Khmer Buddhist Monks, Inc (CKBM) claims to be an advocate of "Engaged Buddhism." Engaged Buddhism is a term attributed to Vietnamese Buddhist monk, Thich Nhat Hanh. According to Queen (2000), socially engaged Buddhism is defined as "the application of Buddhist teachings to solve social problems" (1). Queen argues it is a new phenomenon that grows out of the conversation on human rights, distributive justice, and social progress. Generally, the term applies to Buddhists who wish to apply the insights from meditation practice and dharma teachings to situations of suffering and injustice. One leader of the CKBM is a well-known figure in the Engaged Buddhism movement: Sao Khon.

Venerable Sao Khon

Sao Khon was born April 17, 1934, in a small rural village called Poomo in the province of Siemreab, near Angkor Wat. He was in Thailand in 1975 when the Khmer Rouge came to power. He tried to return to Cambodia but turned back after learning that the Khmer Rouge was killing monks. To escape Thai authorities that were looking for Cambodians illegally staying in Thailand, he went on a silent retreat, to avoid discovery (Kappel 1998). For ten years he remained in Thailand and developed a large following of devotees. He came to the United States in 1985. According to the organization's attorney in Massachusetts, Rick Brody (2004), Sao Khon is the head monk of all the Cambodian monks in the United States

Locally, Sao Khon practiced his Engaged Buddhism by working with the Lowell police department to help gang members choose another path in life.[6] While opponents of Sao Khon state that little good has come from his efforts, he has won praise from the police and journalists who cover these types of stories (Ramirez 2003). One of his supporters, John Massey (a former monk who disrobed himself to take care of his family in 1989 and who has been with Sao Khon since 1985), adds: "Sao works at the Lowell Community Health Center, teaches meditation at the Billerica jail, we have gang kids who came here two times a week. Four gang members cleaned up their lives. That's the kind of stuff Sao Khon does. He's not just some guy sitting on a throne here waiting for money to come in. They criticized him for taking gang members and ordaining them as monks. Buddha took a mass murderer and turned him into a monk" (Massey 2004).

What might be at stake in the conflicts between the Community of Khmer Buddhist Monks and locally run congregational temples across the United States is a debate over this new type of Buddhism. As already discussed, Engaged Buddhism is linked to the idea of interreligious cooperation, Buddhism in a global context, and local social engagement. It is not clear at this time why Engaged Buddhism might be anathema to other Cambodian Buddhists in the United States. It may be that the idea and practice are actually not viewed negatively but because the methods used by the CKBM to come to power *are* viewed so, locally controlled congregational temples associate the philosophical idea with a tainted organization (Warner 1998, 221).[7]

Why the Need for a Cambodian Buddhist Hierarchy?

According to Sao Khon (2004), the Cambodian American community is still suffering greatly as a result of the Cambodian genocide. He believes:

"The Cambodian people [are] still sick. [Suffer from] mental problems. Spiritual problems." Additionally, Sao Khon believes that some monks who have come from Cambodia to serve American communities (such as Chek Choun in the Trairatanaram Temple) are affiliated with political parties in Cambodia. At the Trairatanaram Temple, Sao Khon and his supporters charge that members of Funcinpec, the royalist party in Cambodia, are seeking to use the temple as a means to assist the party: "This place is not for politics. This place is for independence. This place is for a spiritual way, not for politics. This place is a temple. This place is a residence for monks, not a residence of laymen. It's a rule. I want to keep this place for monks, not for laypeople. "

Pere Pen, a longtime Lowell community activist who has ties to Sao Khon but does not hold the CKBM blameless in the current conflict, supports the idea that Cambodia political parties are working behind the scenes to foment dissent. He acknowledges it is very hard to make sense of the parties' motivations or who is affiliated with a particular party as people switch their allegiances to suit their self-interest at the moment. For example, Chek Choun was a member of the ruling Cambodia's People's Party (CPP), led by dictator Hun Sen in Cambodia; Pen claims that Choun switched to the Funcinpec party, the royalist party that was deposed in a July 1997 coup, to get political asylum in the United States (Pen 2004).

John Massey (2004) concurs: "The head of the Funcinpec party in Lowell used to be here all the time. It's money. Money goes from the temple to the party. . . . Venerable Sao Khon is a nice man. He loves everyone. When Chek Choun came to North Chelmsford, he highly hoped that Choun would be his successor because of his knowledge of the dharma. But then Choun Chek tried to control the temple." Sao Khon adds: "I'm not interested in taking Choun Chek away from this temple but members of the Funcinpec party stay around and prepare for meetings with Choun Chek. To me, this place is not for politics."

When asked why the Funcinpec party would want to control this or any temple, Sao Khon and his supporters' reply: money. "This is a conflict that has nothing to do with Buddhism at all," said Pen (2004).

Holy Water Blessing and Making Money

One of the monk's traditional roles is to perform religious services, such as the holy water blessing. Cambodians come to the temple with hundreds and thousands of dollars in cash and leave them in donation boxes to have this ceremony performed. According to Pere Pen (2004), it was when Sao Khon objected to the money-making aspect of the ceremony and decided that the practice of sprinkling holy water to enrich the temple should come to an end that the split at the temple widened and deepened (Pen 2004).

John Massey (2004) said that the crux of the conflict is Chek Choun's desire to fund Funcinpec: "He sends money back to Cambodia. The money is the proceeds from the holy water ceremony, which is done for healing and good luck. For the ceremony a monk will chant and hold a candle over water and let wax drip in. It's like a cleansing thing. I don't really believe in it but I used to do it for people because they believe in it. It's a way to draw people in to the temple. All across the country they have the same problem. It's like a nationwide conspiracy because it's easy to get money. Laypeople who see you with a shaved head and a robe, they bow to you. What do you need? How much?"

Sao Khon (2004) concurred with this version of history: "Faith healing? I didn't want to stop it but I wanted to add more meditation and move it in another direction. Holy water is not true Buddhism. . . . I think the problem of Cambodian people now is they try to use that holy water but holy water never talks. . . . If Buddhist monks work together, step by step, very slowly I think a lot of people will follow me. I want to help them with ideas, not just bless them. Helping with the gang problem is an example of what I would like to see. New monks should respect old monks, it's a rule but he [Chek] breaks the rule" (Khon 2004).

According to Massey (2004), Sao Khon is "trying to be an elder monk who oversees problems. He is the king of the monks in the United States. He doesn't have the final say. It's the sangha council that does. He doesn't have complete control. He's not a dictator. He's very open-minded, believe me. Laypeople cannot make temples. They drink alcohol. They have sex with people. Monks only do one job. He's only had one job his whole life—for fifty-six years he's been a monk."

Sao Khon (2004) believes Chek Choun is trying to build temples in Cambodia while he is trying to build for refugees in the United States. "Chek said he wouldn't listen to Buddhist monks in the U.S., just in Cambodia. . . . Before I tried to talk to him, he said, 'I don't want to talk with an American monk.'"

In sum, it appears that Chek Choun and his supporters seek to build temples and schools in Cambodia while Sao Khon and the CKBM prefer to build temples under their auspices in communities around the United States.

Homeland Politics

The charges of Cambodia party politics infiltrating the Trairatanaram Temple's downstairs' monks activities are unsubstantiated. Nevertheless, they can't be ruled out. One of the downstairs' monks' former spokespeople, Sambath Chey Fennell, was closely aligned with Funcinpec and was widely believed to be the party leader in Lowell. He often led tours of Lowell for Funcinpec officials visiting the city. Fennell dropped out of the temple conflict as a spokesperson for the downstairs monks after Rick Brody filed charges against him for threatening remarks he made toward Sao Khon. According to Brody, Fennell was offered a way out of prosecution: to resign as the downstairs monks' spokesperson, and he promptly did.

There appears to be evidence that the ruling regime in Cambodia, the Cambodia People's Party (CPP) sees the CKBM as a threat.[8] One of their leaders, who is a key figure in the CKBM's attempted takeover of an East Oakland temple, Ven. Tep Kosal, has been decertified by the head of the monks in Cambodia, Ven. Tep Vong, and stripped of his authority as "Provincial Deputy Chief of Monk of Mondul Kiri Province" (Sternfeld 2004). Moreover, all sides in the various temple conflicts claim to be sending money back to Cambodia to build schools and temples, and fund charities. These remittances are important sources of money in Cambodia and show that transnationalism is still a relevant lens with which to view the current Cambodian temple battles in the United States.

To Whom Does a Temple Belong?

Depending upon the version of Cambodian history one chooses to favor, Cambodian Buddhist temples have always been run either by the local community or the temple's monks. The former notion of local control is argued by monks and laypeople who are resisting takeover attempts by the CKBM. The CKBM already claims to control sixteen temples in the United States. Both sides turn to Cambodia history as well as recent past practices in the United States to support their claims.

According to Zhou, Bankston, and Kim's (2002) study of the Cambodian temple in Long Beach, California, there is a lack of lay control over the religious institution. They argue that owing to the Cambodian community's poverty, low education, and home ownership levels, they have sought the direction of traditional religious leaders. The head monk at the Long Beach temple has a doctorate, for example, and is ideally placed to navigate both the English-speaking and Khmer-speaking communities. They conclude, as the community's socioeconomic status rises, so will lay power. Until that occurs, the monks will hold the power.

At the North Chelmsford temple, such is exactly what had occurred. Although the lay community created the organization and board of directors in 1986 and reelected the board in 1990, during the 1990s they acknowledge they took a hands-off stance toward the temple and relied on the monks—particularly Sao Khon—to run the temple's affairs. It was only when the conflict between monks occurred in 1998, that head monk Sao Khon and the congregation divided bitterly.

To the CKBM resistors, the issue is democracy. They say the methods used by the CKBM are undemocratic and their leadership style is paternalistic and arrogant. For Thel Sar (2004), a community activist and public spokesperson for the monks battling the CKBM, the idea that monks are servants of the community, should not own property, should not have money, and should seek charity of the community they reside in, is the authentic practice of Cambodian Buddhism: "The town is the one who built the temple and it seeks a monk to lead the temple, who can help educate the community about Buddhism. Nothing else. Not owning that temple." He continues, "[Sao Khon] became so arrogant. He has insulted people's intelligence and makes people very uncomfortable. He isolated a lot of people from the community. The people said, 'we are trying to communicate with you; we are beginning to lose respect for you. You are a wise monk but let's behave.' He forces people to respect him. Their mentality is not to earn respect from the community but their mentality is to force the community to respect them no matter what they do and that created the whole division."

Another key issue for the downstairs monks' group is the raising of funds at the North Chelmsford temple to be used to create and maintain temples across the country. Benjamin Ronald Phayso (2004), a former monk who studied under Sao Khon and who ran the CKBM's temple in the Bronx, New York, for a few years, was upset about this practice: "He [Sao Khon] doesn't spend money from the community, in that community. Instead he spends money from the temple elsewhere. They spend money for meetings, they spend money for many monks out of state, they pay tickets to monks directly and they spend money without asking anybody. And they spent a lot of money to build the Community of Khmer Buddhist Monks. They tried to do many things because they want to eliminate the board of directors and they want to control it because they don't have money. The monks asked me why I say things about Sao Khon. I told them 'I have to say it. The temple is like a church. It doesn't belong to the pastor, it belongs to the community and to religion.'"

Phayso (2004) recalled the temple in North Chelmsford raising almost $50,000 in two days for the annual Thanksgiving Day ceremony. About $46,000 was spent and there was no accounting of the funds. Thel Sar (2004) believes the temple under Sao Khon had raised more than one hundred thousand dollars.

Sar (2004) does not oppose monks who do well for the community, but he believes it must always be with the democratic control of the people. "We say to the monks, you do your thing. If we earn a lot of money, you want to suggest to open a school and with the people's consent, we support opening that school but it's going to be the people's school and not yours."

In response to the CKBM's argument that in North Chelmsford there was a Sima ceremony in 1989 whereby the Cambodian community gave the monks "ownership" of the temple, Thel Sar states that nobody can give the monks the temple. Even if they did, the monks should not have taken the temple. That would have broken a rule. Moreover, a Sima ceremony in Theravada Buddhism is the way certain areas of the temple are made into places for sangha rituals, and does not necessarily mean the community transfers control to the monks.

The downstairs monks' attorney, Jocelyn Campbell (2004), says a Sima ceremony "doesn't mean they're conveying the temple to them [CKBM]. Absolutely not. If there were a property transfer back in 1996 they would have gone and filed a deed. They would have done what was necessary to transfer their property. The temple people I represent maintained management and control of the temple and their entire properties. They [CKBM] didn't buy the property. They stole the property! They're not even a bona fide purchaser. They have to have done this with no ill will in mind. The CKBM knew about this controversy. What were they thinking?"

Another theme that runs through the critique of the CKBM is their methods for obtaining control of temples. Benjamin R. Phayso (2004) recalls receiving phone calls from Sao Khon when he was a monk, making plans to remove members of the board of directors. When Phayso reported to Sao Khon that they had to wait until the director's term expired, Sao Khon was not pleased: "He kept on calling me and looking for me. They called me too many times" (2004). Sao Khon even recorded these conversations between himself and Ronald Phayso, possibly to use against him. Phayso said he feared "something might happen to my life."

Chek Choun (2004) believes that Sao Khon—the man who had been his teacher and his sponsor to come to North Chelmsford from Cambodia—progressively took over the temple. It began with the creation of the CKBM in 1993 and culminated in the takeover in 1999. Choun believes Sao Khon appointed his friend, Ven. Samboon Kert, as board president, proceeded to dissolve the board by force; and, when the board refused to comply, secretly changed the deed to grant himself ownership. "When I came my goal was to work with Sao Khon in Buddhism. I didn't know that he is a betrayer" (2004).

Part of the conflict, says Choun (2004), was Sao Khon's jealousy of Choun's abilities, in particular his ability to attract followers. " I was able to answer questions and explain about Buddhist education. I was on the Internet, the radio, and people recognized my knowledge. This made Sao Khon jealous because he's been here a long time and he didn't get such attention."

Chek Choun (2004) reinforced the position of Ronald Physo and Thel Sar: monks cannot own temples. "In Buddhist religion, there is no ownership of property for monks. There is no possession, they give up all possessions to be a monk." He believes the ultimate goal of the CKBM is to create a religious hierarchy in America: "He wants to take over all temples in the United States. His by-law was not approved by the head monk in Cambodia. His by-law is to take over the world. There is no head monk in America. Sao Khon is self-appointed. No one elected him. In Cambodia the people elect the head monk and it is approved by the king. Sao Khon elevated himself. Being a monk, you don't want to be a big shot. Buddha does not approve of anybody to become a big shot. All monks are to be in equal position. . . . If you take Buddhist teaching and apply it to Sao Khon, he has committed a lot of sins. He has created division. He has split the monks and also the community itself. He is telling lies. When he dies and he is reborn, he will be born into an animal and he will not have a tongue to tell. Anyone who wants to be a monk has to be truthful. You shouldn't lie to anybody or sabotage anyone's reputation" (Rice 2004).

American Courts to the Rescue?

Interestingly, showing just how assimilated into American political thought these battling monks are, each expresses hope that the American judicial system will resolve their troubles. Most surprising are Chek Choun's comments, as it was he who believed that monks should not even make an appearance in court during a trial. Choun (2004) says: "The court has to decide who is wrong. The court will do justice. If the court decides against them, they will have to find another temple. I like America because of the law, because of justice. They respect people's rights."

Interestingly, Sao Khon is also willing to place his future in the hands of the Massachusetts courts. "If we lose here, we'll appeal and take our case to the United States Supreme Court if necessary. It's our right to do so. I want justice here. I want to stay here" (Khon 2004).

In fact, attorney Rick Brody (2004) has argued before the court in preliminary hearings and briefs, that because the temple is a self-governed entity, with a hierarchical structure (such as the Catholic Church), the Massachusetts court has no jurisdiction. Hierarchical churches have internal tribunals to adjudicate such disputes as this one. According to Brody, when the community and board turned over the temple to Sao Khon in a 1993 Sima ceremony, that transfer created a hierarchical temple structure. Brody says, "It's a religious issue and once it's a religious issue, the courts are going to have a real hard time getting involved with that. How is the United States court system going to get involved in the religious doctrine? They're not. . . . Courts cannot in conformance with the protections of the First Amendment decide who owns the temple by taking a vote. It's completely against the whole idea of what the First Amendment is. Just because some people say they're entitled to the temple means nothing."

Attorney Campbell is hoping the Massachusetts court will find it within its power to decide the case, and cites several Massachusetts law precedents, including the Antioch case, as evidence. In Antioch, the Massachusetts court ruled that if a temple is congregational in nature (meaning it is governed by a board of directors rather than a king or pope), it is a congregational church and the First Amendment to the U.S. Constitution does not bar a civil court from ruling (*Antioch Temple, Inc. v. Parekh,* 383 Mass. 854, 860–862 1981).

Intrareligious Conflict among Cambodian and Cambodian Immigrants: Nothing New

According to Nancy Smith Hefner, temple conflicts in Cambodia and the United States are not new. Immigrants always differ in how they remember the past and how they envision the future. These battles reveal just how complex the process of assimilation and adjustment is. The role of Buddhism and temples in the lives of Cambodian Americans is fluid (Smith-Hefner 1999).

Infighting among immigrant and refugee religious institutions has a precedent in Lowell's history. There were actually two splits in the 1920s involving the Greek Orthodox Church. The first led to the formation of the Transfiguration Church in the early 1920s and arose from political division. A second spilt occurred over whether to use the old versus the new calendar in the late 1920s. Greek churches back then (and now for the most part) were owned by the congregation. The battle was over physical possession of the church. The old calendar adherents rushed the church, which was barricaded by the new calendar contingent. New calendar won and the old calendar people set up a new church, Saint George, in the early 1930s (Nikotopoulos 2005).

Conclusion

The current battle for control of the Cambodian temple in the United States is a multilayered phenomenon. Elements of homeland politics and transnationalism are present in the temple controversies but to an outsider such as myself, it is unclear to what extent they matter.

Charges of Cambodia political party influence in American temples are largely unsubstantiated and may be an effort to smear the opposition with innuendo.

The overarching framework that best contextualizes the current struggle is segmented assimilation. Ultimately what is taking place is part of Cambodian immigrants' attempts to create meaning and value in the context of their experience as refugees. Immigrants and their children tend to "adapt their religious institutions to American conditions . . . and new relationships among its members are forged" (Warner and Wittner 1988, 3). It is more the process of segmented assimilation, or adjustment to American life, that is unfolding in the Cambodian temple in America—especially the use of the courts to solve a matter that might have been dealt with internally in Cambodia. Awareness of civil liberties and civil rights has encouraged previously undeveloped voices within the immigrant religious organization to seek redress in the judicial system.

What does appear to be going on is the process all immigrants face in becoming assimilated Americans. It is a time fraught with conflict over the direction the community should take in all areas of life: generational, religious, civic, educational, and the like. The legacy of the Khmer Rouge and the autogenocide that devastated Cambodian society makes the navigation of these waters even more treacherous; a significant loss of faith in institutions and leaders accompanies the current period. The inability of monks and lay activists to find a compromise, short of going to court, does not speak well for their leadership. In fact, I have heard several key Cambodian American figures say that they no longer bring their families to the Buddhist temple. The longer these conflicts persist, the greater the damage to the legitimacy of Cambodian Buddhism. Already several former members of the Trairatanaram Temple have joined the Glory Buddhist Temple in Lowell's Lower Highlands neighborhood (more centrally located to the Cambodian community), which was founded in 1989 by previous members of the Trairatanaram Temple.

It is ironic that at the same time that some European Muslims are rejecting the values of Western society, more than a few Cambodian American Buddhists are embracing the American judicial system as a solution to their internal problems and perhaps to ease their tough transition to assimilation. Moreover, the issue of centralized control versus local control, Vatican-style hierarchy versus congregationalist lay control, is the same concern under consideration today in the wake of sex abuse scandals in the Catholic Church. In fact, the priest sex abuse cases were the catalyst for one Massachusetts legislator's proposed bill to force religious institutions to disclose their finances. State Senator Marian Walsh called for state intervention to force churches to open their books to the public. Although it was defeated by a vote of 147–3 in the Massachusetts House of Representatives (Americans United for Separation of Church and State, n.d., such a solution would be welcome to many in the Cambodian American community. Pere Pen urges oversight of Buddhist temples by a board of independent trustees, who can investigate corruption and ensure that accepted financial accounting practices prevail—something equivalent to an emergency financial control board, which has been imposed on some cities and towns by state government.

Just as the Cambodian Mutual Assistance Association of Lowell has recognized the need for non-Cambodian board members to help the organization rebound from internal dissension that nearly ruined the fifteen-year-old association, perhaps the temple board should include non-Cambodian civic figures who could bring their knowledge, experience, and—perhaps most important—emotional distance from the Cambodian genocide to assist the fledgling Buddhist temple.

Afterword

In December 2006, a mediator of the Massachusetts Superior Court, Robert L. Burke, brokered a settlement between the contending "upstairs monks" and "downstairs monks" and their respective lawyers and supporters. The highlights of the agreement are: (1) the creation of a new board of directors of the temple consisting of thirteen members, four chosen by each side in the conflict. The eight have already been selected. The additional five members of the new board of directors will be selected by the eight members; and (2) the thirteen new board members and the Venerable Sao Khon as the fourteenth vote will select the head monk for the temple. Ten votes will be needed to select the head monk (Commonwealth of Massachusetts, Lowell Superior Court, 2006).

As one might expect, each side in the struggle has declared itself victorious. Thel Sar believes the downstairs monks have won, as Sao Khon will not be the new head monk.[9] Pere Pen believes the upstairs monks won, as Sao Khon will have a vote in determining whom the new head monk will be. One big question remains: How will the eight new board members agree on the selection of the remaining five? If both parties could not resolve matters similar to this during the last eight years, why should anyone believe they can put aside past differences and select five new board members who are universally considered honorable, independent, open-minded, and fair? Needless to say, further research will be necessary to study the lasting impact of the temple conflict as well as the outcome of this settlement—if it, indeed, holds.

Notes

1. I am indebted to the many figures in this case who were willing to be interviewed and in general cooperated with this study.

2. I thank Pere Pen, Thel Sar, and Sokha Sorn for their transcription and translation assistance. Sar and Pen were especially helpful as gatekeepers to the Cambodian community. Without their support this study would not have been possible.

3. For an example of an anthropologist's approach to the subject, see chapter 7, this volume.

4. A wat is another name for temple.

5. The long-standing Cambodian mistrust of Vietnam dates back several centuries to Vietnam's invasions of Cambodia, which resulted in the loss of life, land, and property in eastern Cambodia. The Khmer Krom, perhaps the most vociferous critic of Vietnam, is an indigenous ethnic Khmer minority living in southern Vietnam. They are ethnically the same as the Khmer people of Cambodia and are descendants of the Khmer that inhabited the delta of the Mekong prior to the arrival of the Vietnamese (Chandler 2000; retrieved December 3, 2006, from http://www.answers.com/topic/khmer-krom).

6. See chapter 7, this volume.

7. Congregational organizations are usually a local religious body constituted by the group itself rather than by geographical or administrative definition. The governance of a congregational body is local rather than in the hands of bishops or regional elders. It is a local voluntary religious association often constituted as a nonprofit corporation and controlled by the laity.

8. Once enemies, the CPP and Funcinpec today have developed a close relationship. A power-sharing agreement in July 2004 allows the CPP to rule Cambodia. In return for supporting the CPP, Funcinpec receives several ministerial and government positions. The Sam Rainsy Party functions as the chief opposition party in the country.

9. The downstairs monks are no longer led by Choun Chek, who, according to his supporters, returned to Cambodia in the summer of 2006 owing to the mental and physical strain of the conflict.

References

Americans United for Separation of Church and State. N.d. Mass. House Rejects Church Reporting Bill. Retrieved February 1, 2006, from http://www.au.org/site/News.

Andrade, K. 2005. Buddhist Temple Fights Civil War, Members Say Assets Were Illegally Transferred to Group in Massachusetts. *Oakland Tribune,* March 22, 2005. Retrieved on August 6, 2005 from http://www.insidebayarea.com/local news/ci_2617463 and http://www.ocbsr.com/oakland.html.

Antioch Temple, Inc. v. Parekh, 383 Mass. 854, 860–862. 1981. Retrieved on December 10, 2005, from http://caselaw.lp.findlaw.com/scripts/getcase.pl?court =ma&vol=sjcslip/sjc May04j&invol=1.

Brody, R. 2004. Personal interview by Jeffrey Gerson and Lewis Rice, June 30.

Buddhist Studies. N.d. Buddha Dharma Education Association & BuddhaNet. Buddhism in Cambodia. Retrieved August 10, 2005, from www.buddhanet .net/e-learning/buddhistworld/cambodia-txt.htm.

Campbell, J. 2004. Personal interview by Jeffrey Gerson and Lewis Rice, July 8.

Chandler, D. 2000. *A History of Cambodia*. 3rd ed. Boulder, CO: Westview.

———, et al. 1987. *In Search of Southeast Asia: A Modern History,* edited by D. J. Steinberg. Honolulu, HI: University of Hawaii Press.

Chhim, T. 2005. Personal interview by Jeffrey Gerson, June 22.

Chigas, G. 2005. Personal interview by Jeffrey Gerson, May 2.

Choun, C. 2004. Personal interview by Jeffrey Gerson and Lewis Rice, August 2.

Commonwealth of Massachusetts. 2006. Lowell Superior Court, C.A. No. 99–04659, Trairatanaram Temple, Inc., Plaintiff, vs. Ven. Sambook Kert and The Community of Khmer Buddhist Monks, Inc., Defendants. Settlement and Stipulation of Dismissal. December 7.

Dictionary by LaborLawTalk. N.d. *Sangha.* Retrieved August 15, 2005, from http//dictionary.laborlawtalk.com/Sangha.

Douglas, T. J. 2003. The Cross and the Lotus: Changing Religious Practices Among Cambodian Immigrants in Seattle. In *Revealing the Sacred in Asian and Pacific America,* edited by J. N. Iwamaura and Paul Spickard. New York, NY: Routledge.

Ebaugh, H. R. and Janet Saltzman Chafetz, eds. 2000. *Religion and the New Immigrants: Continuities and Adaptations in Immigrant Congregations.* Walnut Creek, CA: AltaMira Press.

Eck, D. 2001. *A New Religious America: How a "Christian Country" Has Become the World's Most Religiously Diverse Nation.* New York: HarperCollins.

Encyclopedia of the Nations. 2005. Federal Research Division of the Library of Congress. Cambodia: Role of Buddhism in Cambodian Life, December 1987. Based on the Country Studies. Retrieved on December 20, 2005 from http:// *www.nationsencyclopedia.com.*

Federal Research Division of the Library of Congress under the Country Studies/ Area Handbook Program sponsored by the U.S. Department of the Army, Washington, D.C. area. N.d. Retrieved August 31, 2005, from http://www. country-studies.com/cambodia/buddhism.html.

Gerson, J. N. 2005. The Cambodian-Americans of Lowell, Massachusetts: A Cautionary Tale of New Immigrant and Refugee Political Incorporation. Unpublished paper.

Huynh, T. 2000. Center for Vietnamese Buddhism: Recreating Homes. In *Religion and the New Immigrants: Continuities and Adaptations in Immigrant Congregations,* edited by H. R. Ebaugh and Jane Saltzman Chafetz, 45–66. Walnut Creek, CA: AltaMira Press.

International Network of Engaged Buddhists. N.d. Bangkok, Thailand. Retrieved on July 28, 2005 from www.sulak-sivaraksa.org/network22.php.

Iwamura, J. N. and Paul Spickard, eds. 2003. *Revealing the Sacred in Asian and Pacific America.* New York: Routledge.

Kappel, J. 1998. Spiritual Dimensions: A Buddhist Perspective. Written for Prof. Michael Siegell's Cambridge College course, The Spiritual Dimension: Psychological and Educational Issues. Focus Study 360, summer 1998. Unpublished paper.

Kessler, M. 2005. Personal interview by Jeffrey Gerson, June 15.

Khmer-Buddhist Educational Assistance Project. N.d. Retrieved on August 15, 2005, from http://www.kcap-net.org/project_environment.htm.

Khon, S. 2004. Personal interview by Jeffrey Gerson and Lewis Rice, July 27.

Lien, P. M., M. Conway, and J. Wong. 2004. *The Politics of Asian Americans: Diversity and Community.* New York: Routledge.

Massey, J. 2004. Personal interview by Jeffrey Gerson and Lewis Rice, July 27.

Min, P. G., and J. H. Kim, eds. 2002. *Religions in Asian America: Building Faith Communities.* Walnut Creek, CA: AltaMira Press.

Mitchell, D. W. 1996–97. Asian Social Engagement and the Future of Buddhism. A review essay by Donald W. Mitchell, of *Engaged Buddhism: Buddhist Liberation Movements in Asia,* edited by Christopher S. Queen and Sallie B. King. Albany, NY: State University of New York Press. *Cross Currents* 46, no. 4. *Cross Currents* is the property of Association for Religion & Intellectual Life. Retrieved on August 3, 2005, from http://www.aril.org/engagebuddah.html.

National Crime Prevention Council. N.d. Faith Community and Criminal Justice Collaboration Children and Youth. Retrieved on August 1, 2005, from www.ncpc.org; http://www.fastennetwork.org/Uploads/59CF5363-8BAD-4211-972B-7696D85BCB6B.pdf .

Nikotopoulos, C. 2005. Personal interview by Jeffrey Gerson, June 12.

Pen, P. 2004. Personal interview by Jeffrey Gerson and Lewis Rice, July 7.

Phayso, B. R. 2004. Personal interview by Jeffrey Gerson and Lewis Rice, August 1.

The Pluralism Project. 2006. Cambridge, Massachusetts, President and Fellows of Harvard College and Diana Eck. Retrieved on August 2, 2005 from http://www.pluralism.org/research/profiles/display.php, and http://www.fas.harvard.edu/~pluralsm/98wrb/bu_trir.htm.

Prothero, S. 2004. The Demographic Layout: A Tale of Two New Englands. In *Religion and Public Life in New England: Steady Habits, Changing Slowly,* edited by A. Walsh and M. Silk, 23–40. Walnut Creek, CA: AltaMira Press.

Queen, C. S., ed. 2000. *Engaged Buddhism in the West.* Boston, MA: Wisdom Publishing.

Ramirez, E. 2003. Turning to the Temple: Lowell Police Ask Buddhist Monk to Steer Youths From Violence. *Boston Globe,* June 23, B1.

Rice, L. I. 2004. The Battling Buddhists: A Bitter Feud between Two Monks Divides a Community and its Temple. Literally. [electronic version]. *Boston Magazine* (originally published November 2004). Retrieved on July 10, 2005, from http://www.buddhistchannel.tv/index.php?id=2,363,0,0,1,0.

Sar, T. 2004. Personal interview by Jeffrey Gerson and Lewis Rice, July 10.

Smith, T. L. 1978. Religion and Ethnicity in America. *American Historical Review* 83:1155–1185.

Smith-Hefner, N. J. 1999. *Khmer American: Identity and Moral Education in a Diasporic Community.* Berkeley and Los Angeles: University of California Press.

Sternfeld, D. 2004. Personal interview by Jeffrey Gerson, August 25.

Warner, S. R. 1998. Immigrant and Religious Communities in the United States. In *Gatherings in Diaspora: Religious Communities and the New Immigration,* edited by R. Stephen Warner and Judith G. Wittner. Philadelphia, PA: Temple University Press.

———, and Judith G. Wittner, eds. 1998. *Gatherings in Diaspora: Religious Communities and the New Immigration.* Philadelphia, PA: Temple University Press.

Yang, F. 2000. The His-Nan Chinese Buddhist Temple: Seeking to Americanize. In *Religion and the New Immigrants: Continuities and Adaptations in Immigrant Congregations,* edited by H. R. Ebaugh and Janet Saltzman Chafetz, 67–89. Walnut Creek, CA: AltaMira Press.

Yoo, D. K., ed. 1999. Introduction: Reframing the U.S. Religious Landscape. In *New Spiritual Homes: Religion and Asian Americans.* Honolulu, HI: University of Hawaii Press.

Zhou, M., C. L. Bankston III, and R. Kim. 2002. Rebuilding Spiritual Lives in the New Land: Religious Practices among Southeast Asian Refugees in the United States. In *Religions in Asian America: Building Faith Communities,* edited by Pyong Gap Min and Jung Ha Kim, 37–70. Walnut Creek, CA: AltaMira Press.

Exploring the Psychosocial Adjustment of Khmer Refugees in Massachusetts from an Insider's Perspective

From April 1975 through January 1979, the Khmer Rouge (KR) in Cambodia was directly and indirectly responsible for the death of between one and two million Cambodians, out of a population of eight million. People were murdered, starved, or died from forced labor or a lack of medical care. Many who survived the Killing Fields witnessed the cruelty of the KR; as a result, they now suffer from Post Traumatic Stress Disorder (PTSD). The fortunate ones became displaced and risked their lives to travel through mined jungles to the Thailand border and endured several years of captivity in less than humane conditions in refugee camps. The resettlement process itself, which involved a stop in the Philippines for many and relocation to nations around the globe that would have them, was extremely distressing.

According to the 2000 U.S. Census, Asian Americans are the fastest growing racial group in Massachusetts, having grown by nearly 68 percent since 1990 (Institute for Asian American Studies [IAAS] 2004). This census shows that, as a subgroup, Cambodians comprised 8.3 percent of the total Asian American population, or 19,696 individuals. The actual figure is widely presumed to be much larger. The surprisingly low census figure can be explained in part by Cambodians' distrust of formal institutions. The same study shows that Cambodians had the lowest incomes ($25,000 per year or less) and lowest levels of educational attainment (as measured by their rate of obtaining college, graduate, or professional degrees) of all Asian groups (IAAS 2004). This statistic is confirmed by a U.S. Department of Health and Human Services report (2001) highlighting Cambodians as an especially high-need group compared to other

Asian Americans. Chan (2003) indicated that Cambodians on average fall far below the poverty line in Los Angeles County and rank lower than all other ethnic groups on almost every economic and social adjustment indicator (cited in Daley 2005).

These gloomy statistics reveal the need for a sociological investigation of the association between two key factors: underlying individual traumatic psychosocial effects and adjustment difficulties, and the consequences of those challenges on communitywide functioning. Studying these related phenomena could provide clues into the transition processes Cambodian refugees experience while adapting to life in the United States.

The primary purpose of this research is to discover patterns of culturally pertinent psychosocial adjustment and well-being factors experienced by Cambodian first-generation, adult refugees (ages 30–69) in Massachusetts. Rarely are indigenous Cambodian perspectives and experiences examined from an insider's viewpoint. The researcher as "insider" allows her to view and interact with respondents from a similar social position as that of the recipients of research. This approach permits the observation of coping capabilities in a way that encourages new individual and collective understandings of history and identity for Cambodian refugees; it is hoped that the end result will help them overcome stressful life circumstances and trauma. Of course, the "insider" identity also brings limitations in perspective and view, and, given Cambodian history, issues of trust must be negotiated.

The research team for the project consisted of four Cambodian researchers. I, a female medical sociologist, led the project; I worked with three male research assistants, one in his midforties with a B.A. degree, one in his midthirties working on his B.A. degree, and one in his early thirties with an M.A. degree. One assistant served as senior translator; the other two acted as community liaisons, identifying and recruiting respondents, and one also assisted the senior translator. Although all members of the team currently live in the United States, all were born in Cambodia before or during the Khmer Rouge regime, and all but me, the lead investigator, had firsthand experience of the upheaval and cruelty of the period.[1]

The study seeks to determine the extent to which pre- and postmigration stressors impede people's ability to adjust to life in the United States after experiences with genocide thirty years ago. Violations of human rights, loss of social status, and being uprooted from one's homeland and removed from cultural familiarity highlight the reality of stressors that refugees bring to their new environment. Some authors have noted that Cambodian refugees are particularly at risk for developing serious mental health problems as a result of premigration stressors such as war and genocide, the trauma of escape, and the refugee camp experience, as well as postmigration stressors such as learning a new language, adjusting to new roles, learning new skills, and needing to acquire vocational or educational skills (Daley 2005; Chung and Bemak 2002; Chung 2001; Nicholson 1999; Carlson and Rosser-Hogan 1993).

Methods

The methodological framework of this research has two dimensions. One is to document qualitative reports through focus group discussions on indigenous perceptions and experiences with specific endorsement of stressors, mediators, and psychosocial adjustment (Nou 2006); the second is to quantitatively analyze the stress-health paradigm affecting Cambodian refugees' psychosocial adaptation (Nou in press). Only the most pertinent portions of the research findings will be discussed here.[2] Refugee respondents (N = 80 [64 percent from Lowell, 36 percent from Lynn and Revere], 48 males, 32 females; 30 to 69 years of age; 73.75 percent employed or self-employed fulltime, 26.25 percent unemployed) for the study were survivors of the Khmer Rouge genocide (1975–1979) who currently live in Massachusetts. Focus group respondents (N = 14: 9 males, 5 females) were survivors of Khmer Rouge and arrived in the United States between 1980 and 1988. Some focus group respondents also volunteered to participate in the survey portion of the study. Participants were selected through a quota nonrandom and nonclinical sample based on the participants' convenience, and recruited through grassroots contacts in the Cambodian communities.[3]

Theoretical Model

The theoretical model (see figure 1) for the present study was originally formulated in my doctoral dissertation (Nou 2002) and reconfigured to investigate the stress-health process among Cambodian refugees in Massachusetts. Conceptualization of the stress process model is adapted from the work of renowned stress scholars (Pearlin 1989; Pearlin, Morton, Lieberman, Menaghan, and Mullan 1981). The arrows connecting the domains indicate hypothesized relationships between the variables within each of the three domains (social-structural contexts, stressors, and mediators) and the variables embedded in the psychosocial adjustment domain. This model, along with guiding research questions (for example, What defines Khmer conceptions of physical and mental health/illness? and What are the health-care needs for the Cambodian survivors' population?), was used to analyze the Cambodian stress/health process.

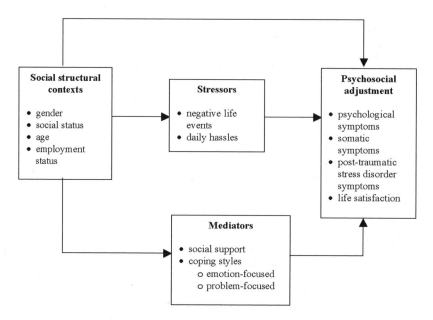

Figure 10.1: Khmer Psychosocial Adjustment Model

Psychosocial Effects of Trauma

Prior to fleeing Cambodia, many Cambodian refugees had firsthand traumatic experiences, such as family separation or loss of loved ones, torture, starvation, and rape. After resettlement, many encountered a loss of status, challenging cultural differences, and racial animosity. Often the failure to cope with previously unresolved post-traumatic stress disorder (PTSD) symptoms and current life stressors led to poor psychological health and well-being.

Marshall and his colleagues (2005) studied the mental health of Cambodian refugees two decades after resettlement in Long Beach, California, and found high rates of PTSD (62 percent) and major depression (51 percent). These rates are much higher than those found in the general population, where the rate of PTSD is 3.5 percent and major depression is 6.7 percent. In a literature review on PTSD in adult refugees, Nicholl and Thompson (2004) noted that specific post-trauma type symptoms within the general refugee population ranged as high as 30 percent to 86 percent. In a study of Southeast Asian refugees, Mollica, Wyshak, and Lavelle (1987) found the Cambodian population to be the most traumatized group, having experienced an average of sixteen traumatic events. These findings point out the urgent need for researchers to investigate and validate culturally relevant Cambodian meanings, perceptions, and manifestations of poor physical health/mental health, and to develop culturally sensitive programs in response.

Ong (2003) aptly describes the use of Western biomedical intervention as a process of control with coexisting good intentions and a desire to manage "diseased" and "deviant" populations, restricted by the availability of limited resources. She asserted: "the diseased bodies of Cambodian refugees . . . spurred the invention of a field called Southeast Asian mental health, that through the systematic naming and ordering of refugee illnesses, has sought to discipline the behavior, beliefs, and grief of Cambodian patients according to the self-evident truths of biomedicine" (93).

Rarely has the meaning or impact of their illnesses as experienced by Cambodian refugees themselves been considered in these investigations. Medical/mental diagnoses and conclusions have been drawn about the well-being of Cambodians without this critical insight, feedback, and validation. One result has been the oversimplified but politically useful notion that being Cambodian essentially meant being medically depressed. Ong (2003) continues to say that "*depressed Cambodian refugees* became a useful term in a number of situations" (96) and that "treating Cambodians became the justification for state and local health clinics to obtain much-needed funding from the federal government, especially when they could furnish charts showing Cambodians and Hmongs scaling the depression stratosphere" (96).

The field of Southeast Asian mental health produced countless studies on Cambodians in the diaspora, all of which pointed to the pattern that Cambodians are likely to suffer from poor pathology or be at the highest risk of developing psychological distress (identified as generalized anxiety disorder, panic, major depression, schizophrenia, and PTSD) as compared to other Asian groups. Selected examples of such studies include Daley (2005); Chung and Bemak (2002); Stevens (2001); Chung (2001); D'Avanzo and Barab (1998); Uba and Chung (1991); and Mollica, Wyshak, Lavelle, Truong, Tor, and Yang (1990).

PTSD symptoms have been cited frequently in research, medical diagnoses, and treatment plans as an underlying cause of Cambodian illness and disease, especially among individuals who had confronted war or actual or threatened death. Individuals suffering from PTSD are likely to report three characteristic types of symptoms (Flannery 1999). First, *intrusive symptoms* involve the persistent reexperiencing of the traumatic event in images, recollections of memories, daydreams, and nightmares. Second, *avoidance symptoms* include avoiding thoughts, feelings, conversations, and interactions with others that could ignite reminders of the trauma. Third, *arousal symptoms* include interrupted sleep patterns, anxiousness, hypervigilance, having poor concentration, and being easily irritated, startled, or angered.

Our focus group respondents reported all three characteristic types of PTSD symptoms (having panic attacks, the inability to concentrate, feelings of hopelessness, suicidal ideations, being easily angered or agitated, and wanting to be alone). In many ways, the poor emotional state of mind and the overall psychological symptoms reported by our respondents reflect the correlates of psychosomatic symptoms found among Cambodian refugees in South Australia (Stevens 2001). In a random sample of 150 male and female respondents 20 to 75 years old, Stevens found that environmental stressors put Cambodians at risk of poor mental health as evidenced by such symptoms as sleeping problems, nightmares, breathing problems, pain, headaches, dizziness, fatigue and lethargy, trouble with concentration, and memory loss.

Findings on stress-related PTSD symptoms from the qualitative portion of this study were confirmed by our quantitative analyses, which yielded significant results highlighting current mental health consequences for Cambodian adult refugees. The quantitative study used four stepwise regression models to predict the respondents' total Brief Symptoms Inventory (BSI) to indicate their level of psychosocial adaptation. The subdimensions of psychological and somatic symptoms for BSI were also examined. Comparisons of multivariate models predicting each of the dependent variables showed that "daily hassles" ($b = 0.471$, $p < 0.001$) and unresolved PTSD symptoms ($b = 0.595$, $p < 0.001$) were significantly related to poor overall scores for the BSI and its subdimensions.

The multivariate analyses from the quantitative portion of this study suggest that the level of PTSD experienced by respondents depends on the degree to which current daily hassles are added to past traumatic life events. In particular, past negative life events increase the stressful impact of current daily hassles; this stress, in turn, increases levels of PTSD. Thus, difficult life histories make it especially challenging for people to adjust; in this way memories of the Khmer Rouge regime continue to haunt many Cambodian refugees.

The findings in this study are consistent with research conducted by Blair (2000), who found that risk factors (such as experiencing a greater number of war traumas and resettlement stressors during the past year) increased the rates of PTSD and depression among adult Cambodian refugees in Utah. According to Blair, current stressors such as anxiety about the future and financial worries were significantly associated with PTSD and depression. Blair's data also indicated that the effects of these disorders were not always immediately apparent, but that they could have long-term, chronic consequences.

Like Blair's research, the Khmer Psychosocial Adjustment Model also raises important considerations for future researchers analyzing Cambodian mental well-being. Respondents in the current study who developed psychosomatic symptoms from the stressors of negative life events and daily hassles without physical/mental health care intervention increased their preexisting PTSD symptoms. Individuals with symptoms of PTSD or other mentally related symptoms (such as anxiety or depression) may be less capable of adapting to life in the host country, and consequently may experience more chronic stress.

These findings agree with a recent study by Marshall, Schell, and colleagues (2005), which reported that many Cambodians still bear traumatic scars from the Khmer Rouge. The researchers found that Cambodians suffer from rates of mental illness six to seventeen times higher than the national average for adults. They also noted that cases of PTSD and depression often overlapped, with 42 percent of respondents reporting both. The more trauma respondents endured, the worse their symptoms were. Their report included strong recommendations to policymakers: "The pervasiveness of psychiatric disorders [among Cambodian refugees] raises questions about the adequacy of existing mental health resources in this community. Addressing this high level of need may require additional research to identify barriers to seeking services as well as efforts at improving treatment for this population" (578).

These findings further complicated the understanding of Cambodians' mental health when community sample data on the rates and correlates of seeking mental health services among Cambodian refugees showed high rates of contact with both medical care providers (70 percent) and mental health providers (46 percent) (Marshall, Berthold, Schell, Elliott, Chun, and Hambarsoomians, 2006).

Similarly, in the quantitative portion of this study (Nou in press), higher social support levels were positively associated with increased BSI symptoms, raising the question of whether access to resources or social support actually results in better physical or mental health. The qualitative and quantitative portions of the current study considered both perceived and received support, including culturally relevant instrumental or emotional forms of social support (for example, seeking support from family, friends, Buddhist monks, or human services providers).

Cheung and Spears (1995) also found that social support and coping did not moderate the relationship between life events/postmigration stressors and general health in a study of psychiatric morbidity among New Zealand Cambodians. In reflecting on their research, Cheung and Spears noted caution on the interpretation of this moderating effect, which can be explained in part by the fact that perceived support is evidently more important than received support. This research further reinforces the need to examine the effectiveness of existing mental health resources in this community.

Gender, Social Status, and Psychological Distress: An Examination of Differential Vulnerability

An ongoing sociological interest regarding "stressful life events" is the attempt to explain associations among different factors such as class, gender, and minority status and the varying rates of psychosocial illness. Findings from early, causative frameworks (for example, Menaghan 1990; Pearlin 1989) indicate that women and low-status individuals had higher rates of disorders due to their disproportionate encounters with harsh life conditions. Often, these elevated rates of disorder were attributed to the lack of access to social, economic, and/or personal resources, which would have enabled these individuals to address difficult life situations constructively (Aneshensel, Lachenbruch, and Rutter 1991).

Our focus group respondents shared their perceptions of stressor exposure in relation to gender and social class differences. They noted that women are likely to suffer more stress because Khmer culture expects them to be silent about personal and family issues; as a result, they are more likely to develop mental health problems. The socialization of Khmer women to take total responsibility for the family's finances, household, and well-being adds to the burden of stressors. Respondents further agreed that women suffer more stress than men because of men's high rates of alcoholism, infidelity, and domestic violence. Khmer women rationalize this behavior by stating that they are expected to tolerate such emotional and physical abuse, while men are expected to be the breadwinners.

Regarding class differences, respondents noted that individuals with more education have greater immunity to mental health consequences that often result from exposure to stressors. Respondents shared their view that people who have attained higher levels of education and training can adapt better to social and life changes. Respondents also indicated that lower-income people are more likely to suffer greater stress because of their lack of food, education, and financial security. Overall, respondents reported that people would have an easier time coping with life stressors if they were better connected to community resources. The socially defined low status of Cambodians substantially limits their access to social resources, including adequate health care, and thereby predisposes them to more numerous stressful life events and higher rates of psychosocial illnesses.

Voices from the Insiders: Contextualizing Social Stress, Institutional
Barriers, and the Politics of Migration

A series of informal, extensive discussions on broadly defined interpretations of social stressors was held at the participants' request.[4] One elderly
Khmer male shared his views of the main problems facing his local
Khmer population. These problems included family disharmony; cultural
clashes between rural and urban lifestyles; racial discrimination by the
police (for example, alleged corruption and perceived slowness in re-
sponding to Cambodian cases); difficulty understanding the legal and immigration policies that affect the Cambodian population; and Khmer ad-
dictions to alcohol and gambling (which he believes are strategically
encouraged by local casinos).

Observations noted by this participant are supported by Asian American scholars studying Cambodians in the United States. The issue of intergenerational conflicts is explained well by Sucheng Chan (2004). Chan's
book, *Survivors,* includes a chapter on the Cambodian crises (increased
rates of gambling, alcoholism, and other forms of substance abuse) mentioned by this participant as adjustment problems. Chan also discusses additional difficulties, including changes or reversals in gender or parent-
child roles; differing rates of acculturation among family members; the
faster assimilation of Cambodian American youth that causes conflicts
within the family unit; and the clash between rural and urban lifestyles.
Observations and experiences with discrimination as reported by this participant also coincide with Hein's (1995) research, which found most
Cambodian refugees in the United States have experienced "severe antagonism" and "perceive extensive prejudice and discrimination" (153).

According to this participant, many of the issues raised reflect a breakdown in Khmer social cohesion and well-being. He personally fears that
the new generation lacks good role models in the community to preserve
Khmer identity, and that the Cambodian population will fall further into
poverty and deprivation as a result. This research found similar group
consensus reports on negative stressors (for example, having limited English proficiency, intergenerational conflicts within the family, lack of
transportation, anxiety over personal safety, and ongoing unemployment
and financial worries). In many ways, negative stressors reported by our
respondents correspond with major postmigration stressor categories
(family, unemployment, job, financial, accommodation, cultural, loneli-
ness, and boredom) found in Cheung and Spears's (1995) study of psychiatric morbidity among New Zealand Cambodians.

Another elderly male respondent identified himself as a former community leader. Our discussion focused on discovering root causes for the

Khmer people's stress and mental illness and contributing factors keeping them sick. According to this respondent, social stress in the Cambodian community is linked to several factors including loss of trust in each other; loss of identity resulting from homeland politics throughout Cambodia's political history (which contributes to problems in contemporary Cambodian-American communities); Buddhism's lack of moral education; and the emphasis on Buddhist ceremonies rather than educational training on morality.

The comments made by this participant reflect historical and cultural context. The fact that the Cambodian genocide was inflicted by certain Cambodians onto their own people created barriers to building and sustaining trusting relationships. For example, the desperate need to survive or receive food during the Khmer Rouge period often led people to betray family and friends; this betrayal often resulted in the named individuals being tortured or killed. The remnants of this survival strategy continue to give rise to a lack of trust among Cambodians. Intrusion by foreigners has been a recurring theme of Cambodian history for centuries. Cambodia and its people have endured invasions, colonial rule, war, devastation, and revolutions.

Respondents also feared persecution for speaking against the Cambodian government, even though they reside in the United States. Consensus reports on homeland politics, issues of identity, and social deterioration included the loss of homeland (stated as "motherland falling into Communist hands"), the personal shame of being a source of community gossip, and lack of trust within the community.[5]

Surprising comments were noted by several Cambodian mental health care providers at an informal meeting to discuss causes of stress in Cambodian communities. These individuals expressed their shared perception that some Western scholars and practitioners exploit, belittle, or humiliate their Cambodian colleagues, or treat them unjustly in other ways, and that little action has been taken to address this issue. These individuals felt undervalued as contributors after working on various Cambodian mental health research projects with non-Khmer researchers. Their personal testimonies reflect their perspective as highly trained Cambodian professionals working within a Western mental health care delivery system serving Cambodian populations in Massachusetts.

The Cambodian mental health care providers also noted that their suggestions regarding issues of cultural sensitivity are rarely taken seriously in the data collection on research projects, and thus these projects continue to project a limited and negative view of Cambodian pathology and psyche. They felt that Cambodian service providers are not always credited in publications for their roles in research projects. While these claims are isolated cases, they are certainly worth noting.

The personal testimonies provided by these Cambodian insiders offer unique community, cultural, and historical insights into the causes of social stress, institutional barriers, and politics of migration on local and national levels. In this study Cambodian researchers as data collectors provided participants the opportunity to claim power and the ability to defend themselves in ways that would have been more difficult had the researchers been seen as outsiders imposing Western values on Cambodian experiences. Research models proposed by social scientists may be designed with bias to satisfy government and funding agencies, and rarely offer Cambodians—or other nonmajority groups—the opportunity to critically examine their own life encounters.

Community Responses to Psychosocial Effects of Trauma among Cambodians

An array of community-based organizations exists to respond to the psychosocial needs of Cambodian refugees in Massachusetts. Some examples of these organizations cited by our respondents include health centers, business associates, and Buddhist institutions. A brief description of one such organization, the Metta Health Center, is provided here to give readers an idea of the culturally relevant services the clinic offers Cambodian Americans in Lowell.[6] The Metta Health Center was reported by many respondents to be one of a number of valuable resources within the community's social networks. Although other community-based organizations and mainstream institutions working with Cambodian Americans were also instrumental in the research project, space limitations preclude our describing them here.[7]

The Metta Health Center is a source of physical and mental health care solace for Cambodians in Lowell. It is a "West-Meets-East Center" that incorporates the best of both cultures (for example, primary care and acupuncture) within a single health care delivery system. As part of the Lowell Community Health Center, the Metta Health Center was established in October 2000 to address the needs of the underserved Asian population and increase their access to appropriate health care resources. Metta served as a critical resource center where our research team and respondents could meet.

The word *metta* refers to the Sanskrit concept of love, kindness, and compassion. The meanings of *metta* resonate with Cambodians, as they reflect both the Khmer perspective and the Buddhist religion. Cambodians seek mental and physical health care from the Metta Health Center to overcome stress or resistance, increase their awareness, and tap into strengths to improve their health and well-being by culturally familiar means.

The staff at Metta consists of a medical team, behavioral health team, alternative medicine team, and support services team. All working members are bilingual and bicultural, coming from a wide variety of cultural and linguistic backgrounds. During October 2006, Metta served approximately 940 patients (76.4 percent Cambodians; 21.7 percent Laotians; 1.7 percent Vietnamese; 0.2 percent others) through 1,233 visits for physical and mental illnesses. Primary care is the most commonly used service, followed by mental health and acupuncture. Various types of comprehensive assistance are also offered, such as social service referrals, transportation to appointments, domestic violence intervention, and community outreach on health education.[8]

The Metta Health Center is an example of an organization that strives to provide culturally appropriate, effective services to the population it serves. By working with researchers on future projects, the services provided by such organizations, including evaluations of the ultimate effectiveness of various programs, could be greatly improved.

Reexamining Cambodian Pathology: Theories of Resiliency

Clearly, although some Cambodian refugees have developed PTSD and other stress-related ailments as a consequence of experiencing traumatic events, others remain resilient in the face of the same stressors. Eisenbruch (1991) emphasizes the need to investigate the meaning refugees assign to their suffering and the coping strategies they use to overcome adversity. He suggests that refugees' psychological distress is quite normal, constructive, and an existential reaction to extraordinarily horrific circumstances. He considers it more appropriate to refer to this condition as "cultural bereavement"; that is, "[the] uprooted person [or] group . . . suffers feelings of guilt over abandoning culture and homeland, feels pain if memories of the past begin to fade, but finds constant images of the past intruding into daily life. . . . It is not of itself a disease but an understandable response to the catastrophic loss of social structure and culture" (673–74).

Similarly, a phenomenological study by Davis (2000) that used open-ended interviews with refugee women, including Cambodians, reveals persistent themes of survival, despite despair and isolation. Davis recommends that health care providers consider cultural bereavement to be a form of psychological resilience rather than a manifestation of PTSD. Davis recommends that by changing our perspective from mental illness to natural grieving and human loss, and by valuing the meaning refugees give to their traumatic experiences, researchers and practitioners can better assist Cambodian refugees with adaptation.

West (2000) investigated the individual, contextual, and cultural factors that promote trauma-related resilience and growth among Cambodian survivors in Lowell, Massachusetts, and Phnom Penh, Cambodia. Having a sense of optimism, social support, access to education, and Buddhist principles were found to be major predictors of resilience and thriving under stress. West's Cambodian respondents reported that resilience and thriving had underlying connections to Buddhist teachings, further underscoring one way Cambodians serve as a resource and social catalyst for each other's healing. The use of Cambodian imagery with historical and symbolic significance (such as photographs of Angkor Wat) also contributed to wellness, resilience, and thriving. Nancy Smith-Hefner (1999) also addressed this topic, discussing the roles of resilience and the social transformation of Khmer identity, focusing on Khmer Buddhist teachings and moral/character education in Khmer adjustment to American society.

Our intent for this study was to investigate and contextualize the insider's perspective of what Cambodian refugees define as stressors, sources of mediators (for example, quality time with friends and family, collaboration with business partners, visiting astrological readers, and finding good health care providers), and psychosocial adjustment, including indicators of quality of life. In so doing, we discovered that our respondents had remarkable intuitive psychological buoyancy toward their current life circumstances in spite of overwhelming adjustment/adaptation challenges.

Policy Recommendations

The results of this study suggest a series of general recommendations for social researchers, practitioners, and policymakers to consider as they seek to understand the underlying cultural factors and precise sociocultural qualities unique to Cambodian refugees and to propose solutions to the challenges faced by them. In order to avoid feelings of exploitation among participants in research studies, researchers are urged to participate in discussions with community leaders and participants on the use of any research or project intended to benefit Cambodian populations. The sharing of research- and practice-based information could be accomplished through a series of educational forums and workshops focusing on how the data might inform policy. One might be the creation of a stress management workshop that highlights symptoms associated with PTSD and depression and offers preventative steps to alleviate negative health outcomes. All supporting research publications and technical reports should be professionally translated and archived as a community resource.

In addition, researchers, practitioners, and policymakers should identify and collaborate with reputable social mediators or institutional gatekeepers within the community, such as Buddhist monks or indigenous health care providers. Community members could be invited to research sessions for data collection, thus providing them with a clear idea of the research process. In turn, researchers, practitioners, and policymakers could attend Cambodian cultural events and celebrations in order to gain further insights into Cambodian culture. Such rapport-building steps are critical to breaking the pattern of distrust found in Cambodian populations.

Finally, researchers, practitioners, and policymakers are encouraged to recognize the importance of family as a source of social support and harmony in Cambodian communities, and to connect with families as the social system that traditionally provides individuals with a sense of belonging. Reaching out to family leaders and urging them to be active participants in research projects or community-based activities will result in greater participation by other community members, while building trust in the formal institutions.

Discussion and Conclusion

The roots of contemporary Cambodian trauma originate in the horrific events suffered by the Cambodian people during the Khmer Rouge genocide. Fieldwork with Cambodians in Massachusetts and elsewhere in the diaspora has shown that lack of trust—both among individuals and as a community—is a pervasive and persistent manifestation of the trauma felt by Cambodian refugees. Many maintain that social detachment is the surest path to safety. Memories have altered their present and future identities, individual and collective psyches. The uprooting from their homeland and the overdue justice for survivors of the genocide prevent Cambodians from making sense of their past and present; in turn, this trauma affects their ability to make plans for their future. The turmoil of a lost past can stand in the way of building healthy relationships in the present at both the individual and collective levels.

Traditional values and social stigma are two strong deterrents preventing Cambodians from engaging in social behavioral research or seeking psychological treatment. Culture is another factor that relates to mental health, as it shapes the expression and recognition of psychiatric troubles. Karmic and fatalistic dispositions can lead people to accept their current psychosocial suffering, believing that they deserve such suffering for having committed bad deeds in their past life. Adding to these challenges is the Cambodian collectivist tradition of discouraging open displays of emotion (in order to maintain social and familial harmony and avoid exposing personal weaknesses). Given cultural and religious deterrents to acknowledging mental illness, it is not surprising that many Cambodians somatize their psychological distress, and then seek treatment for their somatic symptoms. Encouraging individuals to view treatment of mental health problems as part of physical health care might help to break the stigma and contribute to effective interventions, ultimately to enhance personal well-being and functioning and encourage psychoemotional healing.

It is important to note that our respondents understand the negative impact of social stressors on their communities and the inadequate response by the host society, despite its best efforts. Yet there is a critical shortage of Cambodians who are prepared to take on leadership and professional roles within their own communities. The response by Western health care practitioners has not always been respectful to Cambodian clientele or their cultural traditions, resulting in services not being fully utilized by a vulnerable and traumatized population. This problem of underutilization persists even in organizations with the very best intentions, such as Metta. The shortcomings in effectiveness negatively impact the Cambodian community, as evidenced by the high rates of mental and physical illnesses found in this study and others (for example, Nou 2006 and in press; Blair 2000; Marshall, Berthold, et al. 2006; Marshall, Schell, et al. 2005; Stevens 2001; and multiple other sources).

In spite of their difficult histories, many Cambodians have found ways to carry on with life, drawing upon their individual and collective cultural strengths in order to adapt and survive. It is these strengths that must be further defined, nurtured, and incorporated into culturally appropriate programs to rebuild strong and resilient Cambodian ethnocultural identities and social structures. The surfacing of strengths and vital indigenous insights was enhanced in this study by an all-Khmer research team who provided a common linguistic and cultural foundation and an enhanced sense of trust and comfort. The data showed that Cambodians are exceptionally perceptive of their situation as refugees. The level of honesty demonstrated by our Cambodian respondents highlights success. Service providers and policymakers are encouraged to assist Cambodians in becoming proactive in healing the wounds of their past even as they adjust to American life, by drawing upon the indigenous strengths (including resilience and self-awareness) identified in this study.

This research was conducted in part to learn more about the Cambodian psyche and how increased understanding might help Cambodian refugees adjust to life in the United States. It offers a celebration of the resilient spirit of Cambodian refugees and helps them find their historical and collective ethnic voice in contemporary global society. We contend that Cambodians are conscious of their potential and their strength in the face of overwhelming adversity, and their ultimate ability to re-store personal and social homeostasis. Researchers, practitioners, and policymakers should keep these strengths in mind as they explore indig-enous experiences and strive to help Cambodian refugees further en-hance their own resilience and self-awareness, heal the wounds of the past, and thrive as survivors.

Author's Note and Acknowledgment

Correspondence concerning this research should be addressed to Leak-hena Nou, Department of Sociology, California State University, Long Beach, California 90840–0906. E-mail: lnou@csulb.edu. This research was entirely supported by the Institute for Asian American Studies, Uni-versity of Massachusetts Boston.

A special thanks goes to Dr. Paul Watanabe for allowing me to execute and pursue this study with little difficulty. I am especially indebted to the research participants for making this study possible. Thanks are also owed to my core research team: Bou Lim, Kirirath Saing, and Stephen Thong; to members of the Cambodian community, including the Metta Health Center in Lowell; and to mentors and colleagues for their valuable intellectual insights.

Notes

1. The process of researching one's own community is unique and worthy of examination and discussion in its own right. Interested readers are encouraged to refer to my forthcoming work on this topic (Nou in press).

2. As a precautionary procedure to protect human subjects, the study did not proceed until receiving approval from the Institutional Review Board at the Uni-versity of Massachusetts Boston.

3. Readers are referred to the full qualitative (Nou 2006) and quantitative (Nou in press) studies for more detailed descriptions of the participants and the procedures used. The qualitative report is available online at http://www.iaas.umb.edu/ or at http://jsaaea.coehd.utsa.edu/index.php/JSAAEA/article/view/6/3.

4. In order to protect the anonymity of individual respondents, no names are used in this section.

5. See histories by several Cambodian scholars discussing these tragedies (for example, Etcheson 2005; Maguire 2005; Chandler 1999).

6. This description was prepared in consultation with Metta's executive direc-tor, Ms. Dorcas C. Grigg-Saito, and its administrative manager, Mr. Sonith Peou.

7. A number of Cambodian community organizations provided assistance in this research. Readers are encouraged to contact these organizations directly for more information:

Cambodian Mutual Assistance Association (Lowell, MA),
http://www.cmaalowell.org

Khmer Youth and Family Center and Buddhist Temple (Lynn, MA),
ksaing@partners.org

Union Hospital and the North Shore Medical Center (Lynn, MA),
http://www.nsmc.partners.org

8. For additional information on the Metta Health Center, please visit http://
www.lchealth.org.

References

Aneshensel, C. S., P. A. Lachenbruch, and C. M. Rutter. 1991. Social Structure,
Stress, and Mental Health: Competing Conceptual and Analytical Models.
American Sociological Review 56, no. 1:166–78.

Blair, R. G. 2000. Risk Factors Associated with PTSD and Major Depression
among Cambodian Refugees in Utah. *Health and Social Work* 25, no. 1:23–30.

Carlson, E., and E. Rosser-Hogan. 1993. Mental Health Status of Cambodian
Refugees Ten Years after Leaving their Homes. *American Journal of Ortho-
psychiatry* 63:223–31.

Chan, S. 2003. *Not Just Victims: Conversations with Cambodian Community
Leaders in the United States.* Urbana, IL: University of Illinois Press.

———. 2004. *Survivors: Cambodian Refugees in the United States.* Urbana, IL:
University of Illinois Press.

Chandler, D. 1999. *Voices from S-21: Terror and History in Pol Pot's Secret
Prison.* Berkeley and Los Angeles: University of California Press.

Cheung, P., and G. Spears. 1995. Psychiatric Morbidity among New Zealand
Cambodians: The Role of Psychosocial Factors. *Social Psychiatry and Psychiatric Epidemiology* 30, no. 2:92–97.

Chung, R. C. Y. 2001. Psychosocial Adjustment of Cambodian Refugee Women:
Implications for Mental Health Counseling. *Journal of Mental Health Counseling* 23, no. 2:115–26.

———, and F. Bemak. 2002. Revisiting the California Southeast Asian Mental
Health Needs Assessment Data: An Assessment of Refugee Ethnic and Gender
Differences. *Journal of Counseling and Development* 80:111–19.

Daley, T. C. 2005. Beliefs about Treatment of Mental Health Problems among
Cambodian American Children and Parents. *Social Science and Medicine*
61:2384–95.

D'Avanzo, C. E., and S. A. Barab. 1998. Depression and Anxiety among Cambodian Refugee Women in France and the United States. *Issues in Mental Health
Nursing* 19:541–56.

Davis, R. E. 2000. Refugee Experiences and Southeast Asian Women's Mental
Health. *Western Journal of Nursing Research* 22, no. 2:144–68.

Eisenbruch, M. 1991. From Post-traumatic Stress Disorder to Cultural Bereavement: Diagnosis of Southeast Asian Refugees. *Social Science and Medicine* 33,
no. 6:673–80.

Etcheson, C. 2005. *After the Killing Fields: Lessons from the Cambodian Genocide.* Lubbock, TX: Texas Tech University Press.

Flannery, R. B., Jr. 1999. Psychological Trauma and Post-traumatic Stress Disorder: A Review. *International Journal of Emergency Mental Health* 2:135–40.

Hein, J. 1995. *From Vietnam, Laos, and Cambodia: A Refugee Experience in the United States.* New York: Simon and Schuster.

Institute for Asian American Studies. 2004. *Asian Americans in Massachusetts.* Community Profiles in Massachusetts Series. Boston: University of Massachusetts.

Maguire, P. 2005. *Facing Death in Cambodia.* New York: Columbia University Press.

Menaghan, E. G. 1990. Social Stress and Individual Stress. *Research in Community Mental Health* 6:107–41.

Marshall, G. N., S. M. Berthold, T. L. Schell, M. N. Elliott, C. A. Chun, and K. Hambarsoomians. 2006. Rates and Correlates of Seeking Mental Health Services among Cambodian Refugees. *American Journal of Public Health* 96, no. 10:1829–35.

Marshall, G. N., T. L. Schell, S. M. Berthold, and C. A. Chun. 2005. Mental Health of Cambodian Refugees Two Decades after Resettlement in the United States. *Journal of the American Medical Association* 294, no. 5:571–79.

Mollica, R., G. Wyshak, and J. Lavelle. 1987. The Psychological Impact of War and Torture on Southeast Asian Refugees. *American Journal of Psychiatry* 144:1567–72.

———, T. Truong, S. Tor, and T. Yang. 1990. Assessing Symptom Change in Southeast Asian Refugee Survivors of Mass Violence and Torture. *American Journal of Psychiatry* 147, no. 1:83–88.

National Institute of Mental Health. Reliving Trauma: Post-Traumatic Stress Disorder. Retrieved on January 27, 2007, from http://www.nimh.nih.gov/publicat/reliving.cfm.

Nicholl, C., and A. Thompson. 2004. The Psychological Treatment of Post-traumatic Stress Disorder (PTSD) in Adult Refugees: A Review of the Current State of Psychological Therapies. *Journal of Mental Health* 13, no. 4:351–62.

Nicholson, B. L. 1999. Group Treatment of Traumatized Cambodian Women: A Culture-specific Approach. *Social Work* 44, no. 5:470–79.

Nou, L. (2002). *Social Support, Coping, and Psychosocial Adjustment of Khmer University, College, and Technical Students in Modern Cambodia: A Sociological Study.* Ph.D. diss., University of Hawaii at Manoa.

———. 2006. *A Qualitative Examination of the Psychosocial Adjustment of Khmer Refugees in Three Massachusetts Communities.* Occasional papers, Institute for Asian American Studies. Boston: University of Massachusetts.

———. In press. A Sociological Analysis of the Psychosocial Adaptation of Khmer Refugees in Massachusetts. In *Strengths and Challenges of New Immigrant Families: Implications for Research, Theory, Education, and Service,* edited by R. L. Dalla, J. DeFrain, J. Johnson, and D. A. Abbott. Lexington, MA: Lexington Press.

Ong, A. 2003. *Buddha is Hiding: Refugees, Citizenship, the New America.* Berkeley and Los Angeles: University of California Press.

Pearlin, L. I. 1989. The Sociological Study of Stress. *Journal of Health and Social Behavior* 30:241–56.

———, A. Morton, M. A. Lieberman, E. G. Menaghan, and J. T. Mullan. 1981. The Stress Process. *Journal of Health and Social Behavior* 22:337–56.

Smith-Hefner, N. 1999. *Khmer American: Identity and Moral Education in a Diasporic Community.* Berkeley and Los Angeles: University of California Press.

Stevens, C. A. 2001. Perspectives on the Meanings of Symptoms among Cambodian Refugees. *Journal of Sociology* 37, no. 1:81–96.

Uba, L., and R. C. Chung. 1991. The Relationship between Trauma and Financial and Physical Well-being among Cambodians in the United States. *Journal of General Psychology* 118, no. 3:215–25.

U.S. Department of Health and Human Services. 2001. *Mental Health: Culture, Race, and Ethnicity.* Supplement to *Mental Health: A Report of the Surgeon General.* Rockville, MD: Substance Abuse and Mental Health Services Administration, Center for Mental Health Service.

West, C. D. 2000. Pathways of Thriving and Resilience: Growth Responses to Adversity and Trauma in Two Cambodian Communities: A Comparative Study between Lowell, Massachusetts and Phnom Penh, Cambodia. Unpublished manuscript, University of Massachusetts Lowell.

Linda Silka

Transforming Experiences

When Host Communities Become Home Communities

Lowell, Massachusetts has a long history as an immigrant city (Forrant and Silka 2006).[1] Starting in the early 1800s, waves of immigrants have come to Lowell. The original mill girls, who arrived to work in the newly built textile mills, were supplanted by the Irish, and the Irish by Greeks, Italians, and French Canadians, who then were supplanted by additional waves of immigrants and refugees over the subsequent decades.[2] In the late 1970s and continuing today, the largest refugee group is now Cambodian (Lotspeich, Fix, Perez-Lopez, and Ost 2003). Now nearly 40 percent of the youth in Lowell's high school are Cambodian. Many neighborhoods are Cambodian as are many businesses.[3] The Southeast Asian Water Festival has become an annual event attracting thousands from around the country (Silka, 2002c; 2002a). Lowell has won a coveted National Civic League's award as an All American City in part by demonstrating how groups can work together to create events such as the Water Festival (ICMA 2001). Lowell is home to the first Cambodian city counselor in the United States. There are police officers, teachers, nurses, and social workers who are Cambodian. There are artists. And there are gangs, home invasions, and troubled families.

Lowell has a 40-foot wheel in the downtown area, placed there by the Revolving Museum (www.revolvingmuseum.org). This wheel is covered with cloth on which people have hand-printed stories about the paths they have taken that ultimately led them to Lowell. The stories are highly varied but they are all, in one way or another, about arriving in a strange city and trying to find ways to make it their home. And these stories are also about transforming experiences—transforming in both senses of the phrase. First, these stories reflect the fact that experiences need to be made different if the community is to be welcoming. Second, and at the same time, the experiences are themselves transformative: we are all changed as a result of our experiences with each other (see also Chigas 2001; Deaux 2006; Higgins and Ross 2001; LivingLowell 2002; Pho and Mulvey 2003; Silka 2000).

An insightful edited volume entitled *Mistrusting Refugees* (Daniel and Knudson, 1995) captures in its varied chapters the dual nature of these mistrusting views we hold of one another. Many people already living in a community mistrust these newcomers who are moving into their neighborhoods and seem so different. At the same time, refugees who have seen their countries torn apart have every reason to assume that others cannot be trusted (Advocacy Project 2005; Chigas 2000; Daniel and Knudson 1995, Him 2000; Pran and DePaul 1999). The mistrust is pervasive (Higgins and Ross 2001; Silka and Tip 1994). How then do varied, complicated, and accumulating experiences get translated from host community to "home"? From refugees being outsiders to becoming insiders? The New Canadians series in Canada's national newspaper, the *Globe and Mail,* asks and answers these questions intriguingly in their "First Moments: Recent Immigrants Describe When They Realized They Were Canadian" (New Canadians 2003). When do these moments occur, what brings them about, and how are they sustained so that communities truly become home?

Cities all over the country are going through largely the same struggles to change as is Lowell (Bloom 2000; Fadiman 1997; Lehrer and Sloan 2003; Richman 2005; see also New Canadians 2003 for instructive stories from Canada). Consider the community of Lewiston, Maine, for example (Nadeau 2003). As has been widely reported in the press, Lewiston's rapidly growing Somali community has been a surprise (Bouchard 2002; Raymond 2002; Reuters 2003). Lewiston is currently in the throes of ethnic disagreements and misunderstandings, and the assistant city manager said that it was his hope that Lewiston eventually would be able to move beyond these current problems and achieve some of what Lowell has been able to in the way of becoming a home to newcomers. In a recent meeting, the manager discussed with me his questions about how Lowell had been able to change (Nadeau 2004); in trying to learn from Lowell's experiences, he pointed out, what was unclear is the means by which this transformation of Lowell took place. How did it happen? By what steps had Lowell moved closer to being a home community? How did the city go from being host to home?

My vantage point—that is to say, the perspective from which I offer this essay on the puzzling process by which communities move from host to home—is as an academic at a university in the community that is now home to the second-largest Cambodian population in the United States and the third-largest in the world (after Phnom Penh, Cambodia, and

Long Beach, California). For twenty-seven years I have been a faculty member at the University of Massachusetts Lowell, first in the psychology department and most recently in an interdisciplinary department focused on regional economic and social development. I also direct the Center for Family, Work, and Community (www.uml.centers/cfwc) and am a special assistant to the UML provost for Community Outreach and Partnerships. In these roles I work closely with the community in order to make the university's resources available for collaborative problem solving and capacity building (Silka 2002c, 2004b). At the university, we struggle with questions about what our role should be (Silka 1999; 2002c; 2005; Task Force 2005): What should a university's involvement be? What should a university be doing? How should we shape our role? Should we offer an Asian studies program? Programs in Khmer language, arts, and music? Other sorts of programs?[4]

The remainder of this essay offers thoughts on the transformation as seen from a university perspective and draws heavily on my experiences as an academic who has worked closely with many in the community of Lowell during this period of change. The transformation from host to home is not straightforward and perhaps will never be complete. As I note below, we seem as a community to have moved beyond stereotyping one another to a greater complexity of understanding.

On two sides of a cultural divide, we start out stereotyping each other (Esses, Dovidio, and Dion 2001; Horsti 2003; White and Perrone 2001): "Oh, this is what Cambodians are like. They treat their elders this way." "Oh, this is what the 'Americans' are like: they put their elders in nursing homes rather than taking care of them in the home." We seem to want to know enough about each other to classify, to predict what otherwise seems unpredictable: "Oh, these are the likely health problems among those who lived in refugee camps and now live in Lowell." "This is what Cambodian people typically eat for foods and so this is why WIC (Women, Infants and Children) food programs are likely to go unused by Southeast Asians." "This is what Cambodian people believe about teachers and the school system and this is why they aren't likely to become involved in school parent outreach programs." "This is what Cambodian women's roles are like this and so this is what we can predict with regard to domestic violence." "Cambodian children will behave in this way toward their parents." (Rich descriptions of this process by which groups new to a community are stereotyped can be found in Bloom 2000; Fadiman 1997; Nguyen 2003; Um 2003.)

And events are hosted to learn what the newcomers are like (ICMA 2001). In Lowell's case, such events include the Southeast Asian Water Festival, the Cambodian New Year's celebration, the Mogan Center Immigrant Stories Project (http://www.nps.gov/lowe/2002/mogan/whatwedo.htm), traditional Cambodian dances re-created by the Angkor Dance Troupe (http://www.angkordance.org), Cambodian-American operas (such as *Where Elephants Weep*), and presentations of documentaries about Cambodian life, such as *The Flute Player* and *The Monkey Dance*. But unexpected things happen in the act of re-creating these events. These events, intended to share the culture, are changed by taking place in the United States. They are transformed. And they become a part of the city's identity (ICMA 2001; McConville 1999). They are no longer the events of "outsider"; they rapidly become insider events (Silka, 2002a). The Water Festival re-creates what once took place along the Mekong, but here it occurs on the Merrimack and celebrates aspects of making the Merrimack a place for Cambodian recreation and family activities. And to host the Water Festival, groups must obtain permissions, such as from the neighborhood councils near the event site. Leaders in the French Canadian neighborhood adjacent to the river festival grounds saw little connection with the newcomers until they realized that many Cambodians share their love of fishing, and that every new group makes the Merrimack River their own through the ways they use the river. Or, the Water Festival planning group has to explain to the Water Commission the traditions of the Water Festival (the racing of traditional boats and the like), and the Water Commission, by the questions they ask, are themselves changed and change as well how the planning team thinks about the Water Festival. Traditional youth groups such as the Boy Scouts want to be involved in the Water Festival and they too are changed by the process of trying to envision how their programs can be made of interest to newcomers. When groups such as the Boy Scouts become involved, they expect merely to recruit more members. Yet they find through the process of assisting in planning the Water Festival that as an organization they begin to change.

And disagreements emerge on many topics (Silka 2002a). What roles should the monks play in shaping this re-creation of the Water Festival? To what degree should this event adhere to past practices and to what extent can it encompass new roles and new partners? Will this be a religious event or a civic event? An "American" leader of a folk life center in Lowell asserts that the entire event should be an exact reproduction of what once took place in Cambodia before the ravages of the Khmer Rouge. Yet Lowell's Cambodian leaders are puzzled by this apparent interest in freezing their culture "in amber," down to the assertions, for instance, that the traditional racing boats being built for the festival should be created with traditional hand tools even though such tools are no longer used even in Cambodia. Cambodian youth want the Water Festival to include contemporary rap music composed by themselves and to feature a contemporary fashion show; some elders are aghast at the ways such practices go against their recollection of what the festival was once like and what it represented in Cambodia before the Khmer Rouge years. The transformation is about how things change. As conflicts occur within the community, the community can no longer be viewed by "American" outsiders as one in which everyone is the same or speaks with a single voice. The differences among Cambodians become apparent. In effect, the act of stereotyping begins to undo itself through contact that brings longtime Lowell residents into extended contact with many Cambodians all working on the same task.

In Lowell, the initial assumption was commonly that one spokesperson could easily represent all Cambodians on a board or in an organization. Local press outlets fell into the habit of interviewing a mere handful of spokesmen (and they *were* usually men) when some newsworthy event occurred in the Cambodian community. This view that a single spokesperson was sufficient to capture an unfamiliar culture reflects a deep belief in and reliance on stereotype. It seemed to be assumed that Cambodians, for example, were all alike and that therefore one person was capable of reflecting the culture's attributes and propensities. A single young gang member who is Cambodian reflects the problems that all Cambodian youth bring to Lowell's doorstep. A single representative on a board from that culture was assumed to be capable of speaking for the entire community. What this spokesperson says was assumed to be true for all Cambodians (for similar examples and analyses, see Clement, Noels, and Deneault 2001; Zick, Wagner, van Dick, and Petzel 2001).

This reliance on stereotype, however, begins to erode in the face of certain experiences where differences *within* cultures become salient. The Greater Lowell Chamber of Commerce, in order to understand the needs of newcomer business owners, hosted a series of focus groups for local Cambodian business owners. Variations in approaches to business by different Cambodians pointed to the rich diversity within Cambodian culture; after the focus groups, chamber members commented on how much stronger their understanding now was of the diversity. Yet community roles differ in the extent to which they provide these avenues for seeing the diversity within a culture. Police officers who work with gang-involved youth but not other youth from the same cultural background are confronted with the similarities in behavior rather than the differences. Teachers, working closely with individual students in a classroom, have greater opportunities to see the diversity firsthand. And when one works as a physician or nurse, individual differences may be especially salient. In Lowell, we are seeing people transformed when their roles provide opportunities for experiencing within culture diversity.

Metaphors and their transformational significance also seem to be an important expression of the transition going on from host to home (Silka 1999). Consider some of their uses to further community dialogues.

Metaphors have been used to convey to non-Cambodians the impact on elders of being refugees in an unfamiliar country and in an alien culture (Silka 1999). At a community meeting, one Cambodian leader noted: "Our elders are like trees on the bank of a river, trees that have had the soil undercut from around them. They are slowly falling over because their roots are hanging in the air, no longer surrounded by soil. We must do something." Metaphors have been used to capture just how worried leaders are becoming about youth: "Our youth are like a river overflowing its banks. The water goes everywhere and the banks of the river no longer enclose, contain, and guide the water. We need to find a way to guide the water, to rebuild the banks, to guide our youth." This rich reliance on metaphors and analogies has been transforming. They introduce a depth of language. Again and again in our community listeners remark that they now understand what the speaker means; the metaphors overcome differences and point to similarities. And it is not just that metaphors are being used; it is also the particular metaphors that have been drawn upon. The problems may be familiar, but the choice of comparison is often new to the listener. The two together bring listeners up short and cause them to think about the community differently. Metaphors appear to have been a part of the process by which Lowell is moving from a host community to a home community. Metaphors disarm people and bridge differences (Fitzgerald 1993; GudyKunst and Young 1997; Silka 1999; Wood 1998).

The move from host community to home community appears to be reflected in other intriguing ways. A local mutual assistance association in Lowell was recently preparing for an election of its board, and the forms that this preparation took speak to the complex transformation from host to home. American Lowellian leaders were brought in by Cambodian American leaders to talk at a community meeeting about the American election process, about what would be involved in ensuring that the election was not tainted and that candidates did not resort to fixing the election (by, for example, bringing in busloads of their friends to vote). A central feature to ensuring the election was the introduction of an old but still functioning wooden ballot box, a box reflecting American history and the traditions behind it in Lowell. Using this ballot box, each vote was recorded individually and anonymously through a mechanical process that, in effect, loudly announced that the vote had been counted. The outcome of the election in this mutual assistance association resulted in all elected board members being Cambodian; the non-Cambodians were largely voted off the board. Much of the organization is now run by Cambodian Americans, young leaders in their thirties who were born in Cambodia but who have spent much of their early adulthood and formative years as Lowellians. The election, in a curious way, reflects the transitioning from host to home, the mixing of traditions. In the impassioned calls by the new board to create more opportunities for Cambodian businesses, for youth, and for others, we see the bringing together of two cultures that in some sense no longer are two cultures. For more information on these changing patterns, see information on Cambodian Voting Project (http://modelminority.com/article1032.html) and the National Conference of State Legislatures' Building the New American Dream project that led to the creation of the organization OneLowell (http://www.onelowell.net).

Consider yet another example. Lowell is one of the first places in the United States to have an East-West health center devoted largely to Cambodian health care but open to all (Ready 2001; Lewy 2002). The health care center, called METTA (loosely translated as "loving-kindness"), transforms health care and the way it is delivered. It keeps some things the same as at other American health clinics: the same diagnostic tests are given, the same reimbursement procedures are followed. But at METTA different intake forms are used, different questions are asked, and in the waiting area there are materials, photos, and statues from Cambodia and in the Khmer language. METTA reflects the importance of meeting the health care needs of Cambodians through changing the ways that health care is delivered. Places like METTA move Lowell closer to a home community, and the home itself is transformed as a result.

In a similar way, large-scale projects are assisting with this transition: the Cambodian Community Health 2010, funded by the Centers for Disease Control to find new ways for health care to meet the needs of Cambodian elders in preventing diabetes and cardiovascular disease (Fernandez 2002; CDC 2005); or the Southeast Asian Environmental Justice Partnership (Coppens, Silka, Khakeo, and Benfey 2000; Silka 2000), funded by the National Institute of Environmental Health Sciences to change the ways environmental health issues such as asthma are addressed (Reece, Silka, Chao, and Phan 2002). These projects change how environmental health and other health problems are conceptualized (Silka 2002d; see also DeSantis 1997). The result is a transformed community, a community that no longer views itself in the same ways. Consider education. Chath pierSath, a young Cambodian leader in Lowell, worked as a Cambodian parent liaison with most of Lowell's middle schools for the U.S. Department of Education–funded GEARUP initiative, facilitated through UML's CFWC. PierSath notes that he was repeatedly told that he should not expect Cambodian parents to become involved in the schools. Cambodians, he was reminded by his elders, traditionally do not participate because of their respect for teachers. Out of respect, parents turn their children's education over to teachers and then avoid any activities that might be seen as interference or overstepping bounds. In the face of such comments, pierSath began pointing out to parents and others that those are the old traditions, and while important in the past, it was now time for Cambodians in Lowell to create new traditions, traditions that fit with American educational systems and that would help Cambodian children succeed in school. He said that the old traditions were what we were like in Cambodia; this is what we will be like here at home in the United States. Traditions can change. New traditions can be created.

In these transitions from host to home, then, what roles has the University of Massachusetts Lowell, played and what might these roles be in the future? Universities have traditionally played the role of studying things, dissecting them, in effect, doing their best to place them "under amber" so that such traditions might be preserved. University faculty have played the role of rescuing traditions before they are lost: music, master artists, and the like. Universities have played other roles as well. At the University of Massachusetts Lowell, we have become engaged in capacity building and technical assistance roles that are reflected in our work on educational projects to encourage youth to aspire to college (http://ecommunity.uml.edu/gearup), capacity building for refugee and immigrant leaders (see http://www.uml.edu/centers/cfwc/; Silka and Eady 2007), projects on urban aquaculture that draw on the Cambodian experience (Silka 2002a, 2002b), projects to improve relations between the police and the community (Silka 2004a), and assorted other roles intended to foster regional economic and social development (ICMA 2001). The question continues to be, can universities blend together these diverse and paradoxical roles, as communities move from host community to home community? In universities, we write, we bring people together, we host conferences, we try to create a neutral ground for discussions, and we attempt to take the long view (Nyden 2005; Sandy and Arguelles 2005; Levenstein, DeLaurier, and Silka 2001). Yet as individual faculty we also see events through the narrow lens of our individual disciplines, we transmit knowledge and are storytellers, but of an unusual but highly constrained sort. The result is opportunity but only if universities and faculty change. As the above suggests, UML as a university is in the act of being transformed.

Final Thoughts

In the book *For Those Who Come After* (Krupat 1989), the discussion focuses on the difficult questions of how the practices of Native American tribes will be preserved. Native Americans come from oral cultures; thus, writing down their traditions was not a cultural practice. Anthropologists who were non-Indian were those who were engaged in recording. This process of outsiders choosing to record the culture created all kinds of paradoxes: people who are not a part of the culture played the role of preserving cultural information in important ways; yet as outsiders they could not entirely capture its nuances. Moreover, the act of recording cultural information exposed those private cultural practices to the scrutiny of outsiders. The information was recorded and therefore preserved; by the very act of having the facts written down, however, the culture itself was transformed. Similar issues about recording difficult histories, about exposing troubling cultural experiences to the view of outsiders have been a point of discussion and reflection within communities such as Lowell.

Consider the discussion going on about the Emmy-nominated documentary *The Flute Player.*[5] This film follows Arn Chorn-Pond from Lowell back to Cambodia to confront the culture and his demons. The film documents the ways in which Arn Chorn-Pond was forced as a youth to collaborate with the Khmer Rouge in order to stay alive; it describes his forced collaboration in using flute playing to survive when those same musical talents were the "rationale" behind the Khmer Rouge murder of all of the other musicians in his family. Chorn-Pond returns to Cambodia to locate any elder master musicians who may still be alive and who can provide a link to the past, a past that is nearly lost. As Chorn-Pond meets with these elders, the film captures the complications of these relationships and reflects the ambiguities back to us. The film reflects the ambiguities that come with transformations, the sense that no place is really home, or that *all* places perhaps have the potential to become home (see also the documentary *The Monkey Dance,* which raises similar issues about the ways in which Cambodian youth in Lowell struggle with their dual identity and with the question of which culture represents home to them as opposed to which culture does so to their parents). In Lowell we continue to try to come to terms with how this history becomes a part of what is discussed in schools, in temples, and in homes.

Notes

1. Elements of this analysis were originally presented at the Association for Asian Studies 2004 annual meeting, San Diego, California, March 2004 and at the Southeast Asian Workshop, Lowell, Massachusetts, June 2005. Research and partnership work reported here is based on work carried out under grants from National Institute of Environmental Health Sciences, U.S. Housing and Urban Development, U.S. Department of Eucation, U.S. Environmental Protection Agency, and the National Science Foundation.

2. For detailed descriptions of this history from the Patrick J. Mogan Cultural Center, Lowell National Historical Park, and the Tsongas Center for Industrial History, see http://www.nps.gov/lowe/2002/home.htm.

3. See Cambodian Neighborhood Walking Tour, University of Massachusetts Lowell Library, Center for Lowell History, http://library.uml.edu/clh/cam/Cam bw1htm.

4. An ad hoc UML committee has undertaken deliberations on what the university's role might become. Minutes from these deliberations are available from the author at Linda Silka, Center for Family, Work, and Community, 600 Suffolk Street, 1st Floor South, Lowell, MA 01854 or Linda_Silka@uml.edu.

5. Discussions can be found at Public Broadcasting System, http://www.pbs.org /pov/pov2003/thefluteplayer, http://www.thefluteplayer.net/; National Public Radio, http://www.npr.org/templates/story/story.php?storyId= 1344101; Human Rights Watch, http://wwwhrw.org/iff/2004/boston/flute.html; and Cambodian Masters Project, http://www.cambodianmasters.org/cmpp/flute_player.htm.

References

Advocacy Project. 2005. Available online at http://www.advocacynet.org.

Bloom, S. G. 2000. *Postville: A Clash of Cultures in Heartland America.* New York: Harcourt.

Bouchard, K. 2002. Lewiston's Somali Surge. *Portland Press Herald,* April 28.

Centers for Disease Control and Prevention (CDC). 2005. Racial and Ethnic Approaches to Community Health (REACH 2010): Addressing Disparities in Health. National Center for Chronic Disease Prevention and Health Promotion. Available at http://www.cdc.gov/nccdphp/aag/aag_reach.htm.

Chigas, G. 2000. The Trial of the Khmer Rouge: The Role of the Tuol Sleng and Santebal Archives. *Harvard Asia Quarterly (wi*nter).

———. 2001. Cambodian Experience and Literature. *Bridge Review II.* Available at http://ecommunity.uml.edu/bridge/review2/.

Clement, R., K. A. Noels, and B. Deneault. 2001. Interethnic Contact, Identity and Psychological Adjustment: The Meditating and Moderating Roles of Communication. *Journal of Social Issues* 57, no. 3:559–78.

Coppens, N. M., L. Silka, R. Khakeo, and J. Benfey. 2000. Southeast Asians Understanding of Environmental Health Issues. *Journal of Multicultural Nursing and Health* 6, no. 3:31–38.

Daniel, E. V., and J. C. Knudson, eds. 1995. *Mistrusting Refugees.* Berkeley and Los Angeles: University of California Press.

Deaux, K. 2006. *To Be an Immigrant.* New York: Russell Sage Foundation.

DeSantis, L. 1997. Building Health Communities with Immigrants and Refugees. *Journal of Transcultural Nursing* 9, no. 1:20–31.

Esses, V. M., J. F. Dovidio, and K. L. Dion, eds. 2001. Immigrants and Immigration. Special issue of *Journal of Social Issues* 57, no. 3.

Fadiman, A. 1997. *Spirit Catches You and You Fall Down: A Hmong Child, her American Doctors, and the Collision of Two Cultures.* New York: Farrar, Straus, and Giroux.

Fernandez, S. 2002. *Cambodian Health 2010.* Paper presented at the National Leadership Summit on Eliminating Racial and Ethnic Disparities in Health, Washington, D.C., July 10–12, 2002.

Fitzgerald, T. K. 1993. *Metaphors of Identity: A Culture-Communication Dialogue*. Albany, NY: State University of New York Press.

Forrant, R., and L. Silka. 2006. Inside and Out: What's It All About. In *Inside and Out: Universities and Education for Sustainable Development*, edited by R. Forrant and L. Silka, 1–14. Amityville, NY: Baywood Press.

GudyKunst, William B., and Yun Kim Young. 1997. *Communicating with Strangers: An Approach to Intercultural Communication*. New York: McGraw-Hill.

Higgins, J., and J. Ross. 2001. Fractured Identities. *Bridge Review I* 1. Available at http://ecommunity.uml.edu/bridge/review2/.

Him, C. 2000. *When Broken Glass Floats: Growing Up under the Khmer Rouge*. New York: Norton.

Horsti, K. 2003. Borders of Strangeness: Multicultural Discourse in Journalism. Paper presented at the What's the Culture in Multiculturalism? Conference, University of Aarhus, May 22–24, 2003. Electronic copy available at http://www.politicaltheory.dk/conference/res/papers/5202003143637/tanskapaperi percent20(Horsti).pdf.

ICMA. 2001. Lowell Massachusetts: Reweaving an American Community. In *Brownfields Blueprints: A Study of Brownfields Showcase Communities Initiatives*, 231–53. Washington, DC: International City/County Management Association.

Krupat, A. 1989. *For Those Who Come After: A Study of Native American Autobiography*. Berkeley and Los Angeles: University of California Press.

Lehrer, W., and J. Sloan. 2003. *Crossing the BLVD: Strangers, Neighbors, Aliens in a New America*. New York: Norton.

Levenstein, C., G. F. DeLaurier, and L. Silka. 2001. What Do Regions Want? A Report on the Millennium Breakfast Series of the Council on Regional Development. *Bridge Review IV*. Available at http://ecommunity.uml.edu/bridge/review4/cita/levenstein_delaurier.htm.

Lewy, J. 2002. West meets East in Massachusetts: Love, Kindness and Compassion at Lowell's METTA Health Center. Integrative Medical Alliance Newsletter, issue 23. Available at http://www.integrativemedallian.org/projects_news letters_archive.asp.

LivingLowell. 2002. http://www.livinglowell.com. Web site of Living Lowell: An American City.

Lotspeich, K., M. E. Fix, D. Perez-Lopez, and J. Ost. 2003. *A Profile of the Foreign Born in Lowell*. Available at http://www.urbanorg/DanPerezLopez.

McConville, C. 1999. It's Official: Lowell an All-American City. *Lowell Sun*, June 27.

Nadeau, P. 2003. The Somalis of Lewiston: Community Impacts of Rapid Immigrant Movement into a Small Homogeneous Maine City. Paper presented to the Brown University Center for the Study of Race and Ethnicity.

———. 2004. Lewiston assistant city manager, personal communication.

New Canadians. 2003. Twelve Part Series in *Globe and Mail*. Available at http://www.theglobeandmail.com/series/newcanada/index.html.

Nguyen, T. 2003. Working with Linguistically and Culturally Isolated Communities: The Cambodian Outreach Project of Merrimack Valley Legal Services. *Journal of Poverty, Law, and Policy*, 79–83.

Nyden, P. 2005. The Challenges and Opportunities of Engaged Research. In *Scholarship in Action: Applied Research and Community Change*, edited by L. Silka. Washington, DC: U.S. Housing and Urban Development.

Pho, T.-L., and A. Mulvey. 2003. Southeast Asian Women in Lowell: Family Relations, Gender Roles and Community Concerns, *Frontiers* 24, no. 1:101–29.

Pran, D., and K. DePaul, eds. 1999. *Children of Cambodia's Killing Fields: Memoirs by Survivors.* New Haven, CT: Yale University Press.

Raymond, L. T., Jr. 2002. Mayor Raymond's Letter to the Somali Community. *Portland Press Herald.*

Ready, T. 2001. Healing Traditions Americans Have Only Recently Begun to Experiment with Body Work, Herbs, Acupuncture, and Other Forms of Oriental Medicine. Cambodians Have Been Doing It Forever. *Boston Phoenix,* June 21, pp. 1–3.

Reece, S., L. Silka, K. Chao, and P. Phan. Cultural Interpretations of Asthma: Exploring Explanatory Models of Families, Key Informants, and Health Care Providers within Lowell's Cambodian Community. Paper presented at the 2002 CITA Conference on Sustainability, November 2002. Available at http://www.uml.edu/com/CITA/asthmapaper,pdf.

Reuters. 2003. White Supremacists Plan Anti-Somali Rally. *Reuters,* January 11.

Richman, K. 2005. *Migration and Vodou.* Gainesville: University of Florida Press.

Sandy, M., and L. Arguelles. 2005. Fusing Horizons through Conversation: A Grassroots Think-tank Approach to Applied Research. In *Scholarship in Action: Applied Research and Community Change,* edited by L. Silka. Washington, DC: U.S. Housing and Urban Development.

Silka, L. 1999. Paradoxes of Partnership: Reflections on University-Community Partnerships. In *Research in Politics and Society: Community Politics and Policies,* edited by N. Kleniewski and G. Rabrenovic, 335–59. Stamford, CT: JAI Press.

———. 2000. Strangers in Strange Lands [invited essay on award-winning work with newcomer communities]. *Journal of Professional Service and Outreach* 5, no. 2:24–30.

———. 2002a. Combining History and Culture to Reach Environmental Goals. *New Village: Building Sustainable Cultures* 3:4–11.

———. 2002b. Environmental Communication and Refugee and Immigrant Communities: The Lowell Experience. *Applied Environmental Education and Communication: An International Journal* 1:107–14.

———. 2002c. Immigrants, Sustainability, and Emerging Roles for Universities. *Development* 45:119–23.

———. 2002d. *Rituals and Research Ethics: Using One Community's Experience to Reconsider the Ways that Communities and Researchers Build Sustainable Partnerships.* Case study prepared under National Institute of Health, National Institute of Allergies and Infectious Disease Grant Program for Research Ethics, D. Quigley, principal investigator. Available at http://researchethics.org/uploads/pdf/ritual_case.pdf.

———. 2004a. Race Relations in the Immigrant City. Paper presented at the symposium *From Cambodian Killing Fields to the Streets of Lowell.* Presented at American Psychological Association annual convention, Honolulu, Hawaii, July 2004.

———. 2004b. A University Enters into Its Regional Economy: Models for Integrated Action. In *Universities and Regional Economic Development,* edited by Jean L. Pyle and Robert Forrant. Northampton, MA: Edward Elgar Publications.

———. 2005. Partnerships within and beyond Universities: Their Opportunities and Challenges. *Public Health Reports* 119, no. 1.

———, and V. Eady. 2007. Diversity: Welcoming Multiple Cultures into One Community. In *Preserving and Enhancing Communities: A Guide for Citizens, Planners, and Policymakers,* edited by Elisabeth M. Hamin, Linda Silka, and Priscilla Geigis. Amherst, MA: University of Massachusetts Press.

———, and J. Tip. 1994. Empowering the Silent Ranks: The Southeast Asian Experience. *American Journal of Community Psychology* 222:497–529.

Task Force on UML Community Outreach and Partnerships. 2005. Available at http://www.uml.edu.

The Monkey Dancer. N.d. Description and analysis can be found at http://www.mfn.org/newsandevent/newsletter/MassHumanities/Fall2001/monkey.html.

Um, K. 2003. A Dream Denied: Educational Experience of Southeast Asian American Youth. Washington, DC: Southeast Asian Resource Action Center.

White, R., and S. Perrone. 2001. Racism, Ethnicity, and Hate Crimes. *Journal of Transnational and Cross-Cultural Studies* 9, no. 2:161–81.

Wood, J. T. 1998. Celebrating Diversity in the Communications Field. *Communications Studies* (summer).

Zick, A., U. Wagner, R. van Dick, and T. Petzel. 2001. Acculturation and Prejudice in Germany: Majority and Minority Perspectives. *Journal of Social Issues* 57, no. 3:541–58.

Part III

REFLECTIONS

Sylvia R. Cowan, Jeffrey N. Gerson,
and Tuyet-Lan Pho

Conclusion and Recommendations for Future Research

This selection of essays is a modest but important contribution to grow-ing interest in Southeast Asian Studies. Together they illustrate a city's people and institutions meeting newcomers, grappling with the issues each face, and seeking solutions and ways to thrive.

Many questions were raised and authors searched for insights and un-derstanding. What is the impact of resettlement on refugees and immi-grants' lives—their families, education, business or work and overall well-being? What is the effect on the community and how does it re-spond? What missteps occurred and what lessons can other cities and towns currently experiencing secondary migration (Lewiston, Maine's re-cent influx of Somalis, for example) learn from the Lowell case? Can the Lowell experience contribute to an understanding of economic, political, and social incorporation? How do policies such as national immigration impact local communities such as Lowell? How do continuing social, cul-tural, and political links between newcomers and their countries of origin impact their current lives in the city? What social problems continue to bedevil the community and what solutions exist to solve them? What are the city's and the community's greatest accomplishments in the thirty-year process of transformation of both groups? Sometimes insights into these questions have appeared. At other times layers of complexity emerged to reframe the questions. Some solutions were posed, some rec-ommendations made, and areas for additional research identified.

In recounting the history of migration to Lowell, Hai B. Pho found that in the early days sponsors, federal, state, and local programs, and fi-nancial support made a difference, and favorable economic conditions in the city contributed to early settlers becoming economically self-sufficient and independent relatively quickly. Later arrivals had to contend with stretched and reduced resources, recession, and rising anti-immigrant sentiment. Now that the influx of Southeast Asians to Lowell has leveled off and newer immigrants continue to arrive, a quandary remains: how can relationships between public officials and communities of immigrants—and among immigrant communities themselves—develop in a mutually beneficial fashion?

Jean L. Pyle examines key questions: What are the effects of the second migration on the particular areas in which immigrants settle? How will any proposed changes in national immigration policy affect these localities? She asserts that policymakers must understand, and build into their policies, the wants and needs of those migrating secondarily. In the future, research teams could survey households and businesses to construct a community network analysis. Concrete studies of this type are needed to provide well-informed and integrated policies.

David Turcotte and Linda Silka examine the paradoxes presented by contrasting perspectives of immigrant communities: are they needy recipients of services, or are they vital resources? They ask what strengths of the newcomer community typically go unrecognized, and what clashes in community economic development models arise between immigrants and planners. They raise important questions about differing results that are obtained when cities use models of development that ignore potential contributions of immigrant communities. We need to look carefully at existing models of economic and community development in order to recognize and move beyond their inadequacies. Community planners need to tap the ideas of the community members themselves, for in that process new ways of thinking about development, ways unimagined in familiar models, may emerge.

Tuyet-Lan Pho asks how cultural values and family systems of support interact with educational institutions and if they affect achievement? The relationship between family education and school achievement is more intricate than two factors. Issues that need to be addressed in future research include: What changes have taken place in Southeast Asians' family education since their resettlement in the United States? How can parents, students, and teachers work together to improve family education and school learning? Further research that addresses these complex interactions could enhance teacher education, sustain strong family tradition, and may bring benefit for students and their parents.

Khin Mai Aung and Nancy Yu wonder whether Cambodian youth are being supported in their educational advancement in the public schools. They found high dropout rates, low economic status, and linguistic and cultural factors to be barriers. They acknowledge important contributions of community support programs for youth, and highlight the need for intervention programs for youth already involved in gangs. They see continued research with the communities themselves as important, including research to assess Lowell's past bilingual education program.

Susan Thomson wonders if traditional Theravada Buddhist practices contain the basis for civic engagement with the larger Lowell community. She finds in a program for runaway teens and in traditional community celebrations that sense of responsibility to and connection with others. Through expanded partnerships inclusive of a broader spectrum of the city's residents, Thomson envisions the potential for strengthening the political and social fabric of the city and the sense of belonging of the immigrant communities.

Sylvia Cowan asks how past history and memory affect attitudes and the ability to form a cohesive group among immigrants in the receiving community. She finds that ties to the homeland continue to influence relationships in the here and now, and different interpretations of the past and visions for the future emerge within a richly diverse Lao community. More detailed study of connections among those in the Diaspora needs to be undertaken.

Jeffrey N. Gerson wonders how conflicts in the temple can be resolved as religious communities establish themselves in the new land. He finds that Cambodian Americans have deep differences over the structure, authority, and emphasis in values of their temple. The question remains whether turning to the host country's judicial system will help resolve an intractable conflict, when homeland ties continue to influence the players.

Leakhena Nou explores what Cambodians themselves experience as stressors and adjustment difficulties, how these influence development of their communities, and how Khmer use resilience to overcome a traumatic past and establish new lives. She highlights the importance of cultural factors in the provision of services. Additional research needs to include central involvement of the indigenous community.

Linda Silka asks, when do host communities become "home"? In collaborations and partnerships, she finds that both immigrants and the larger community are transformed, and new forms emerge. She discovers ambiguities that come with transformations, and that in a sense no place is home— or perhaps all places have the potential to become home. Silka names a number of artistic events that occur in the city to celebrate the cultures of origin and to serve as a means to create a sense of "home" in Lowell.

A number of themes recur in this collection of diverse articles. The need to belong (through religious institutions, mutual assistance associations, youth gangs); keeping traditions alive (through celebrations at temples, dance troupes, water festivals); bridging worlds (through homeland ties, board membership across ethnic lines, partnerships); issues of identity (underscored in language and culture passed down, hyphenated identities, visits "home"); conflict (within and among communities and institutions); resilience (survival, economic successes, expression in the arts). All these emerge as salient features in these stories.

The communities and the city have attempted to find solutions, sometimes encountering barriers, sometimes emerging victorious, sometimes riding the ups and downs as they uncovered new layers of complexity. The receiving community's education systems and labor markets were challenged and were found not adequately prepared for the newcomers. Failure to address inadequacies of existing systems sometimes results in social unrest and the involvement of the criminal justice system.

We have seen missteps; yet there have also been accomplishments along the way. Many successful partnerships between members of the immigrant communities and the host community have emerged. A number of alliances and collaborations have been highlighted; in some cases these ventures have been transformative for all involved. Considered by many in the community as an organizational success that blends East and West, the Metta Health Clinic provides one example of merging cultural knowledge and practices to tackle health challenges.

While attempting to address issues from many perspectives, this volume falls short by not adequately including the views of those in existing structures and institutions in the city: perspectives of leaders and workers in city hall, the criminal justice system, educational administrators, and policymakers. Future research should explore these perspectives. Future studies should continue to take into account the cultures and social structures of the immigrant communities, and substantively involve members of these communities. Further investigation into the cultural influences of home culture in the adaptation process needs to be explored. Perspectives of majority and minority groups within an immigrant community, as well as second and third generations, gender, and race need more in-depth analysis. The influence of homeland connections in present-day migrant communities especially requires further exploration. Relationships of Southeast Asians' experiences with that of other immigrant groups in the city could provide both interesting and insightful comparisons.

The Prospects For the Future

The challenges faced by the Southeast Asian community of Lowell are still great: poverty, high dropout rate, post traumatic stress disorder, youth gangs, and generational, civil, and religious conflict. Nevertheless, the authors of this volume remain upbeat; by and large they are inspired by the resilience they found in both the City of Lowell's ability to incorporate the newcomers, and the abilities of the Southeast Asian groups, while remaining diverse, to organize for communal improvement. Examples of the latter are found in every corner of the community.

In several states, especially in impacting local politics, Southeast Asians are now emerging as a cultural and political force. The recent rise of naturalization and the growth in registration and voting among Southeast Asians has been noted. (Asian American Legal and Education Defense Fund (2005).[1] Moreover, community activists are addressing local social problems on a national level. For instance, the National Cambodian American Health Initiative (NCAHI, a national Cambodian American health advocacy organization whose service area covers 50 percent of Cambodians in the United States) issued a declaration of a health emergency in the Cambodian community. "This statement was issued in response to indicators which suggest that the prevalence of Post Traumatic Stress Disorder is increasing at a time when resources for survivors are diminishing. . . . Data regarding diabetes and cardiovascular disease in the Cambodian community paint a picture of escalating health problems that are dramatically impacted by PTSD. . . . Another issue contributing to the health emergency is the upcoming trial of the Khmer Rouge slated to begin in 2007. The trial of perpetrators is associated with an increase in PTSD symptoms in victims and requires a support system to aid not only witnesses but other survivors who will be exposed to testimonies" (Mass Media Distribution, April 10, 2006, p. 277). The long-term political and emotional ramifications of the Tribunal for Cambodian-American communities will be great and needs to be carefully studied (Human Rights News 2006).

Likewise, the "American War"/"Vietnam War" and its aftermath is still having a huge impact on Lao communities in the United States. Some Lao Americans are attempting to understand the implications through the Legacies of War project (Legacies of War, n.d.). The exhibit is traveling the nation and, with the assistance of the Lowell National Historical Park, the Brush Art Gallery of Lowell, and the University of Massachusetts Lowell, is slated to visit Lowell during the winter and spring of 2008.[2] The International Lao Studies Conferences (2005, and 2007) and the International Hmong Studies Conferences (2006, and scheduled for 2008) illustrate increased attention to these communities at the international level. In Minnesota and Wisconsin, Hmong have become active in the local communities and run for political office. In 2002 a Hmong American woman Mee Moua was elected to the Minnesota State Senate, becoming the first Hmong American state legislator in the United States. About her victory "we may also say that Mee Moua helped make Hmong Americans care about politics, and more Hmong candidates have stood for public office since her election. In 2002 Cy Thao was elected State Representative in Minnesota, and Dr. Tony Vang became the first Hmong member of the California School Board" (Yoshikawa 2006, 18). In 2006, Mee Moua was reelected to Minnesota State Senate for a second term with 69 percent of the vote (Yoshikawa 2006).

In the past thirty years, most Vietnamese Americans were and continue to be drawn back to the issues of deep concern in their homeland. They voice questions about Vietnamese authorities that have committed gross violations of human rights, including the suppression of religious freedom and oppression of ethnic minorities in Vietnam. They closely and publicly scrutinize the authorities' police powers, including the violation of civil rights of Vietnamese citizens, who seek to exercise their rights to freely promote democracy and the right to a multi-party system as guaranteed in the regime's Constitution. Wherever there is a large concentration of Vietnamese Americans there are also ethnic newspapers, radio programs, and political actions seeking to mobilize public opinion against the current Vietnamese government.

On the other hand, the strategy of the Vietnamese government seems to aim both at pacifying overseas opposition and maintaining domestic order. The authorities charge political activists within the country with subversive activities and conspiracy to overthrow the state. They put opposition leaders, including religious freedom advocates, under extended house arrests or long term jail sentences after well-managed court trials. The authorities commit those persons with extensive international visibility to permanent overseas exile that, with time, neutralizes the effectiveness of their advocacy. Future studies could continue to examine the Vietnamese-American communities perspectives on the homeland, and explore possibilities and conditions under which Vietnamese-Americans might be able to reconcile the current regime.

Taken together, all the chapters in this volume illustrate the complex interaction of multiple factors for three Southeast Asian communities in Lowell. Inherent in the experience of immigration to a new country are many challenges along with new opportunities. Their struggles are long and may leave psychological scars that take many years to heal. Yet for many the struggles afford a chance to know their strength and resilience at a new depth, a chance to tap into their resources for surviving and thriving. It is not enough to look only at the immigrant communities, themselves, in isolation. We must also examine how the current situations in the homelands of immigrants impact how their local communities develop, and what conflicts arise or what collaborations become possible.

Additional research can help provide broader understanding of: (1) immigrants' attempts to create meaning and value in the context of their experience as refugees; (2) the impact and direction policy decisions take at both the national and local levels; and (3) the meaning of "diaspora" in a global economy. The editors and authors encourage continuing exploration of these issues, not only for the welfare of new immigrants themselves, but also for the emergence of a richer, fuller, vital society in which all can contribute their talents, knowledge, and experience.

Notes

1. See also Deepa Bharath, Asian-Americans making their voices heard. The most ever Asian-Americans were on November ballot, observers say. *Orange Country Register.* Wednesday, January 3, 2007; retrieved January 4, 2007, from http://www.ocregister.com/ocregister/news/homepage/article_1405139.php.

2. The devastation of U.S. bombing in Laos is now said to have occurred in Cambodia as well, according to new research, recently published by the Yale University Cambodia Genocide Project: Bombs Over Cambodia: New Information Reveals that Cambodia Was Bombed Far More Heavily than Previously Believed (mapping done by Taylor Owen, October 2006).

References

Asian American Legal and Education Defense Fund. "The Asian American Vote 2004: A Report on the Multilingual Exit Polls of the 2004 Presidential Election." Retrieved December 13, 2005, from http://www.aaldef.org/voting.html.

Human Rights News. Retrieved December 30, 2006, *from Human Rights News, Cambodia: Government Interferes in Khmer Rouge Tribunal,* http://hrw.org/english/docs/2006/12/05/cambod14752.html.

Legacies of War. N.d. Retrieved March 23, 2007, from http://www.legaciesofwar.org/low_main.html.

Mass Media Distribution. Press release, April 10, 2006. Retrieved April 10, 2006, from http://mmdnewswire.com/content/view/277.

Owen, Taylor, and Ben Kiernan. Yale University, Cambodia Genocide Project. Retrieved December 8, 2006, from http://www.yale.edu/gsp/publications/index.html.

Yoshikawa, Tacko. 2006. "From a Refugee Camp to the Minnesota State Senate: A Case Study of a Hmong American Woman's Challenge." *Hmong Studies Journal* 7:1–23.

Contributors

Khin Mai Aung is a staff attorney at the Asian American Legal Defense and Education Fund in New York City, where she runs an educational equity and youth rights project. Issues she has worked on include school discipline, access to bilingual education, language access, anti-Asian violence in public schools, post-9/11 and gang profiling, and school testing policies. Previously, Ms. Aung was the director of policy and civic engagement at Youth Leadership Institute, a staff attorney at Asian Law Caucus, and an associate in the litigation department of Morrison and Foerster, all in San Francisco. Ms. Aung is a 1996 graduate of Boalt Hall School of Law at the University of California, Berkeley, and holds a bachelor's degree in international politics from Georgetown University.

Sylvia R. Cowan is associate professor and program director for the Intercultural Relations Program in the Graduate School of Arts and Social Sciences at Lesley University in Cambridge, Massachusetts. With more than twenty-five years of experience in the international and intercultural fields, Dr. Cowan has provided seminars for educators and professionals on intercultural understanding and conflict. Her special interest in immigration studies has taken her to Latin America, Europe, the Middle East, and Asia. She is currently working on a research project with Cambodians who have returned to their homeland. Her scholarly interests include issues of identity and culture, arts and education, and conflict transformation.

Jeffrey N. Gerson is associate professor of political science at the University of Massachusetts Lowell. He teaches courses in ethnic and racial politics, urban politics, state and local politics, American politics, and the politics of popular culture (sports, music, and film). His most recent book is *Latino Politics in Massachusetts: Struggles, Strategies and Prospects*, coedited with Carol Hardy-Fanta (2002). His recent studies have been of the Southeast Asian and Latino communities of Lowell, Massachusetts, and professional and amateur hockey.

Leakhena Nou has specialized clinical and research training in mental health and holds a master's degree in social work from Columbia University. She taught in the School of Social Work at the University of Illinois at Urbana-Champaign, and organized an international conference on the meaning of community in Cambodia for the Social Organization Working Group (SOWG). She also acted as dean of the College of Social Sciences at the University of Cambodia. Dr. Nou joined the Institute for Asian American Studies (2004–2005) as a postdoctoral fellow at the University of Massachusetts Boston, in which she conducted research on the psychosocial well-being of Cambodian communities in Massachusetts. Currently, she holds a position as assistant professor of sociology at California State University, Long Beach.

Hai Ba Pho (Pho Ba Hai) is political science professor emeritus at the University of Massachusetts Lowell. He holds a B.A. in American history from Boston College, an M.A. in history from Rutgers University, and a Ph.D. in political science from Boston University. Dr. Pho taught for thirty-two years at the University of Massachusetts. He has given lectures at several institutions, including Clark University and the University of Rhode Island and, from 1973 to 1975, taught as a visiting professor at the University of Saigon. He taught in several areas including international relations, modern diplomacy, comparative Asian politics and Southeast Asian refugees in America. He has published several articles including "The Politics of Refugee Resettlement in Massachusetts," in the journal *Migration World, 1955–1975,* and the book, *Vietnamese Public Management in Transition: South Vietnam Public Administration,* (1990), which has recently been translated into Vietnamese and published in a bilingual edition in Hanoi. He has served on several councils and state boards, and, as a Humanity Scholar for the National Endowment for the Humanities, he helped to publish the Fitchburg Ethnic Audio-Visual Program Series. He also contributd the introduction to James Higgins and Joan Ross's *Southeast Asians: A New Beginning in Lowell* (1986).

Tuyet-Lan Pho is director emerita of the Center for Diversity and Pluralism at the University of Massachusetts Lowell. She has conducted several studies on the experiences of Southeast Asians in the United States and has written extensively on Southeast Asian youth and their education. She also taught courses on contemporary American culture, educating newcomers in American schools, and women in higher education at the Graduate School of Education. During the past thirty years she has devoted time and effort to volunteer work with social service agencies and community-based organizations in the resettlement of Southeast Asian refugees and immigrants at the state and national levels. She was president of the Indochinese Refugees Foundation in Massachusetts and chair of the Board of Directors of Indochina Resource Action Center in Washington, D.C. She was a visiting professor of ethnic studies at the University of California, San Diego, during the academic year 2005–2006.

Jean L. Pyle is a senior associate at the Center for Women and Work and a professor emerita in the Department of Regional Economic and Social Development at the University of Massachusetts Lowell. She holds a Ph.D. in economics and her recent work examines globalization, transnational migration, and gendered care work. Her writings expose the growing care deficits in the lives of women who migrate transnationally to provide care services to others as nannies, domestics, or health care workers. Her ongoing research examines how globalization has contributed to the rise of types of work (sex work, domestic service, and production in subcontracting networks) that are gendered, span the globe, and increasingly involve the migration or trafficking of women. She has also analyzed the impact of state policies on women's economic roles in Singapore and Ireland and coauthored a set of journal articles that examines factors constraining the effective use of diverse peoples in U.S. workplaces. She coedited (with Robert Forrant) *Globalization, Universities, and Issues of Sustainable Human Development and Approaches to Sustainable Development: The Public University in the Regional Economy* (2002).

Linda Silka is a University Professor in the University of Massachusetts Lowell's Department of Regional Economic and Social Development. She directs the UML Center for Family, Work, and Community and is special assistant to the UML provost for community outreach and partnership. Silka's recent publications include three coedited volumes: *Inside and Out: University Education for Sustainable Development* (2006), *Citizens as Planners* (2007). She has won numerous awards for her partnership work with immigrant and refugee communities, including the University of Massachusetts Award for Professional Service.

Susan Thomson is a cultural anthropologist and currently an adjunct faculty member at Middlesex Community College, as well as an associate at the Center for Women and Work at the University of Massachusetts Lowell. Her earlier research included a political and artistic analysis of a traditional masked dance performed in Jharkhand, India; her recent research centers on civic engagement—especially its implications for immigrants and women—in the Lowell area. She is a researcher and planning team member for the Lowell Civic Collaborative, and holds a Ph.D. in anthropology from Harvard University.

David Turcotte is a program manager at the University of Massachusetts Lowell's Center for Family, Work, and Community. He has a master's degree in Community Economic Development and more than twenty years of nonprofit and community development experience. Dr. Turcotte managed the CIRCLE (Center for Immigrant and Refugee Community Leadership and Empowerment) Program at the University of Massachusetts Lowell; this program provided technical assistance and capacity-building training to leaders of the minority and immigrant community. He is an adjunct faculty member of the University of Massachusetts Lowell's Department of Regional Economic and Social Development and chairs the Non-Profit Alliance of Greater Lowell. In 2006 Dr. Turcotte received his doctoral degree in work environmental policy/clean production/pollution prevention at the University of Massachusetts Lowell's Department of Work Environment.

Nancy Yu is a policy analyst at the Asian American Legal Defense and Education Fund, where she provides strategic research, mapping, and data analysis to support the organization's organizing and advocacy efforts. She focuses on a range of policy issues, including voting rights and redistricting, immigration reform, and community and economic development. Prior to joining AALDEF, Ms. Yu had been an analyst and consultant to several public interest organizations and policy think tanks, including the Asian Pacific American Legal Center in Los Angeles and Demos: A Network of Ideas and Action in New York City. She is a graduate of the University of Southern California.

Index

Family life *(continued)*
secondary migration, 34; resettlement disruption of connections,
136; support for healing from traumatic stress, 186. *See also* Intergenerational issues; Parents,
immigrant
Federal government: and Lao/Hmong
immigrants, 132–35, 136, 211; resettlement role of, 11, 12, 14, 15,
22, 25, 33, 34; support for immigrant education, 109n22; and undocumented immigrant control, 19,
22
Fennell, Sambath Chey, 162
Financial capital: host community
sources, 61, 62, 63; informal
sources for, 13, 52, 62; lack of funding for youth programs, 105–6; and
transnationalism, 54–55
Flag controversies, 143–45, 149n31
Flora, C., 51
Flora, J., 51
The Flute Player, 200
Forbes, Susan S., 34
Foreign-born population. *See* Immi-
grant community
For Those Who Come After (Krupat),
199–200
Four Noble Truths, 118
French Canadian neighborhood in
Lowell, 195
Funcinpec Party, 57, 160, 162, 169n8

Gangs, ethnic, 15, 102–3, 120–21,
126
Gardner, C., 51
Gateway states/cities, 19
Gear-Up, 109n22
GED (General Education Develop-
ment) certificate, 96
Gender: and academic performance,
76; and stress disorder rates, 180;
and traditional differential treat-
ment, 80
General Education Development
(GED) certificate, 96

Gibson, J., 51
Glory Buddhist Temple, 120, 167
Goodman, Michael, 16
Government, U.S. entities. *See* Federal
government; Local government; So-
cial services; State government
Governor's Advisory Council for Ref-
ugees and Immigrants, 13, 14

Hanson, Gordon H., 23
Hate crimes against Asians, 15, 16n5
Health issues, 173–88, 198, 210, 211
Hein, Jeremy, 140, 181
Heritage State Park, 13
Higgins, James, 71
High-tech economic boom in Lowell,
12–13, 22, 25, 29, 89
Himelblau, Linda, 71
Hmong immigrants: ethnic background in Laos, 132–33; initial resettlement of, 11, 148n13; as military agents in Indochina Wars, 134,
135–36; political activism, 211
Hmong Veterans Naturalization Act
(2000), 136
Holy water blessing, 160–61
Host community: advantages of Asian
communities for, 15; and Cambodian psychosocial adjustment, 182–
83; future prospects for, 210–12;
immigrant transformation of, 192–
200; immigration pressures on, 12,
13, 20, 33, 35, 88–89, 93, 94, 136,
210; and initial refugee resettlement,
11; and Laotian immigrants, 137–
42; law and order concerns, 15; politics vs. homeland, 155; and rural
vs. urban lifestyles, 181; tolerance of
diversity in, 13–14; values differences and education, 69–84. *See
also* Economy, host community;
Lowell, Massachusetts
Hun Sen, 160

Identity and group formation: and
Cambodian resilience, 185; and
cultural preservation, 142; and